九典 BaF

聯 合 建 築 師 事 務 所

Bio architecture Formosana

Produced by:

九+ Research and Innovation

Bio-architecture Formosana
Taipei, Taiwan
www.bioarch.com.tw
arch@bioarch.com.tw

Published by ORO Editions
www.oroeditions.com
info@oroeditions.com

Authors: Ying Chao Kuo, Ching Hwa Chang
Editor & Graphic Design: Ana Coelho
ORO Project Coordinator: Kirby Anderson

10 9 8 7 6 5 4 3 2 1 First Edition

Library of Congress data available upon request. World Rights: Available

ISBN: 978-1-943532-98-8

Color Separations and Printing: ORO Group Ltd.
Printed in China.

International Distribution: www.oroeditions.com/distribution

Nine design modules
for non-linear interactive design flow
inspired by Biological Intelligence

FOREWORD

For the last 20 years, Bio-architecture Formosana (BaF) has produced an incredible body of work within Taiwan's architecture scene. It has become one of the country's most prestigious architecture firms and one of the forerunners for international recognition in Taiwanese contemporary architecture. The partnership was penned in 1999 by Ching Hwa Chang and Ying Chao Kuo; both experienced academicians, talented creative architects, and recipients of several individual and collective architecture awards.

Sustainable practice is their leading priority and it is this concern for sustainability that lead them to spearhead buildings such as the Beitou Public Library, the Pavilions for the Flora Expo both in Taipei, and the Taijiang Visitor Center.

This publication explores the concept of Biological Intelligence: which can be defined as an attempt at understanding nature's *life* forms systems and replicating them within the architectural realm. The goal here is to create a sustainable cycle of design by first learning the way life works in the natural world in order to achieve a circular design.

BaF's creative flow is a design process inspired by Biological Intelligence based on three key elements: origin, form, and interface, which in total contain nine different modules. Although it seems to be a complex system it is actually a simple, straightforward, and efficient design methodology. It is a structured design approach where the nonlinear connections between its simple modules leads to an information flow shelled by a circular design envelope that uplifts the standards for creative architectural design.

At the core of the practice's principles there is a devotion to high-quality international standards in architectural environmental and sustainable design, in order to ensure that the buildings are places that are welcoming to everyone. This devotion disseminates throughout all their projects and acts as a sort of motto for BaF.

On the whole, this book is a celebration of a fresh approach to new ideas and explorations into sustainable, responsible design that can be a useful teaching tool for other architects, professors, or architecture students. It naturally stands out as a perfect example that good practices lead to excellent buildings.

Tiago Costa, DArch
Assistant Professor, NTUST

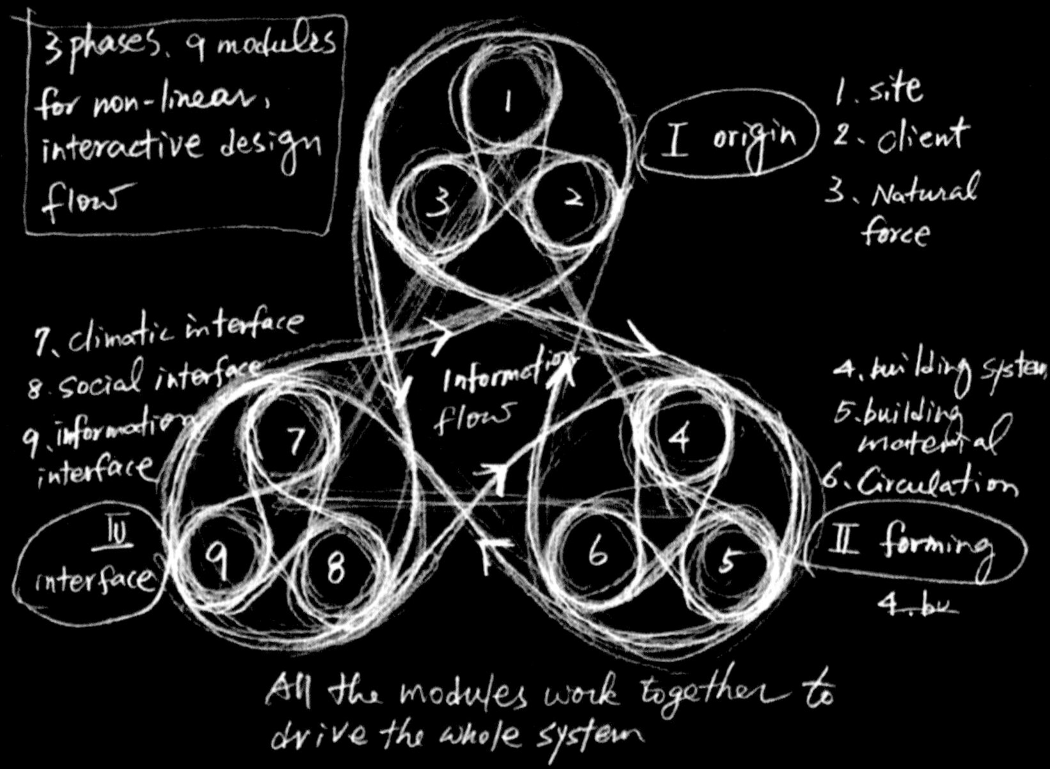

Initial draft of the modules that determine the design process.

THE "MIND" BEHIND NATURE'S CREATIVITY

Nature never intends to be creative, while its mere creativity never stops engaging our admiration. Not only does it create millions of life forms that exude absolute beauty and delicacy, but all its creations fit into a ceaselessly elaborate network that begs the question of how such engineering could even exist.

The "mind" behind all this we call: Biological intelligence. There is a great similarity between architecture and life form. They are both made of skin, supporting structures and life-sustaining organs. They are both interconnected and driven by intrinsic energies as well as external pressures. Life itself is originated from single cell organism that eventually evolved into tens of millions of species through genetic mutations (intrinsic energies) and nature's selections (exterior pressures). Architecture began with the fundamental principal of providing shelter with primitive materials and evolved, through main selection, into metropolises with varieties of functions that can accommodate tens of millions of people. It is the response to the needs of an ever-evolving human civilization that fuels the evolution of architecture. In this book, we seek to explore the underlying mysteries of this billion-year-old intelligence and learn to create architecture that parallels how nature creates itself.

Ying Chao Kuo, Ching Hwa Chang
Founding Partners

INTRODUCING A ROADMAP FROM BI TO ARCHITECTURAL CREATIVITY

Architectural creativity, like Charles Darwin noted in *On The Origin of Species* is "the mystery of the mysterious." The scope of architecture is vast, all of the requirements and considerations are correlated and interact as a complex system which is almost impossible to be formulized or simulated, therefore the process of architectural design is so often like a walk in thick mist: hard to see what's in front of you. This aspect not knowing is what makes architecture so engaging, and also why so many unnecessary mistakes are made.

Nature is a much more complex system than architecture, but through the relentless effort of many generations of naturalists and scientists, we are able to understand the "architecture of the organic world." The mystery of the mysterious is largely solved in this aspect. Inspired by the architecture of the organic world, we hope, in a humble and not hasty way, to have a sketch of the "architecture of architecture," which can be used as a map of the maze that is the architectural design process for the less-experienced staff of BaF, as this book is originally intended, and for anyone who also appreciates our perspective.

The first section of this book refers to our view of "Biological Intelligence" based on very primitive insight that is currently acknowledged by the academia and the general public, from that six principles: informationization, circulization, evolution (fundamental of life), inclusive, passive, adaptive (strategy for sustainability) are extracted as a possible link, through philosophical means, between the biological world and architecture. Furthermore, we examine "16 patterns of life" from Mahlon and Bert Dodson's book *The way life works* to provide more physical relevance between life and architecture. The 16 Patterns are then re-organized into four groups—origin, form, interface, circular—to lay the ground for four design modules that are universal for the design of all types of building. Each design module contains multiple, smaller modules: site, program, natural force for origin, circulation, structural system, building material for form, hard, soft, social for interface, city, nature, temporal, and interior for circular. Even though throughout the design process, in a traditional way, these modules seem to work in sequence, they are intrinsically nonlinear, interactive, driven by information which is constantly expanding, transformed, and restructured.

The second part of the book features 35 of BaF's projects from the past 20 years, to explain in more detail the meaning of each module and to illustrate how each design module works in architectural practice. Even though all of the projects should implement every concern in all of the design modules, some projects have stronger traits to correspond to certain design modules than the others, due to their specific conditions; that should not lead to an assumption that they are weaker in implementing the other modules.

As nature never intends to be creative, architecture creativity is generally not achieved through intentional action, but by thoroughly dealing with the elements contained in the design modules, exactly like how life struggles for existence, accumulates varieties, then achieves creativity.

THE ROAD MAP FROM BI TO ARCHITECTURAL CREATIVITY

1 BIOLOGICAL INTELLIGENCE

p.12

The "mind" behind nature's creativity

2 3x2 6 PRINCIPLES OF BI

p.16

ICE: Fundamentals of Life
IPA: Strategies for Sustainability

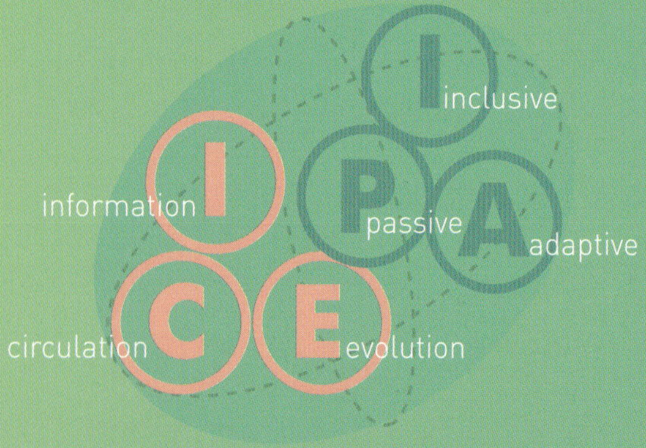

3 4x4 16 PATTERNS OF LIFE

p.18

16 patterns in 4 groups: OFIC
(Origin, Form, Interface, Circular)
As interface for BI and architecture

4 3x3
9 DESIGN MODULES

p.26

work together and improved by the information flow, very much like "struggle for existence" and "nature's selection."

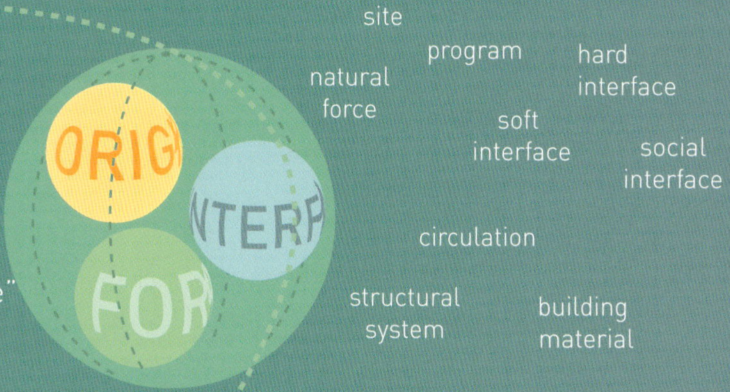

5 +1 CIRCULAR LOOP

p.290

how nature renews itself and how architecture achieves sustainability.

6 ARCHITECTURAL CREATIVITY

creative design solution emerges through the exercise of the design modules, as beautiful life forms emerge from a few simple rules in nature.

BI: BIOLOGICAL INTELLIGENCE

Nature has given us a colorful yet delusive expression on the surface of earth: day and night, seasonal changes, droughts and floods, not to mention thunder and lightning, earthquakes and tsunamis, tornados and hurricanes. This interchanges of phenomena form an enormous complex system. But for every complex system, there's always simplicity residing deep within in order to stabilize and sustain the system. Some simple patterns and principles can always be found beneath the bewildering surface of natural phenomena, that is the reason why we are able to forecast the weather and the rhythm of the tidal change; and because of it, life gets an opportunity to develop under relatively more predictable conditions.

Life seems to take the same footsteps as nature: organic beings acquire complex systems to respond to the multiple challenges from nature, and the same simplicity is also needed to make the complicated life-sustaining tasks imaginable. One of the perfect examples is the hereditary information of all organic beings which is recorded by merely four bases, ATCG. The other example is all of the trillions of cells of hundreds of specialized types from one single origin: the fertilized egg; Nature does not design a complex system, instead it uses some simple rules and the complex system emerges naturally. For us, this could be the true meaning of BI, that gave birth to the diversity of ecosphere we admire today.

Homo sapiens are arguably one of the most successful life form in our ecosphere, a part of this can be attributed to our ability to explore, identify, and understand the simple rules well veiled within the complex environment to improve our chance in the struggle for existence. In some respects the advancement of technology unshackled us from the limitation of evolution. We use technology to create materials that don't exist in nature and products that are designed to satisfy our endless desires.

Unlike nature, we did not invent technologies that can restore man-made substances back to their original state, and as a result, we have exhausted resources and polluted our environment simultaneously. Among the pollutants, architecture has to be the greatest source in terms of quantity, scale, and potential risks.

Life is mostly composed of carbon, hydrogen, and oxygen; just as architecture is mostly composed of concrete, steel, aluminum, glass, and other non-organic materials. Even though organic materials such as lumber or bamboo are common, its usage amount is still not comparable. Architecture needs to function like a life form in order to satisfy the variety of needs during its minimum 50-year lifespan and be able to recycle into other building materials or back as raw materials in order to enter the lifecycle of another building. As such, the design and construction of a building is very much like the creation of life. The intention of BI is to understand how life is structured, deconstructed, and to follow the principles of evolution so architecture can also enter a sustainable cycle of design, construct, operate, and disassemble. Similar to how life will evolve in all directions and not be constrained by a particular appearance, BI is also able to freely express itself based on a set of environmental stimulants.

In sketching the scope of relevance between the biological world and architecture, six principles of biological intelligence are induced as stepping stones in understanding the relation between the patterns of life and patterns of how architecture works:

I **Information** – for construction and reproduction of life
C **Circulation** – for renewing life with limited resources
E **Evolution** – for external challenges that result in the variation of life

I **Inclusive** – cooperation for more benefit
P **Passive** – maximizing resources and energy efficiency
A **Adaptive** – modification for existence and prosperity

ICE: Fundamentals of Life
IPA: Strategies for Sustainability

As life moves up the scale from molecular level to ecological level, there are six repetitive themes that are organized into two major categories.

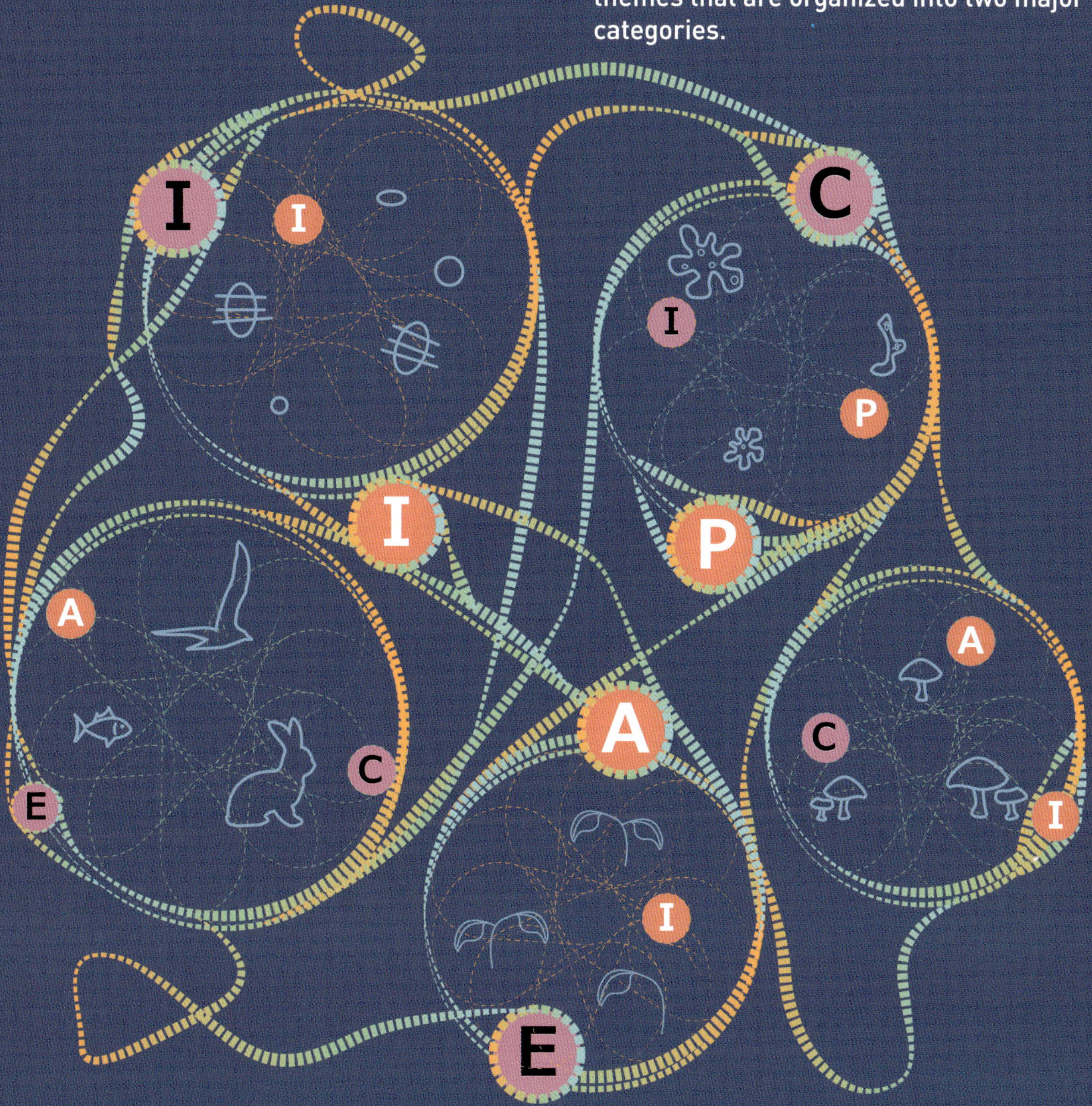

SIX PRINCIPLES OF BIOLOGICAL INTELLIGENCE

ICE: FUNDAMENTALS OF LIFE

1 Information

It is understandable to say that a life's chapter consists of only four letters: the four nucleotides that constitute the information chains of DNA. Tens of thousands of proteins, responsible for the proper function of life, can be created through only about 20 types of amino acids that are composed from these four letters. Information is the essential core for the creation and function of life, its perseverance, duplication, and distribution is the source of life's self-consciousness as it gets stimulated externally while commanding bodily functions through the distribution of messages internally.

2 Circulation

For every life form, there is a network structured by a circulatory system that is responsible for organizing and transporting life-sustaining resources, and the expulsion of the waste created during this transportation process. However, there is no difference between resources or waste in an ecosystem, as the waste of one species can be the nutrition of another. All matters are confined into a continuous cycle of oxidation, decomposition, and re-composition, allowing the ecosystem to sustain itself indefinitely.

3 Evolution

As life evolves from a single-cell organism through the exchange and integration of genetic information, the ability to harness the light as life-sustaining energy and the capability to be mobile came to fruition. Evolution is not unlike a great musician who composed a magnificent symphony with only a limited amount of notes to work with.

IPA: STRATEGIES FOR SUSTAINABLITY

4 Inclusive

An ecosystem and its life forms contain a closely connected network that is dynamically balanced. The relationship inside of this network is both self-serving and mutually beneficial, competitive and cooperative, cruel and pleasant. As more members are included into the network, the more resources will be available and the more complex the system will become. However, as a result the network will become increasingly more stable.

5 Passive

As a self-organized system, life forms—and their ecosystem—are driven by the power provided by the sun; life forms use such power to produce elements and energy necessary to sustain life. On the other hand, an ecosystem can utilize the solar power to activate the mechanism of composition, decomposition, and distribution; or as others would call it, a sustainable cycle. Taking full advantage of the energies provided by nature—such as solar, heat, wind, and hydro—is the fundamental ability for all living creatures.

6 Adaptive

Evolution allows for life forms and ecosystems to transform according to its external condition. By transforming we are referring to the ability to efficiently acquire external resources for the purpose of sustaining life, and to reflect this ability on the external appearance, internal transmission of messages, management of bodily function, and self-perseverance mechanism.

16 PATTERNS OF LIFE AND ARCHITECTURE

Mahlon Hoagland and Bert Dodson in their book *The Way Life Works* explain the "Sixteen Things You Should Know About Life." We believe these sixteen patterns are extremely useful in perceiving each living thing (from the tiniest cell) as a part of a whole, complex system and also in understanding a new perspective about building.

ORIGIN

	Life		Architecture
1	"Life builds from the bottom up. The influence of small things."	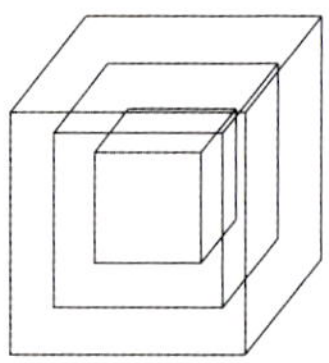	A man on a chair, a chair in a room, a room in a house, a house in a neighborhood, a neighborhood in a city, a city on the planet, the planet feeds the man.
2	"Life occurs in water. The all-purpose molecule."	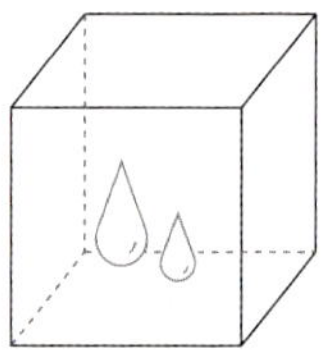	A building without water (supply) is simply not habitable.
3	"Life runs on sugar. A molecule to burn."	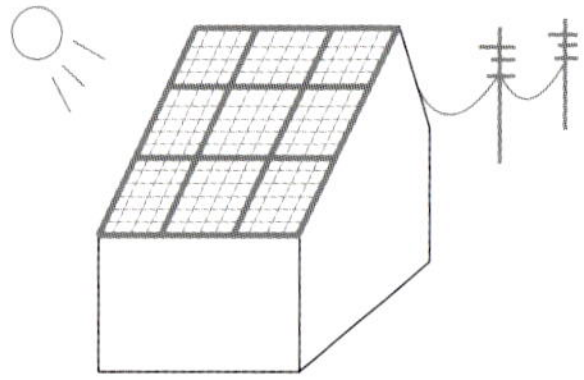	Modern buildings run on electricity, from renewable or non-renewable sources.
4	"Life is opportunistic. Making the most of what is."	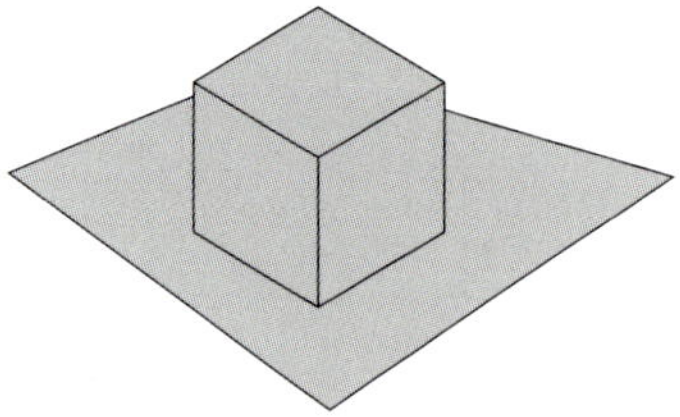	What's around you? What resource is most available?

FORM

Life | Architecture

5 "Life creates with mistakes. Accidents ensure novelty."

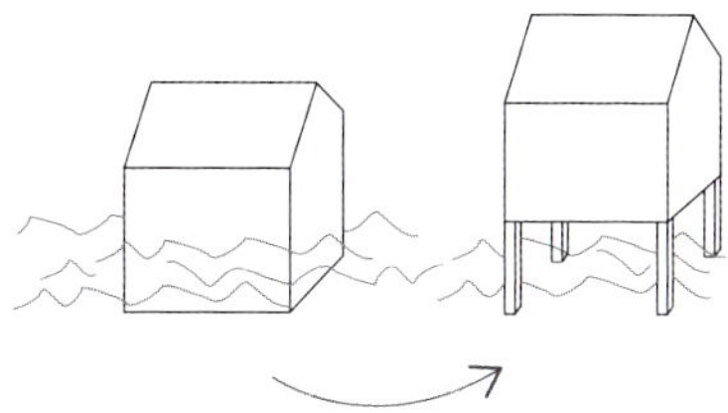

Traditional architecture is the foundation of learning.
Lifting a building is a response to previous mistakes.

6 "Life assembles itself into chains. When difference becomes information."

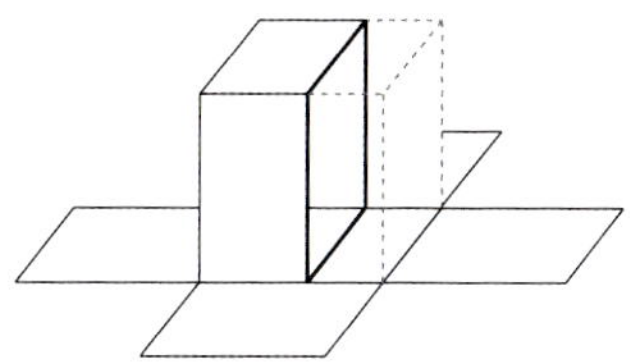

Chains of information DNA (BIM) transmitted by plans, sections, façades, diagrams, renderings.

7 "Life uses a few themes to generate many variations. The inward similarity of outward diversity."

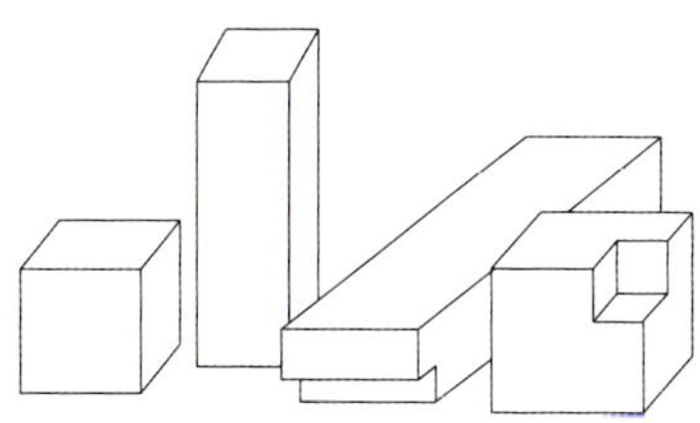

Architecture uses a few geometric forms to generate great diversity.

8 "Life encourages variety by reshuffling information."

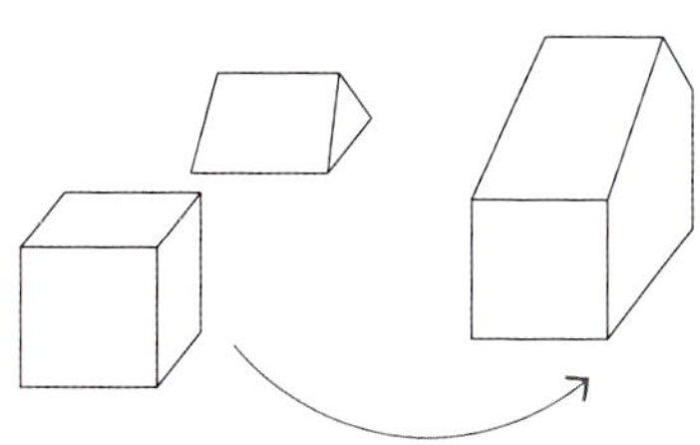

Architecture is in constant creativity renewal, based on the information/ influence acquired.

INTERFACE

	Life		Architecture
9	"Life tends to optimize rather than maximize—when less is better."	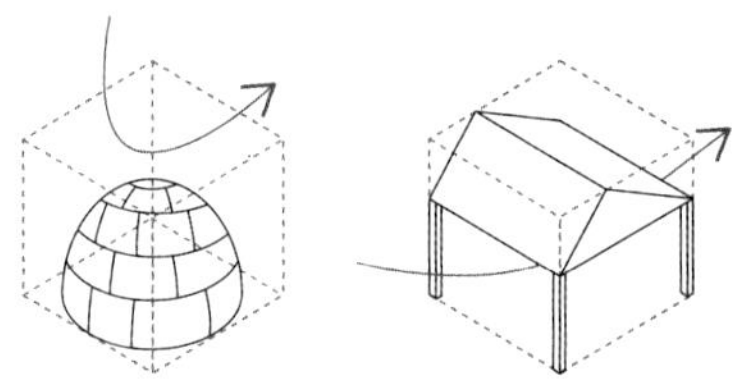	Architecture looks for minimum envelope in cold climate and minimum walls in the hot climate.
10	"Life needs an inside and an outside."	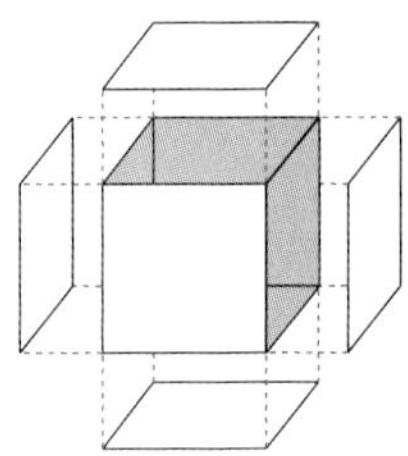	Building envelope is the necessary protective skin membrane that defines the interior from the exterior.
11	"Life competes within a cooperative framework. 1–Every creature acts in its own interests. 2–The living world works through cooperation."	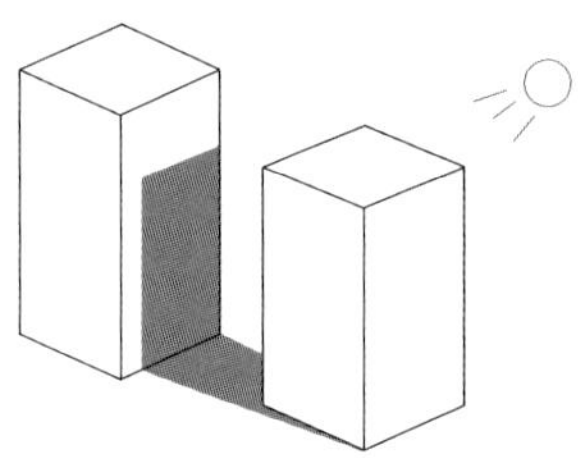	Neighboring buildings compete for sunlight but provide shading at the same time.
12	"Life is interconnected and interdependent."	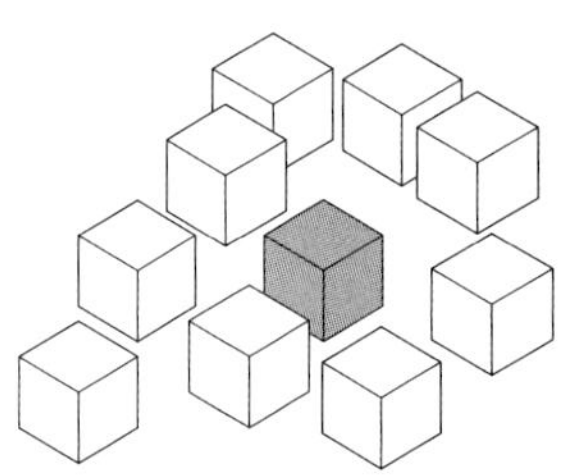	Inclusive. All things considered.

CIRCULAR

	Life		Architecture
13	"Life organizes with information. Making the parts that make the whole."	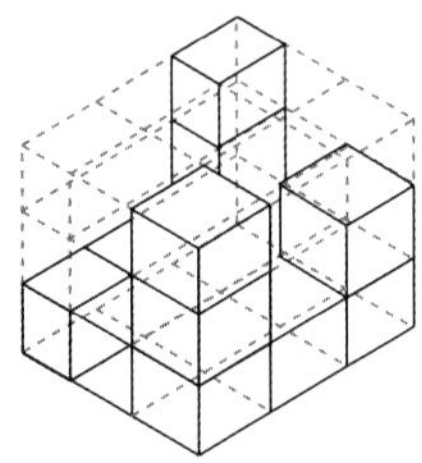	Simple blocks are assembled to become a building through BIM.
14	"Life works in cycles."	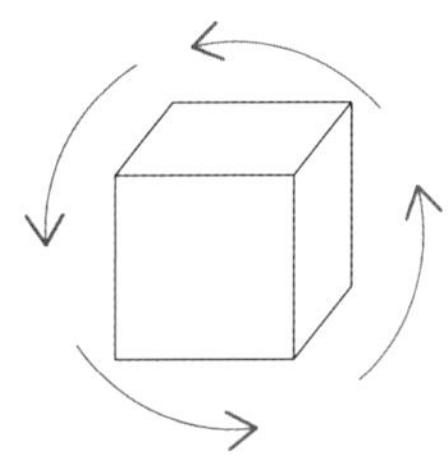	BAMB, buildings as material banks.
15	"Life recycles everything it uses. A circular flow of materials."	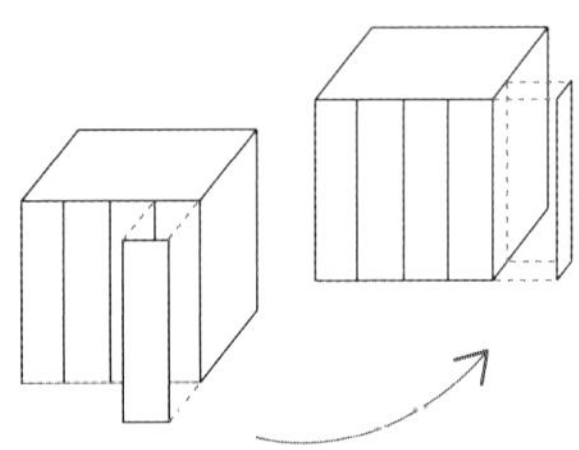	Architecture assembles, uses, disassembles, reuses.
16	"Life maintains itself by turnover. Put it together—take it apart."	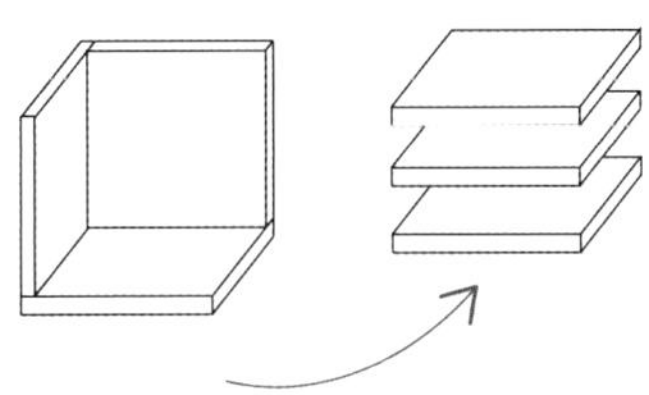	Architecture assembles and disassembles, assembles, disassembles.

IN NATURE...

ORIGIN

There are beetle species for any environment, but the majority live on land. Generally they prefer a humid location with availability of food.

FORM

Beetles don't have an internal skeleton, their main structure is composed of an exoskeleton, which is their large shell, that provides support and protection. They have an opened circulatory system and their composition can be separated into three major parts: the head, the thorax, and abdomen.

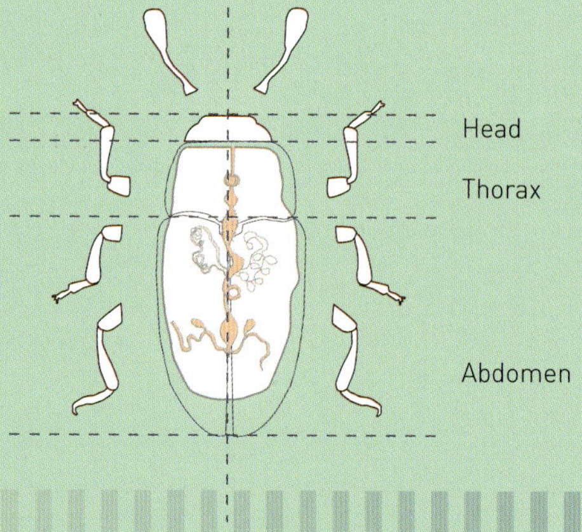

INTERFACE

Some beetles share their habitat with other species such as ants or termites. In order to be socially accepted they produce attractive secretions that please their co-habitants. Also, the adaptation to this habitat modifies their interface needs, causing them to lose their wings.Their exosleleton works as their protective shield.

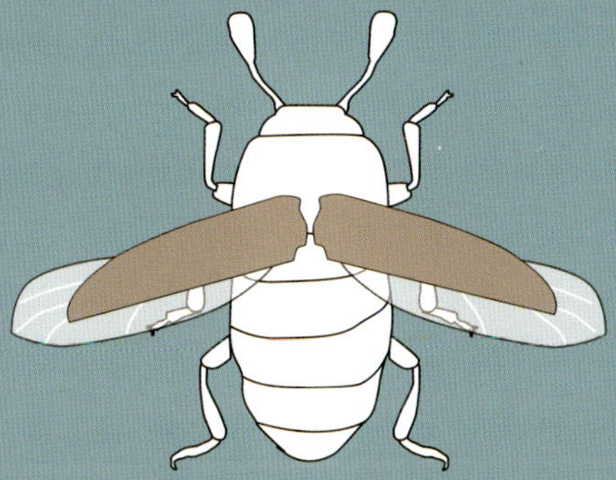

CIRCULAR

After going through four life stages in their development (from egg to larva to pupa to adult) just like any life form, the beetle becomes soil and fertilizer for new life.

IN ARCHITECTURE ...

ORIGIN

The birth of life: Three core issues corresponding to the design proposal phase: the condition of the site, the needs of the client, and the condition of the surrounding environment.

site
program
natural force

FORM

The evolution of life: Three core criteria corresponding to the design development phase that transforms abstract concepts into actual architecture: circulatory system, building system, and building material.

circulation
structural system
building material

INTERFACE

The relationship between life and its external surrounding: how architecture negotiates itself in a contextual setting; from its immediate surroundings, community, to a greater urban context.

hard interface
soft interface
social interface

CIRCULAR

The circular flow of life: the balanced loop of give and take, using prefabrication modular systems.

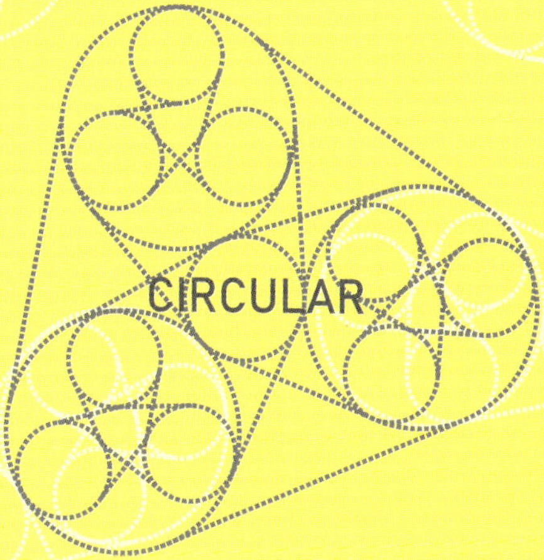

temporal
city
nature
interior

CREATIVE DESIGN FLOW INSPIRED BY BI

nine design modules for non-linear interactive design flow

As we look closer at how organic beings are constructed and function, we can find the significance of the hierarchical structure of modules. Modules from small to large: amino acids constitute protein, which is in charge of the operation of cell, cells constitute organs, organs constitute systems (such as the digestive system, the cardiovascular system, the respiratory system, the skeletal systems) which collaboratively constitute and sustain life. Arguably, life relies on modules to run daily operations, in so that modularization would simplify the preservation and duplications of genetic information and contain the risk of modification within the module.

The design process of transforming special requirements into physical form is a similar process to how life is formed. This is a highly complex design process that weaves together various needs, limitations, and abstract values into a seamless balance between estheticism, sociology, culture, and environmental concerns. To use nature as a teaching model, learning from the principle of hierarchical modular structures of organic beings, we can establish a hierarchical structure of interconnected modules within the complex architectural system that can enable us to create rich, diversified architecture.

A BI-inspired (Biological Intelligence) design process can be categorized into three steps and nine modules, which are driven by the 6 principles of BI: Information, Circulation, Evolution, Inclusive, Passive and Adaptive.

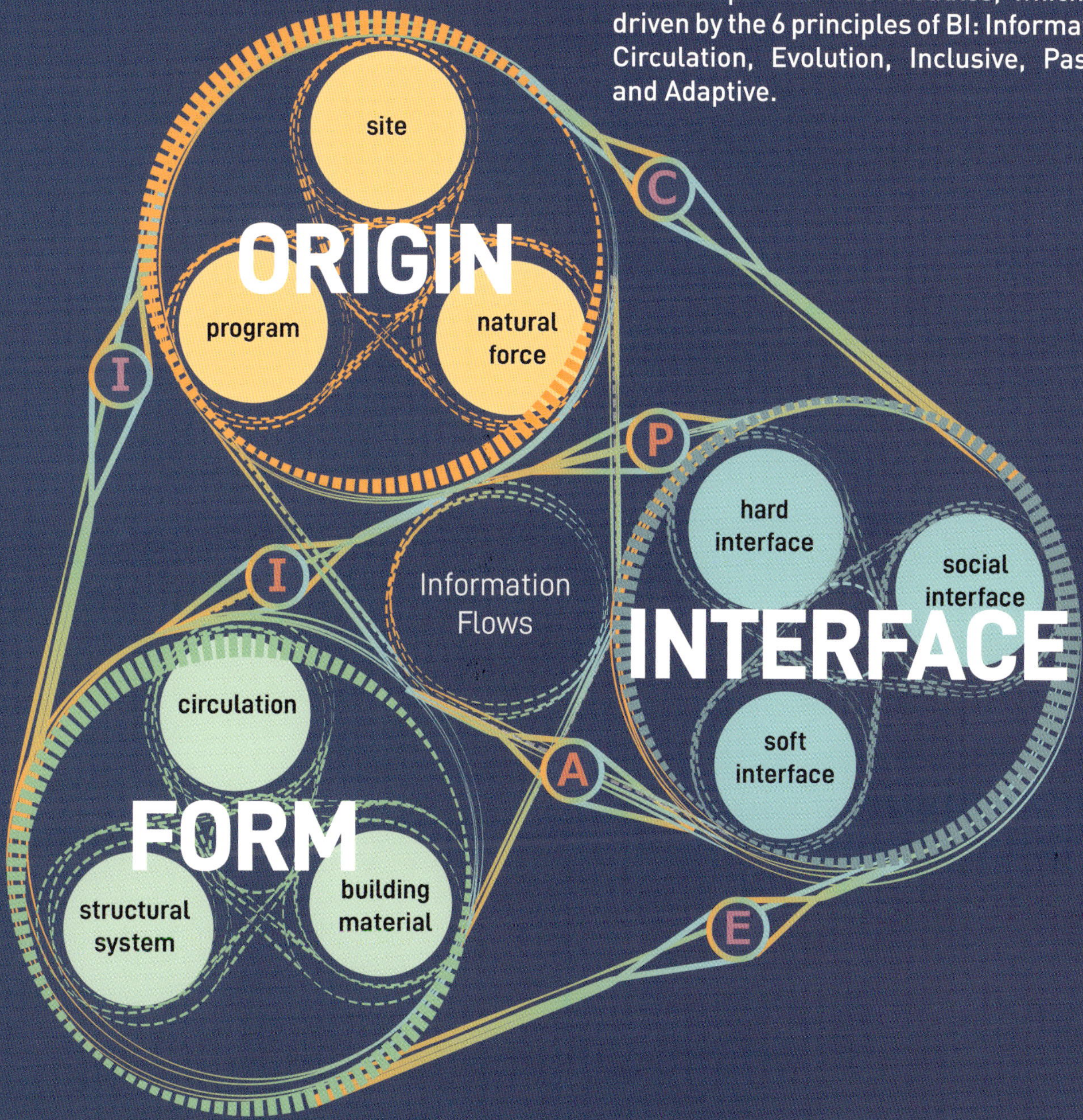

All lives originate from the same cradle and are based on different external environments and evolve into their own unique life forms. The rich and heterogeneous ecosphere surrounding us today is mainly driven by the condition of their habitat and external forces, including the climate of their habitat, the availability of their food, and the threat of predators.

Architecture is no exception to this method of operation. The varieties of architectural exhibitions we see today are a collective accumulation from centuries of external challenges architects have responded to and dealt with. No matter the type of architecture, they have to meet three fundamental requirements: the condition of the site, the needs of the client, and the force of the natural environment. Responding to these challenges presented by these fundamental requirements is the basis of architectural creativity.

ORIGIN

ORIGIN
site
program
natural force

site

Life surveys both resources and threats to its habitation, while maximizing the benefit from both. Architects initiate a project with site analysis in order to identify the resources it may offer and the potential hidden threats, therefore, the following elements are essential in diagnosing: landform, soil type, underground water level, orientation, existing objects, source of pollutants, adjacent neighborhoods, road traffic, as well as invisible elements such as local community awareness, demographic structure, and local business and culture.

Whether the site elements are tangible or not, they interact with one another to form an intricate and dynamic relationship. The more complex the site gets, the more stimulant it can provide to foster the creativity of the design. Therefore, the goal behind site analysis, aside from understanding the limitation of the site, is to explore and respond to the complexity and richness of it in order to fuel the drive for design originality.

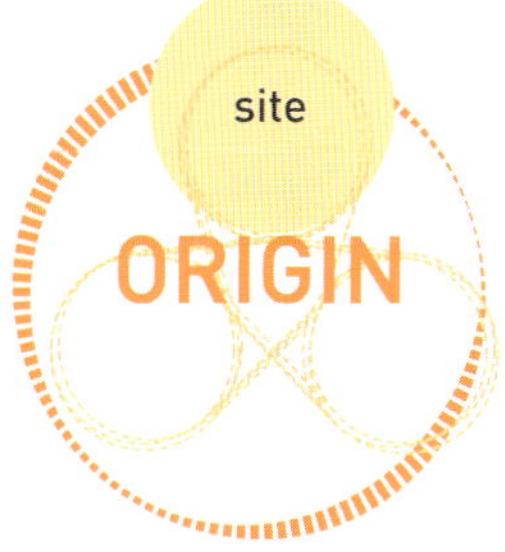

TAIPEI FLORA EXPO PAVILIONS

TAIPEI, 2008

Taipei Flora Expo Pavilions (Dream, Future, and Life) represents a long-awaited desire of integrating architectural art with technology. Built as eco-friendly buildings these expo pavilions were created to house the exhibition of a wide variety of products and technologies from Taiwan's horticultural industry.

This project has turned the existing trees in Xinsheng Park into a mystical driving force that invites buildings to extend, either high or low, among the trees, offering visitors scenic views.

The building mass was carefully positioned on site in order to control the winds and preserve the trees. The larger building mass was strategically blocking northern winds and the southern, smaller mass allows the permeability of southern winds. The preservation of the trees was also key in controlling the northeast winds, and possible typhoons, as well as reducing the hours of direct sunlight.

Three pavilions integrate the qualities of "green building, contemporary green house, and intelligent building." The green roof helps soften the skyline and reduce the urban heat island effect, while intelligent energy saving systems adjust comfortable, internal air conditioning by detecting external weather with central monitoring systems.

The building's mass is carefully positioned on site in order to preserve the trees.

Rooftop view showing a seamless merge between architecture and nature.

DESIGN CONCEPT

1.The building is positioned in order to embrace the trees.
2.Preserve the openness of the central courtyard. Maintain the existing scale of the newly-designed park.
3.Spatial hierarchy and human scale—minimize the sense of constraint caused by the architectural massing.
4.Sustainable architecture—bio-diverse, energy efficient, minimal waste, and healthy lifestyle.
5.Soft architecture—utilize natural building materials.
6.Resistant against northeastern seasonal wind.

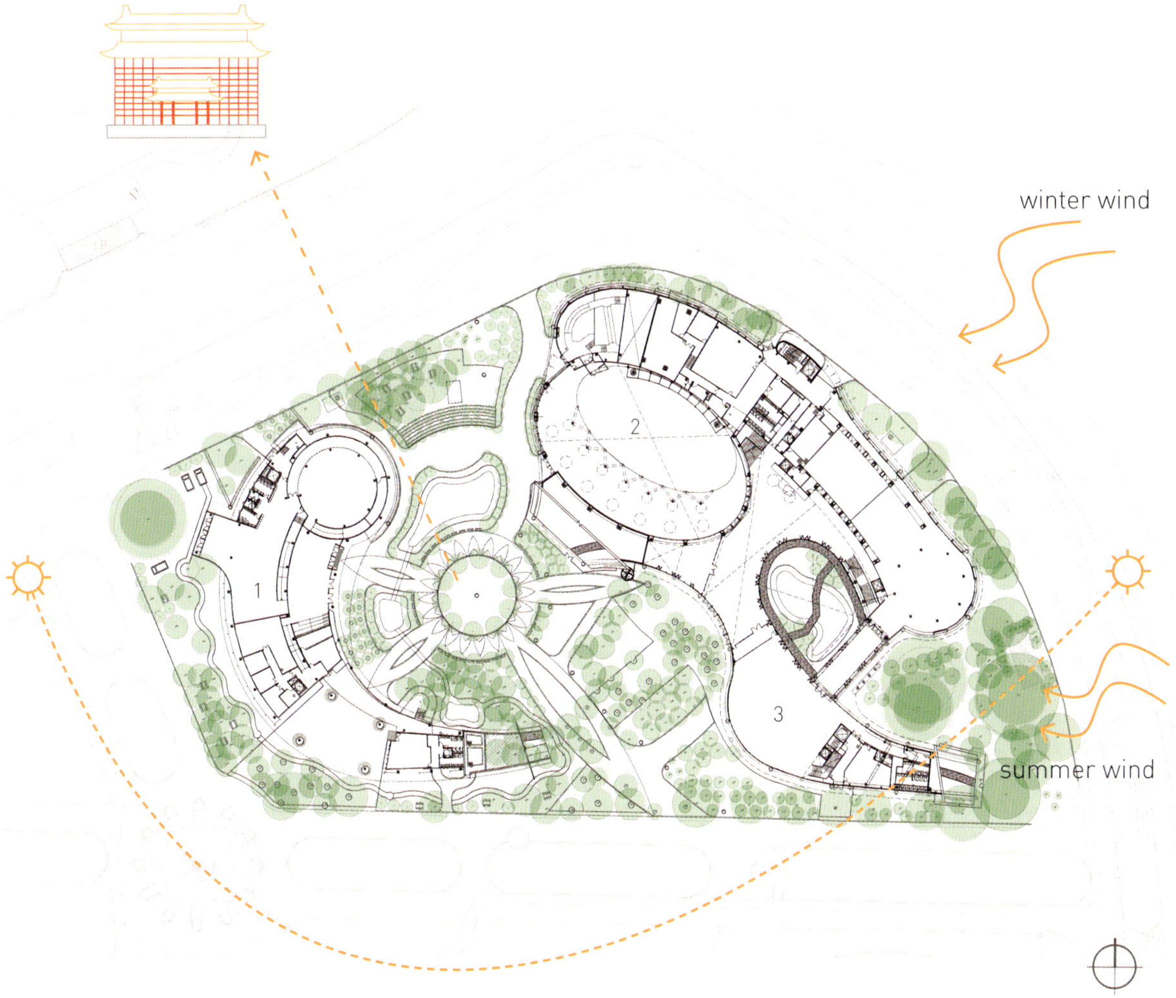

Above: The architectural massing forms an open courtyard inspired by the existing park, captures summer wind, and blocks winter cold breeze. Ground-floor plan of the three Pavilions: 1) Dream; 2) Future; 3) Life

Left: The green façade and wooden material blends with the preserved trees on site.

Above: Close-up view from the green roof and green house.

Left: The walkable green roof with the background mountains that surround the city of Taipei.

SONGSHAN PUBLIC HOUSING

TAIPEI, 2017

This site was originally the home for Fulian Village 5; a village reserved for military veterans and their relatives. An essential design proposal sought to combine both existing architectural elements with the new building design; thereby, not only express due respect and protect this historical place as well as its past identity but also achieve a good understanding of the current urban context.

The linear site, extremely elongated and narrow, raised a challenge from the design perspective. The idea of building a long, massive block would break the community in two. In order to avoid that, the design allows and even encourages a permeable connection between both sides of the site. The building responds to this need by having a porous-pierced ground floor followed by a low, three-story main volume that acts as the base for the four towers that peacefully interact with their surroundings and allow more sunlight into the community at the northside of the site.

The preservation and implementation of green spaces back into the community was always a priority as was the usage of on-site resources. This sustainable design used recycled-building materials and prefabricated construction methods.

The final design is a combination of distinct horizontal and vertical movements, set in a proportional manner in order to preserve the surrounding community views, the southern sunlight, and the green areas, thus acting as a linking mechanism between the building and its surrounding urban environment.

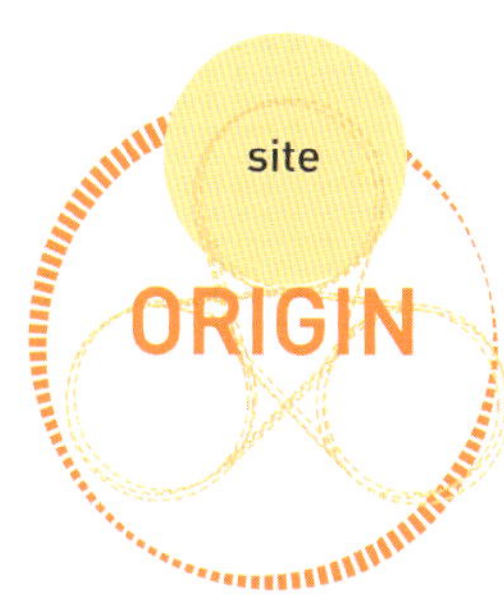

Site analysis

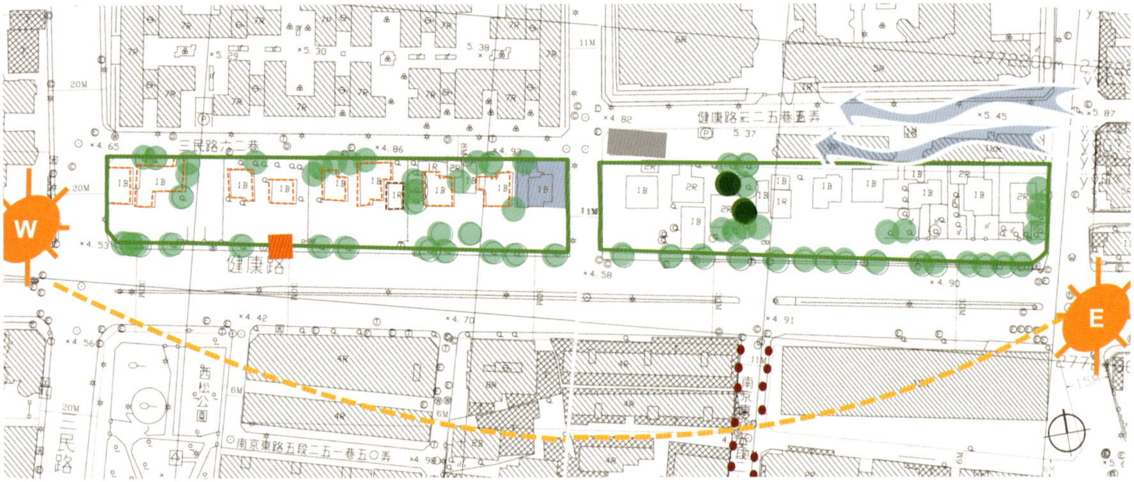

Ground floor plan

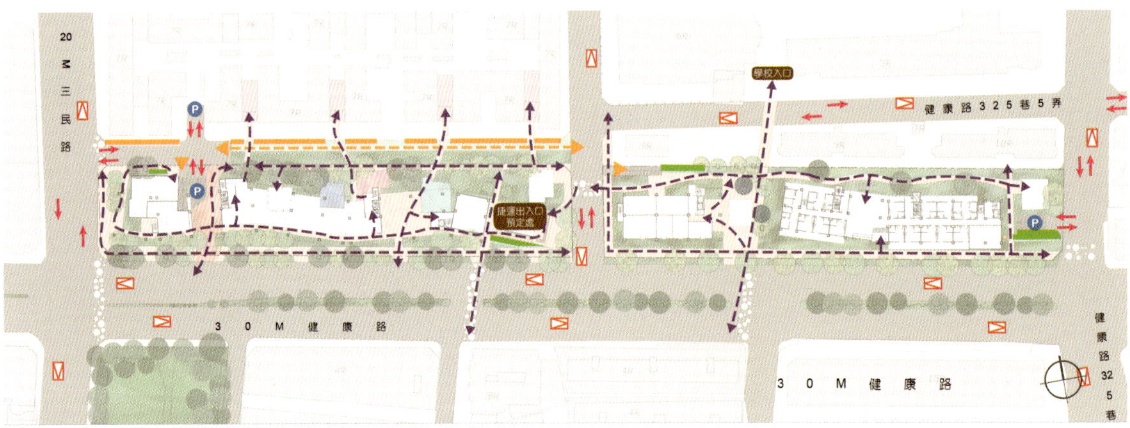

Left: The design allows a permeable connection between both sides of the site.

Right: Street view of one of the four living blocks.

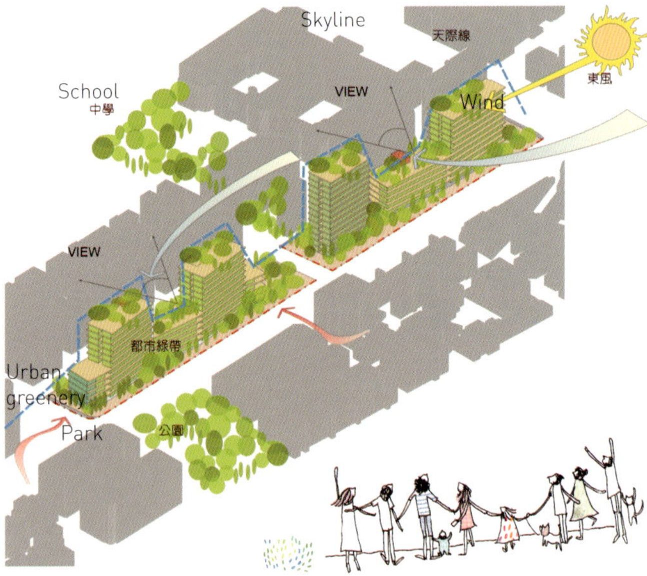

Above: Strategy for distribution of floor areas to allow more sun light through to the community at the north side.
Below: Historical old gate from the Fulian Village 5.

Above: New urban courtyard embracing the existing trees.
Right: Illustration of the intent: to create a co-living, community space of different ages.

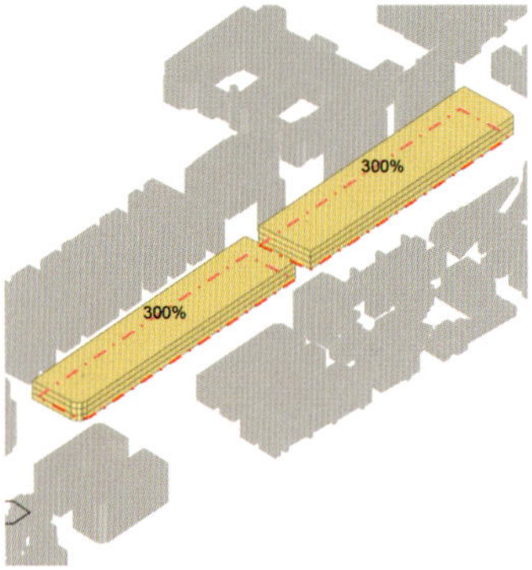

Floor area ratio – 300%.

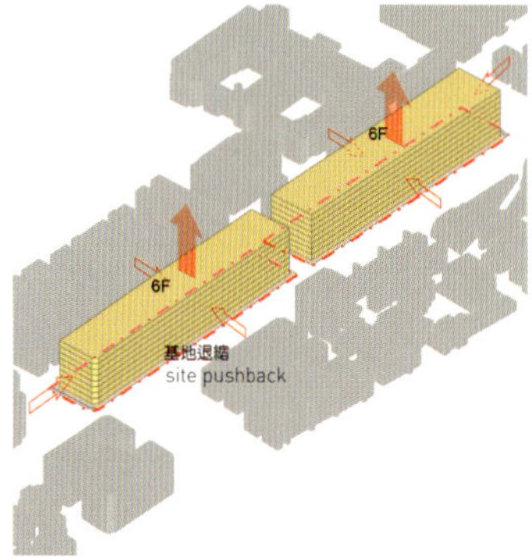

Building coverage ratio 45%.

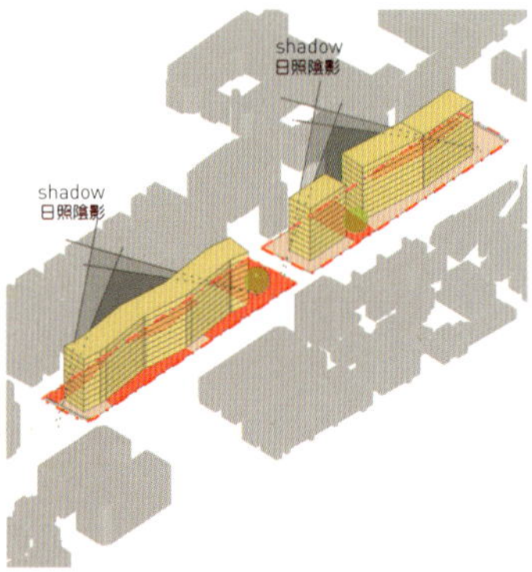

Relationship between shadow and adjacent buildings.

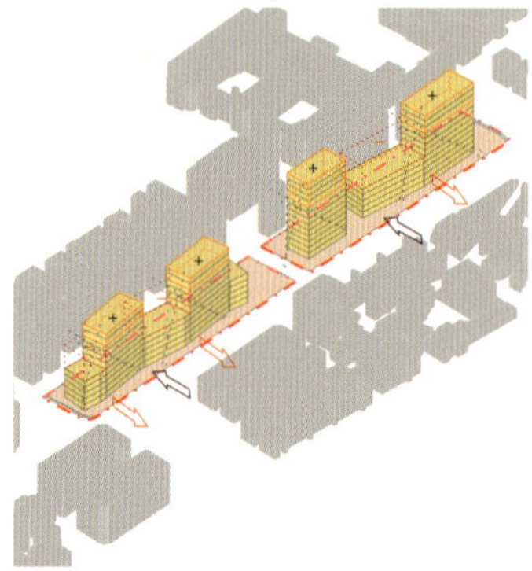

Relationship between building and open space.

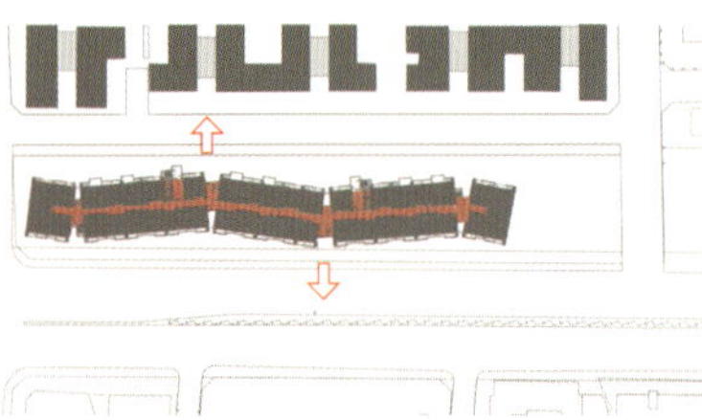

Maintenance of original path.

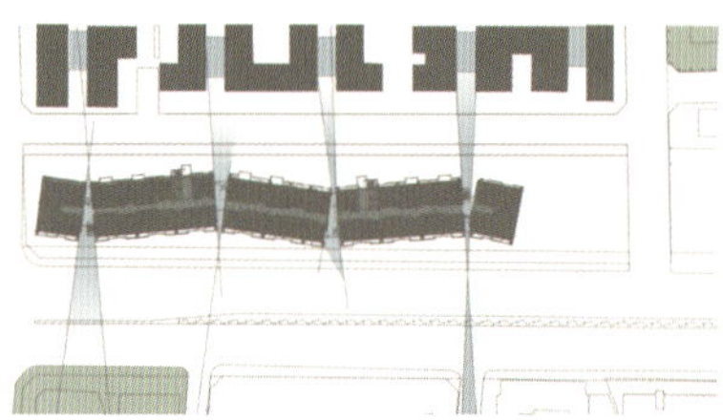

Building responds to the neighboring courtyards.

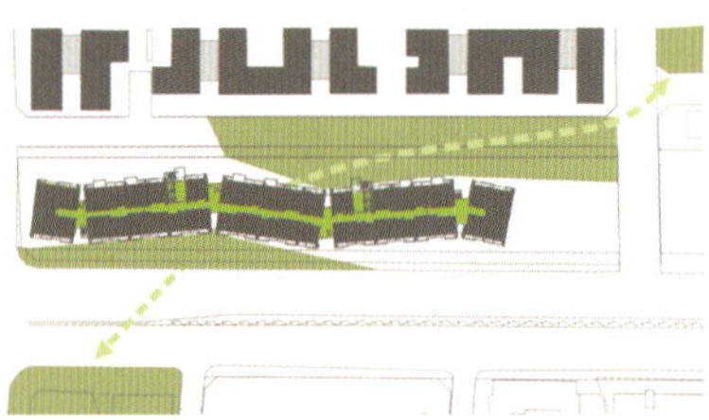

Connecting green spaces.

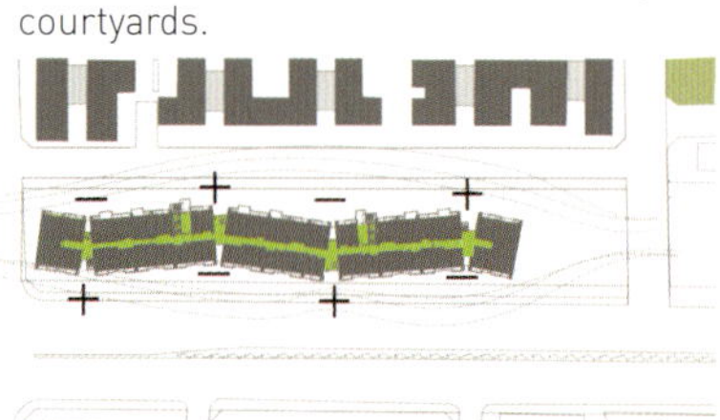

Building shape creates convection wind.

The new urban courtyard is one example of the green spaces brought back into the community.

HUWEI ARTS CENTER AND LEISURE PARK

NEW TAIPEI CITY, 2013

Tamsui is the first port to encounter the great Western sailing era in northern Taiwan, rich in cultural heritage. The intent for the Huwei Arts and Cultural Leisure Park was to seamlessly integrate the unique natural landscape, historical monuments, local arts and festivals, while establishing Tamsui's own cultural scenery. Additionally aiming to transform Tamsui into a creative cultural platform, encouraging various types of arts to flourish. In prospect, this development would also collaborate with other types of activities, and inspire further growth in neighboring regions, and was therefore designed to work as a social activator.

The site is located along a bustling tourist route, effectively linking historic sites and various attractions in Tamsui, expanding the economic benefits from the development to the communities in proximity.

The design concept mirrors the natural topography nearby, shaping unique characteristics for leisure and recreational environments. Due to their different operating hours, the market is located at the bottom level whilst the hotel is on the upper part of the site, with the purpose of enjoying the roof of the market as a garden overlooking the river.

Contemporary functions of the architectural space correlate with the local culture and provide a relaxed atmosphere, establishing convergence of art communities.

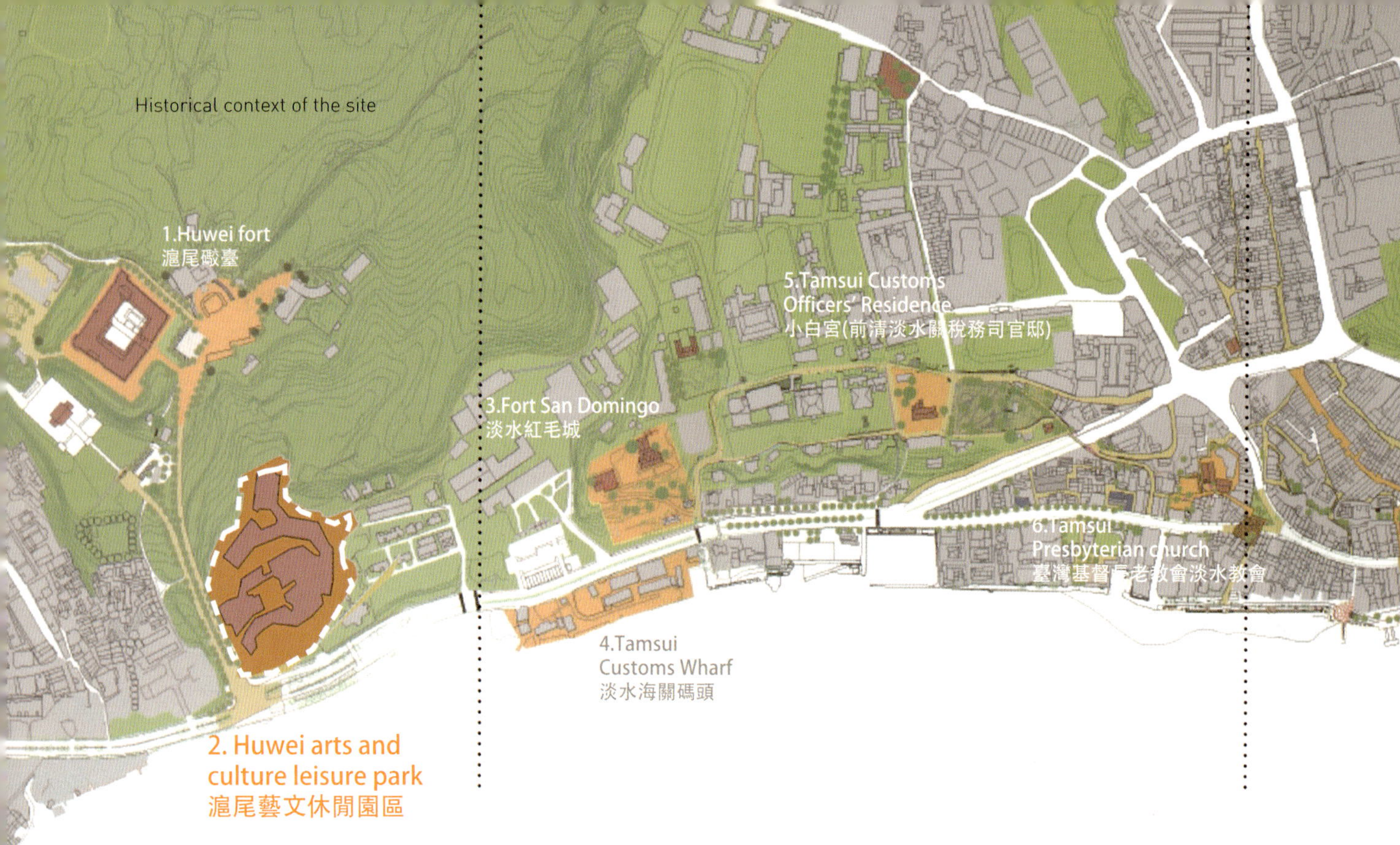

1884 Battle of Tamsui
1884 Guerre Franco-Chinoise

中法古戰場區

Pu-ding Area

埔頂地區

West elevation.

Street Area

漢人市街區

the Heritage Area of Tamsui Pi-A-Tou

鼻仔頭史蹟園區

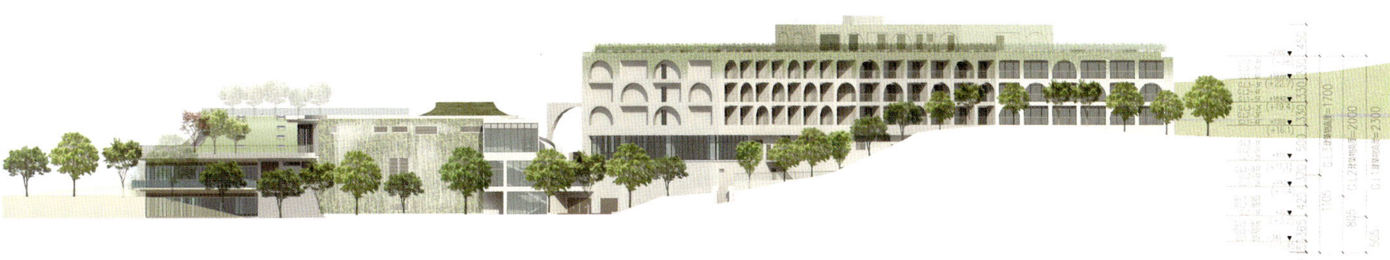

East elevation.

Green roof overlooking Tamsui river and Mount Guanyin.

Huwei Fort + Natural slope + Tamsui Village

Aerial view of the entire complex where the design mirrors the natural topography.

Detailed view of the façade.

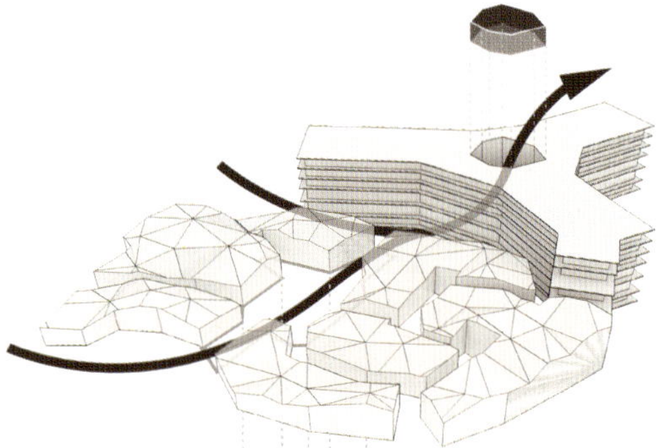

Air circulation in the atrium.

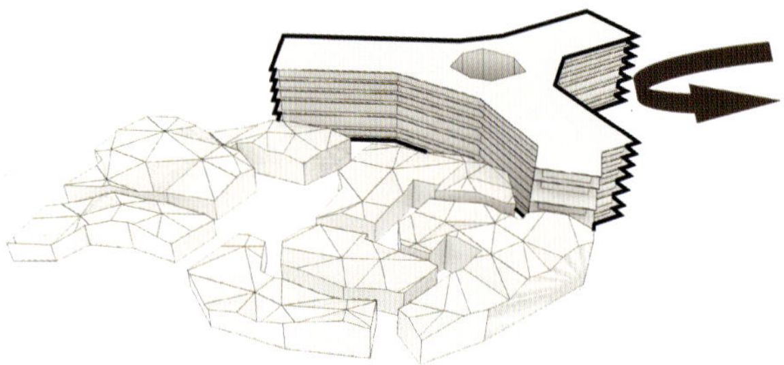

Winter northeast Monsoon

Wind analysis of the site

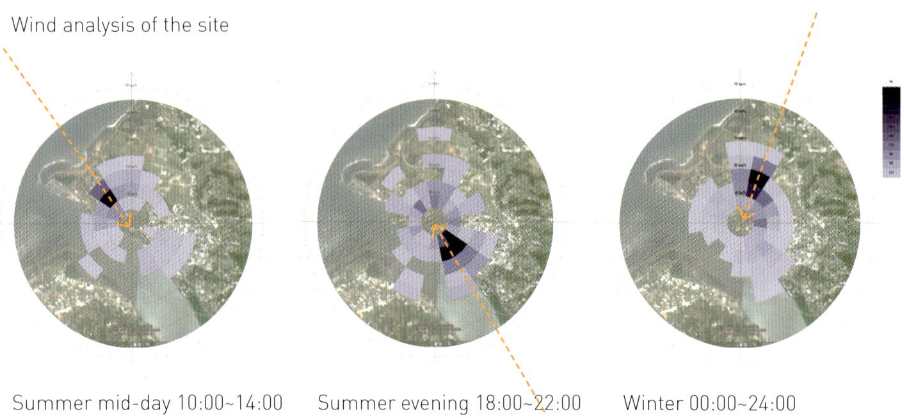

Summer mid-day 10:00~14:00 wind from the river bank

Summer evening 18:00~22:00

Winter 00:00~24:00 wind from northeast

Above: The daily and seasonal wind pattern inspired the massing concept.

Right: Arched façade inspired by nearby Fort San Domingo and Huwei Fort.

Above: The light shaped by the arches bathe the interior of the hotel reception lobby.

Left: Five-story-high atrium at the center of the hotel supports natural ventilation of the building.

program

Individual species fight for their niche in their habitat and become an inseparable part of the ecosystem. The space requirement provided by clients are the named areas and the number of rooms needed; they should be organized, structured, and transformed to a coherent network of spaces to serve as the habitat for people.

These requests from clients can be categorized into tangible and intangible. Tangible requests include: spatial functions, spatial relationship, area, quantity, cost, and timetable. Intangible requests, on thc other hand, include: spatial efficiency, wellbeing of the user, management and maintenance, and public images.

At times the requests from clients can be clear-cut, however, some projects can be ambiguous when it comes to what clients want. Therefore, architects will need to analyze and interpret client's requests in a professional manner by re-assessing and re-integrating spatial requirements in order to develop a unique spatial network. The creation of a relational network, the elevation of usage efficiency and, at the same time, the satisfaction of the client's intangible requests, are all part of the process of developing design ideas.

消防栓
HYDRANT

ABORIGINAL GALLERY AND INNOVATIVE INCUBATION CENTER

TAITUNG CITY, 2016

The design process behind this project was deeply influenced by the indigenous architectural practice of Eastern Taiwan and its peculiar climate. The architecture, furthermore, should celebrate the presence of the seven Aboriginal tribes from this region, scattered between the mountains and the sea.

The design of the Incubation Center encompasses old traditions and existing buildings into new dynamic spaces. The shadow produced by the canopy transforms this hot arid space into a comfortable, ventilated plaza. The incorporation of a terrace overlooking the ocean creates a comfortable space for relaxation in the middle of the plaza turning it into the linking element for the whole project.

The existing building, which functioned as a bus-maintenance garage, has been transformed into a place for multiple workshops that can work flexibly to accommodate different demands.

The program of this project aimed to make the best of the conjunction between old and new. The creation of building elements such as bridges allow for the learning experience to be shared between a mature professional and a young entrepreneur.

ORIGIN

program

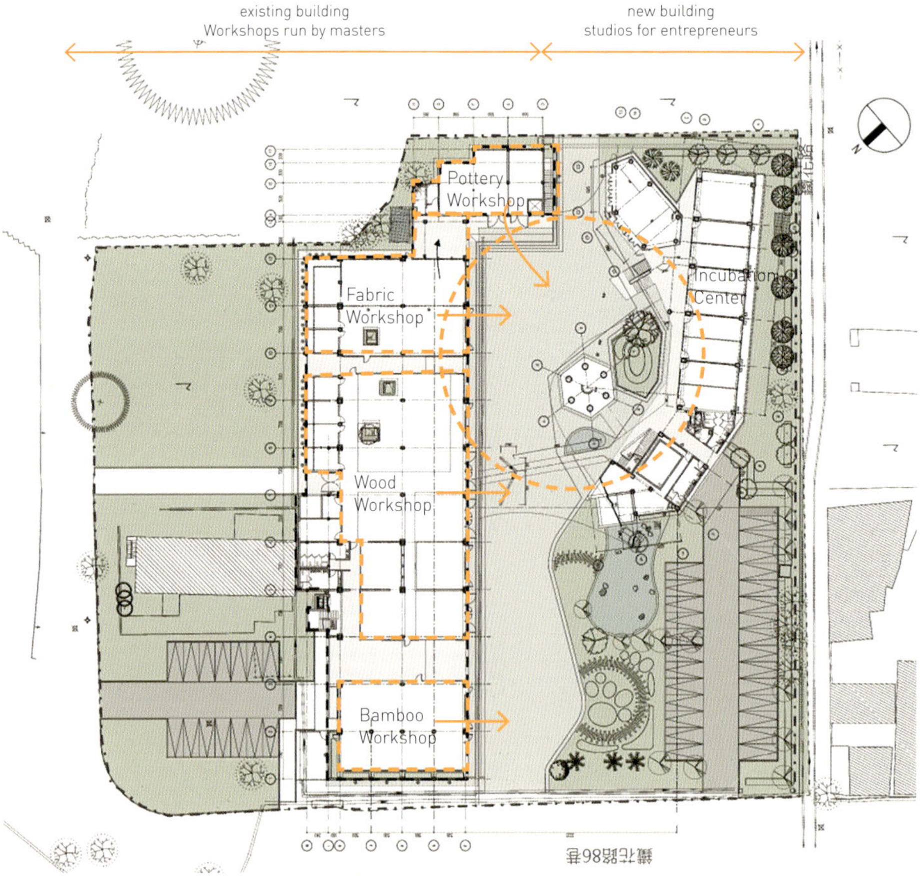

Above (top): Program configuration diagram.
Above (bottom): Strategy used to incorporate old and new.

Right: The interior of the workshop classrooms and the "barn."

Discussion Room

The bridge connects the old and the new part of the complex.

Above: The "barn," which symbolizes prosperity in the tribe, functions as an outdoor meeting room.

Right: The courtyard space sheltered by the canopy.

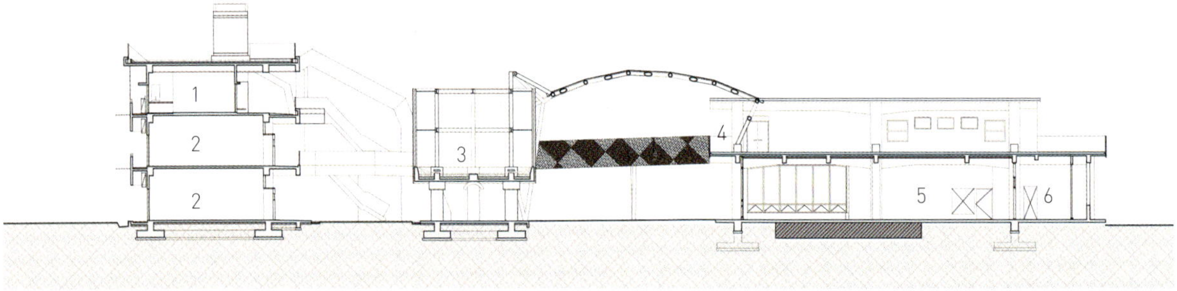
1
2
2
3
4
5
6

Above: The old partition and wood window frame is preserved, to loosely provide boundaries for different workshops.

Left (above): The weathered paint on the existing building was purposely preserved as a reminder of the complex's past.
Left (below): Section through the three different structures.

1 - Teacher's Dormitory Units
2 - Training Offices
3 - Terrace
4 - Connecting Corridor
5 - Wood Art Workshop Classroom
6 - Woodwork Workshop Office

TAIJIANG NATIONAL PARK AND VISITOR CENTER

TAIJIANG, 2016

Taijiang is the oldest settlement for Chinese migrating from mainland to Taiwan. Taijiang National Park was established in 2015 to preserve the landscape and cultural heritage of the region. The site of the visitor center is on a seven hectare fish farm, which houses the tourist service facilities, administrative spaces, the national park police station, and dormitory for the staff.

The building was raised from the ground above the fish farm, acknowledging the on-site natural context. Its design was determined by different factors: the buildings functionality, the public accessibility, and the relationship between the multiple masses and building height were the criteria that decide the outcome of its shape. The alleys and water network break the building masses into smaller forms in order to allow enough ventilation and reduce solar heat.

A connected waterway was established to join individual fish farms on site and to the nearby Taijiang river system. The configuration of the water network system is responsible for reducing the level of evaporation, thus decreasing water salinity and introducing a wider range of biodiversity.

The boundary between public and private was made to be ambiguous due to the openness of the building program. Its inclusivity mirrors a traditional village where the different elements perform together as a whole.

The natural environment becomes the additional program. The re-shape of the bank, which used to be steep, is now the perfect set for new species to live in. All building boundaries, roof, floor, and walls, were planned in order to create a better living space for species like birds and fish.

ORIGIN program

1. Space requirement from the client

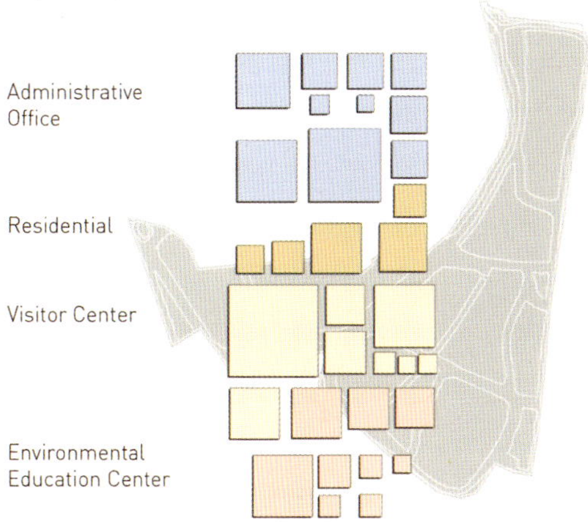

3. Water Program

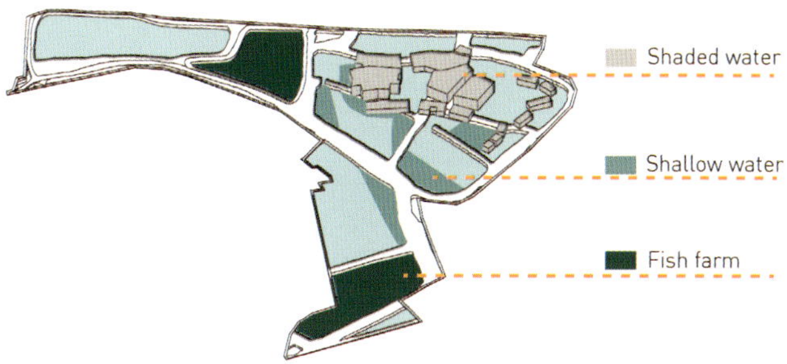

2. Reinterpreted program – Taijian Campus

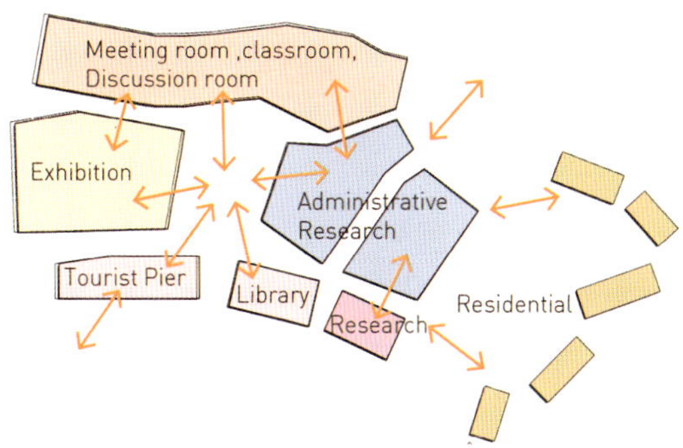

4. Public to Private space

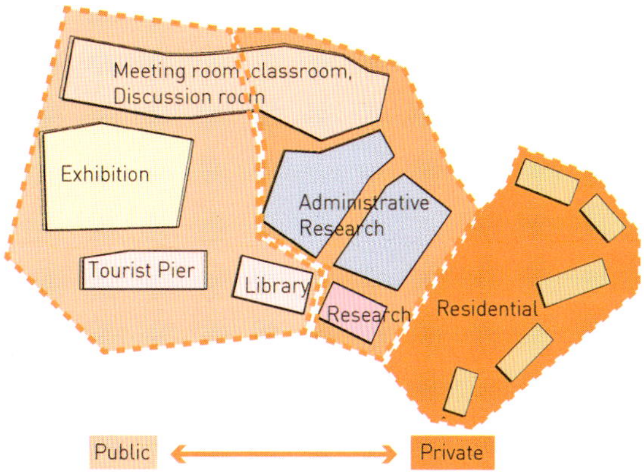

Above: The spatial requirements from the client were regrouped and rearranged to form a village like Taijiang Campus.

Left: Façade made of white oyster shell waste from local farms provide a porous habitat for very small birds and insects.

The residential blocks, mainly north facing, have very small openings along its corridor to protect people from unpleasant north wind during winter.

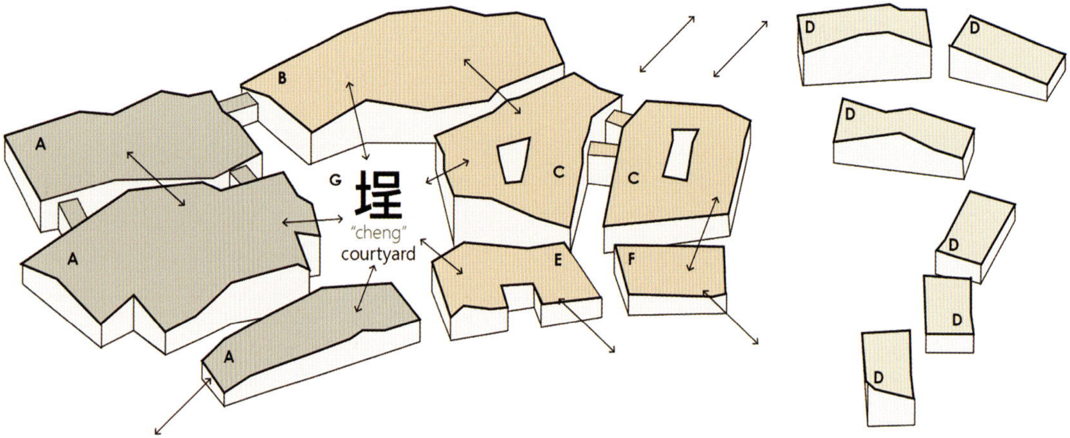

Program configuration diagram.

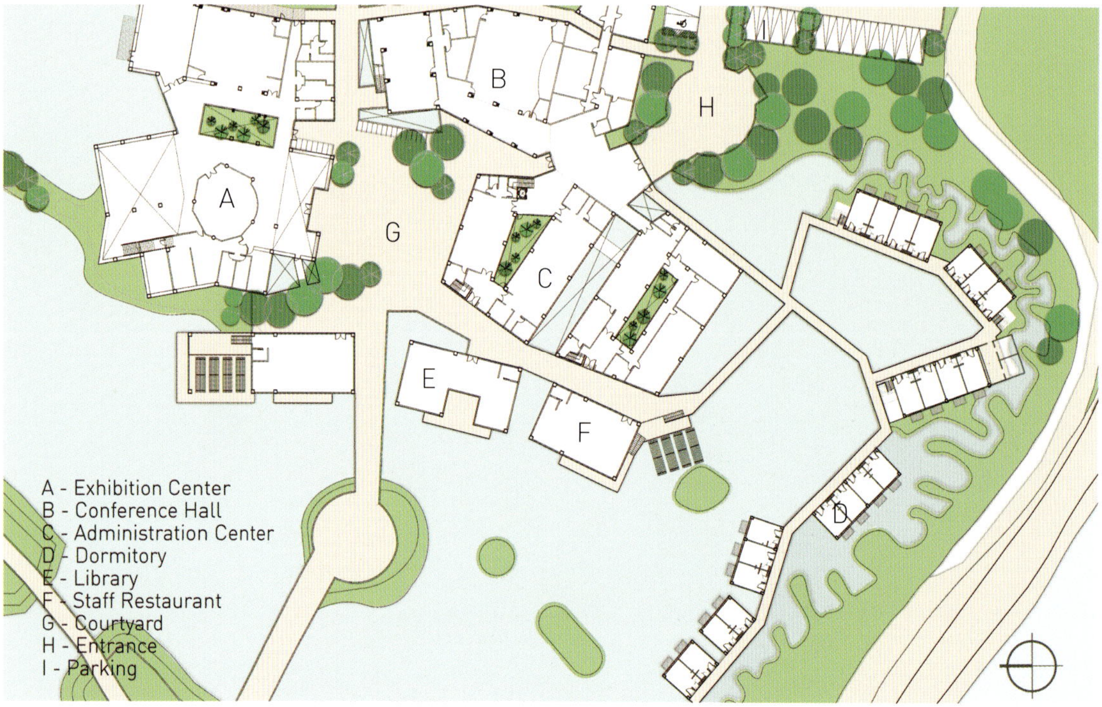

Ground-floor plan with the program description.

Above: As approaching the village, one can easily identify the building which houses the main program for environmental education.
Right: Early sketch of the design.

Above: The Taijiang campus not only is programmed to serve people, but also programmed to serve various species by creating a porous habitat on the roof, walls, and water banks. Animals such as milk fish, mud crabs, white egret, and black-faced spoonbill found a home around the building.
Below: Rethinking the function of traditional building roof: a habitat for the birds.

Left: Salvaged driftwood from a nearby beach provides a natural isolation layer of the roof and nesting site for birds.

Oyster shell waste.

Oyster shell paint.

Above: Shaded spaces are provided by the central plaza.

Left: The interior space bathed with natural light provided by the multiple skylights.

ZHONGSHAN PUBLIC HOUSING

TAIPEI, 2019 (COMPETITION)

This site was part of the Taipei jail during the Japanese colonization, some stone walls and officer's residences still remain on site. This public-housing-project design was inspired through the study of the relations between the historical parts and the old apartment complex on Jinhua Street, one of the oldest streets in Taipei City.

This proposal attempted to preserve the community spaces while simultaneously maintaining a dialogue with its proposed vertical settlements and programs that are relevant to our time. The purpose was to emphasize the spirit of co-living and community assistance, proposing a new generation of public housing.

Due to site restrictions the strategy to implement quality public spaces had to be placed every five floors, compared with the traditional centralized community space. The 5th floor takes cues from the nearby activity facilities, such as the plaza dance class in the neighborhood park and chess in the pavilion, to create a co-playing space that will produce vitality in the surrounding neighborhood within this vertical settlement. The 10th floor features a shared space in the center of the building that combines the needs of different age groups to promote opportunities for generational communication. The 15th floor combines creative and teaching spaces, allowing community residents to share and exchange ideas and learn from each other. The roof-top on the 20th floor not only overlooks the Chiang Kai-shek Memorial Hall and Taipei 101, it also combines sports, runways, aquaponics greenhouses, organic farms, and shared kitchens as a multi-functional floor.

ORIGIN

program

Lin & Li:

Thousand-year-old community concept in China.

Lin: 5 households.

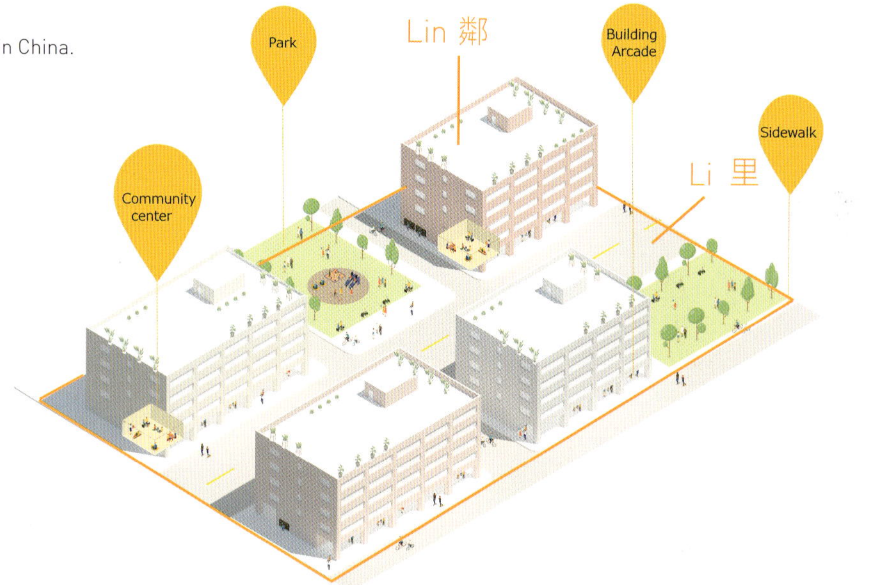

Pattern of housing and public space in Jinhua community.

Li: 5 Lin.

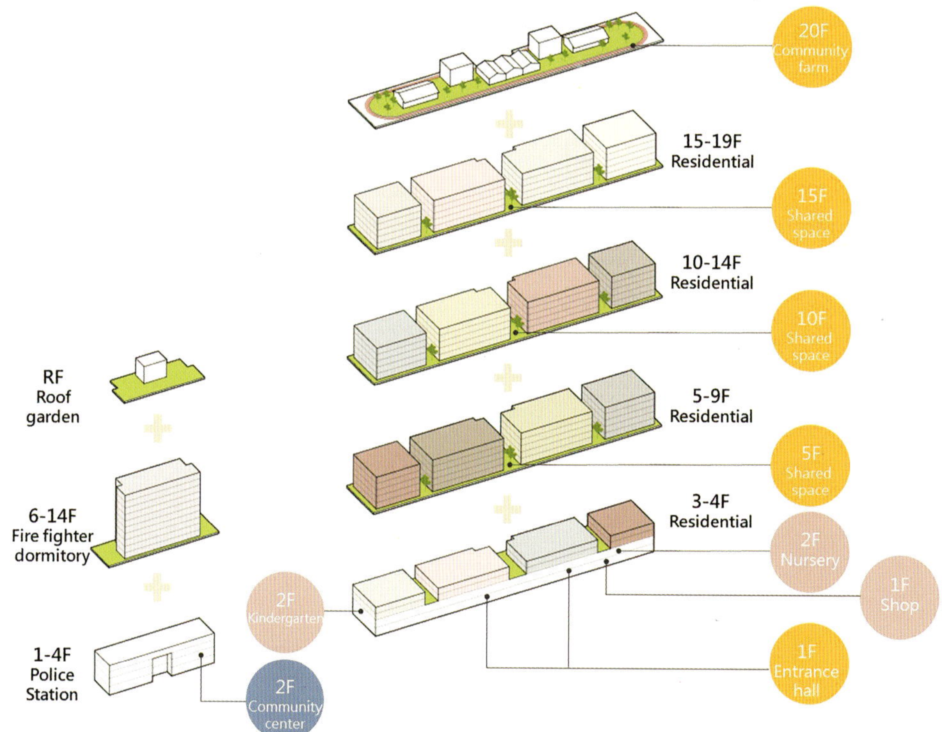

Vertical variation of the Jinhua community.

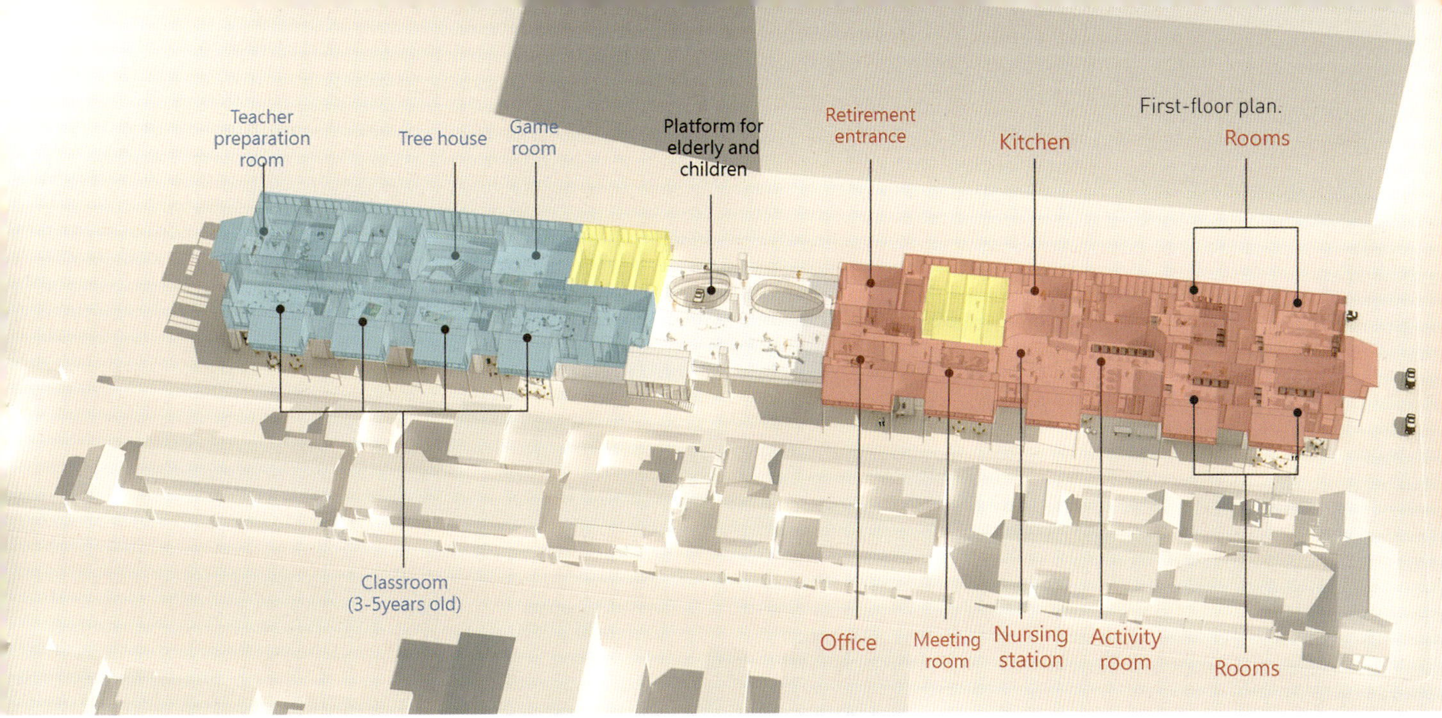
First-floor plan.
Teacher preparation room
Tree house
Game room
Platform for elderly and children
Retirement entrance
Kitchen
Rooms
Classroom (3-5years old)
Office
Meeting room
Nursing station
Activity room
Rooms

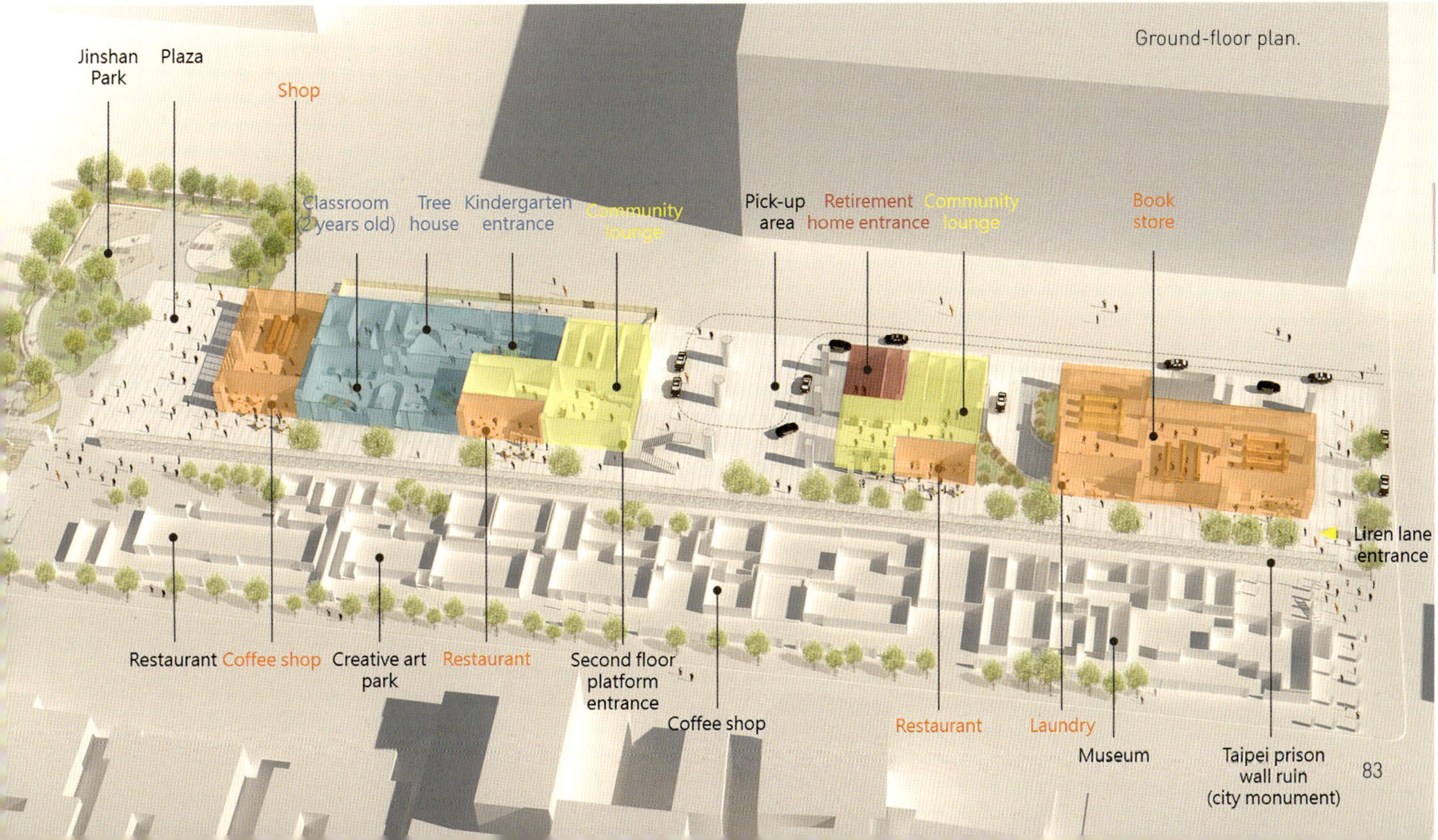
Ground-floor plan.
Jinshan Park
Plaza
Shop
Classroom (2 years old)
Tree house
Kindergarten entrance
Community lounge
Pick-up area
Retirement home entrance
Community lounge
Book store
Liren lane entrance
Restaurant
Coffee shop
Creative art park
Restaurant
Second floor platform entrance
Coffee shop
Restaurant
Laundry
Museum
Taipei prison wall ruin (city monument)

The historical residences for Taipei jail officers.

The historical wall from Taipei jail.

The alley to the entrance of the housing.

Small shops. Stores.

Above: Sectional perspective sketch of the new building communicating with the old.

Right (above): The new, lively Liren Lane.
Right (below): Views of the green community terraces located in between the building blocks.

natural force

The appearance of our land mainly comes from the impulsion, accumulation, erosion, and gravity of the natural forces; while, the appearance of life form mainly depends on its adaptation to natural conditions such as sunlight, water, wind, temperature, and life-sustaining biomass. The characteristics of architecture are somewhere between inorganic landmass and organic biomass, natured and restricted by the same natural forces.

Aside from gravity, natural forces are considered to be architecture's prime restrictor; be that as it may, they can also prove to be a great benefactor just as well. The consensus of the primary benefit for architecture is solar energy, followed by wind energy. In order to provide energy-efficient and comfortable spaces in architecture, the orientation of a building is crucial in avoiding solar radiation, while still accommodating winter sunlight. The acquisition of solar energy will compel the design to tilt the building mass facing south. The high building mass will help block out chilling winter wind while guiding summer wind into the building through well-positioned openings. Design can also take advantage of a sloping roof and the site's topography to retain water during raining days. These responses to natural forces are the deciding factors in shaping and composing the noted architectural mass. In addition, a flexible utilization of the natural forces can also shape a variety of outdoor spaces, semi-outdoor multi-functional spaces, roof top areas, as well as healthy, sustainable indoor spaces that are both well ventilated and lit. The occupants can also be benefited from the bio-diversity of the design. The ever-evolving landscape driven by these natural forces is a mesmerizing source for architectural creativity that can help us shape our design, just as it can shape the earth as well.

ORIGIN natural force

PUBLIC LIBRARY: BEITOU BRANCH

TAIPEI, 2003

The site of Beitou Library is on the western end of Beitou Thermal Valley with Beitou Creek running through the north side of the site, the water from the creek is rich in sulfur, which can cause serious erosion to steel, which is why timber seems to be an obvious choice for building material.

The Beitou Park is rich in nature and history, mainly due to its renowned Hot Springs phenomenon. Hence Beitou Public Library's design approach respects the importance of the site by achieving harmony with nature and consideration of the local ecological environment.

This strategy was meant to make the least impact to the natural environment of the park and to adapt an eco-friendly design approach. The form of this design was the result of considering the natural forces and is strategically positioned on a north-south axis. The lowest and least façade surface was turned toward the west where it houses the equipment space to avoid heat exposure. The façade on the east bears the most openings and utilizes the surrounding trees for shade. The north-side façade connects to nature by opening itself to the park. Encompassing the building is the balcony which permits windows to be opened freely allowing natural ventilation and shade in order to reduce solar-heat radiation. The selection of timber for the building structure not only efficiently withstands the sulfur water from the creek that crosses the whole linear park but also helps create a warm and welcoming atmosphere into the inside reading space. The green roof also does a great job at blending the entire building in with the surrounding natural environment. Last but not least, the materials used for the outdoor pavement were carefully selected in order to allow permeability.

Ecoroof cultivation area for the regional vegetation to grow freely
Ecoroof (extensive type)
Solar panel (16,000 watt)
Rainwater collection system
Natural ventilation and lighting
Timber walkway and stair to the rooftop
Rainwater collection filter tank
Wooden veranda and outside reading space

Above: First-floor plan.

Left: Aerial view of the Library building within Beitou Park.

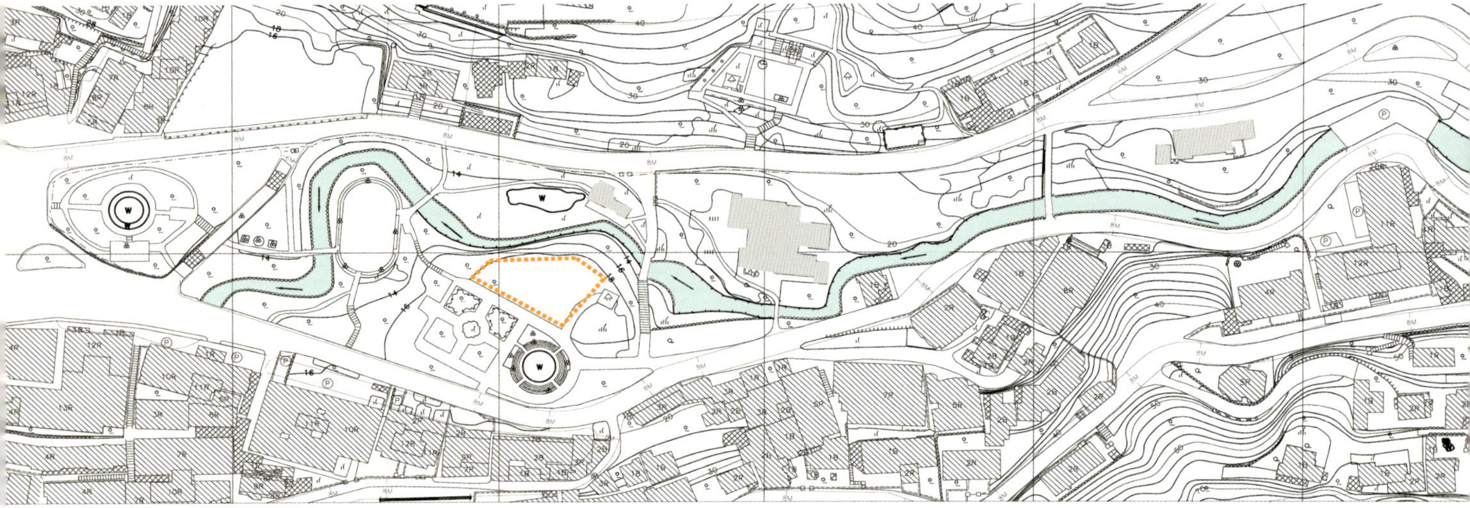

Above: Beitou Creek runs through the north side of the site.
Below: Section.

Right (above): The roof is designed to harvest the rain water while the slope is gentle enough for wheelchair accessibility.
Right (below): The warm wooden interior space.

1.Open-stack room
2.Newspaper/periodical
3.Open-air reading space
4.Children's reading room
5.Rainwater collection tank
6.Roof activity area

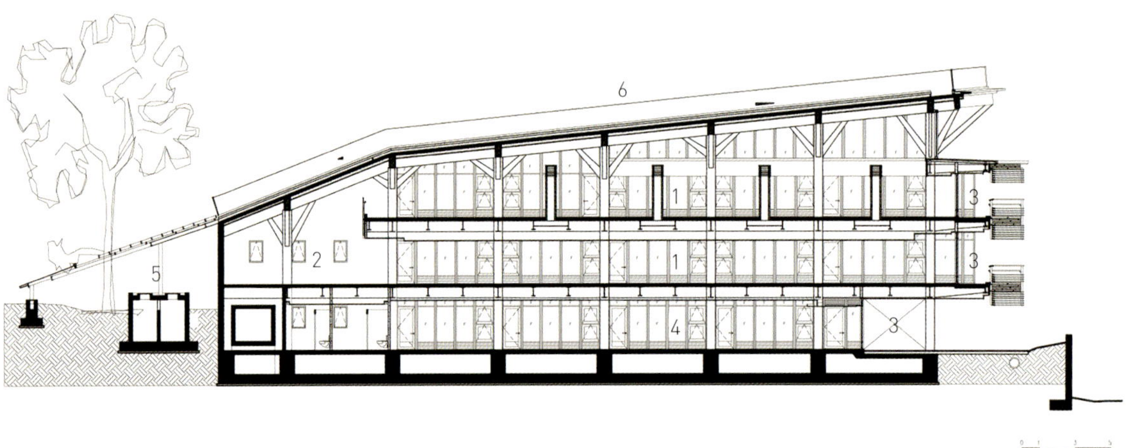

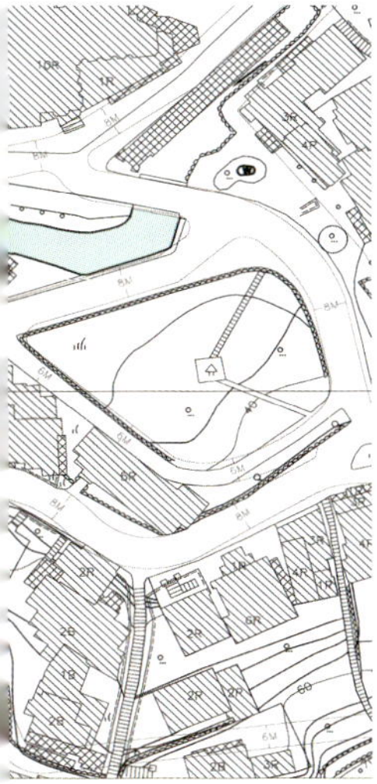

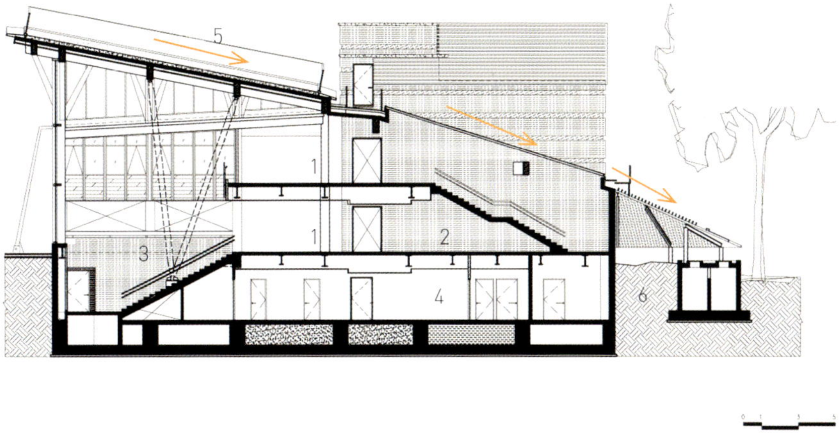

1.Open-air reading space
2.Newspaper/periodical
3.Story-telling room
4.Children's reading room
5.Roof activity area
6.Rainwater collection tank

Left: East façade with large openings protected by the existing trees.

Right: Balcony on the north side provides shading in the summer and users can read outdoors overlooking the surrounding nature.

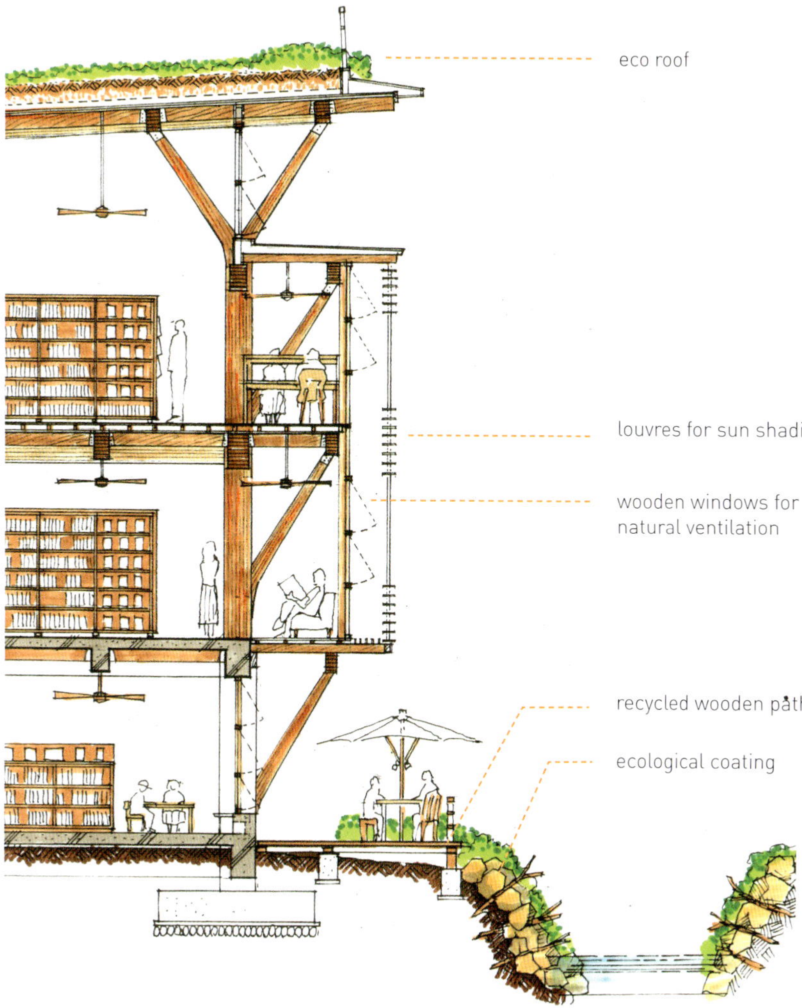

Above: Section drawing showing the relationship between the building's façade and the Beitou Creek.

Left: The openings allow for generous natural light to get in for a more comfortable reading experience.

SHALUN GREEN ENERGY DEMONSTRATION CAMPUS
TAINAN, 2017

Solar energy is abundant in southern coastal Taiwan. This building complex develops solar energy technology and provides facilities for PV field testing. Besides that, the campus will work as an incubator for public education, which will be crucial in narrowing the gap between the consumer and this growing industry.

The program consisted of a research building, testing warehouse, demonstration and education center, energy center, demonstration houses, smart parking building, and a dormitory for scholars. The design of the building was the result of various local micro-climate analyses. Therefore, the intention was to preserve a large, green landscape area and various courtyards. As the open space scheme was carefully crafted, an eco-pond was created on the south side to ease the gruesome southern wind during the summer.

Appropriate exterior openings were designed to guide cool air into the interior to achieve low-energy consumption. After heat-radiation simulations, suitable materials are selected for the exterior façade and roof in order to achieve a higher heat-resistant rating that will translate into a cooler interior effect. The implementation of trees were made along the courtyards and paths to provide shade to these outdoor areas.

ORIGIN
natural force

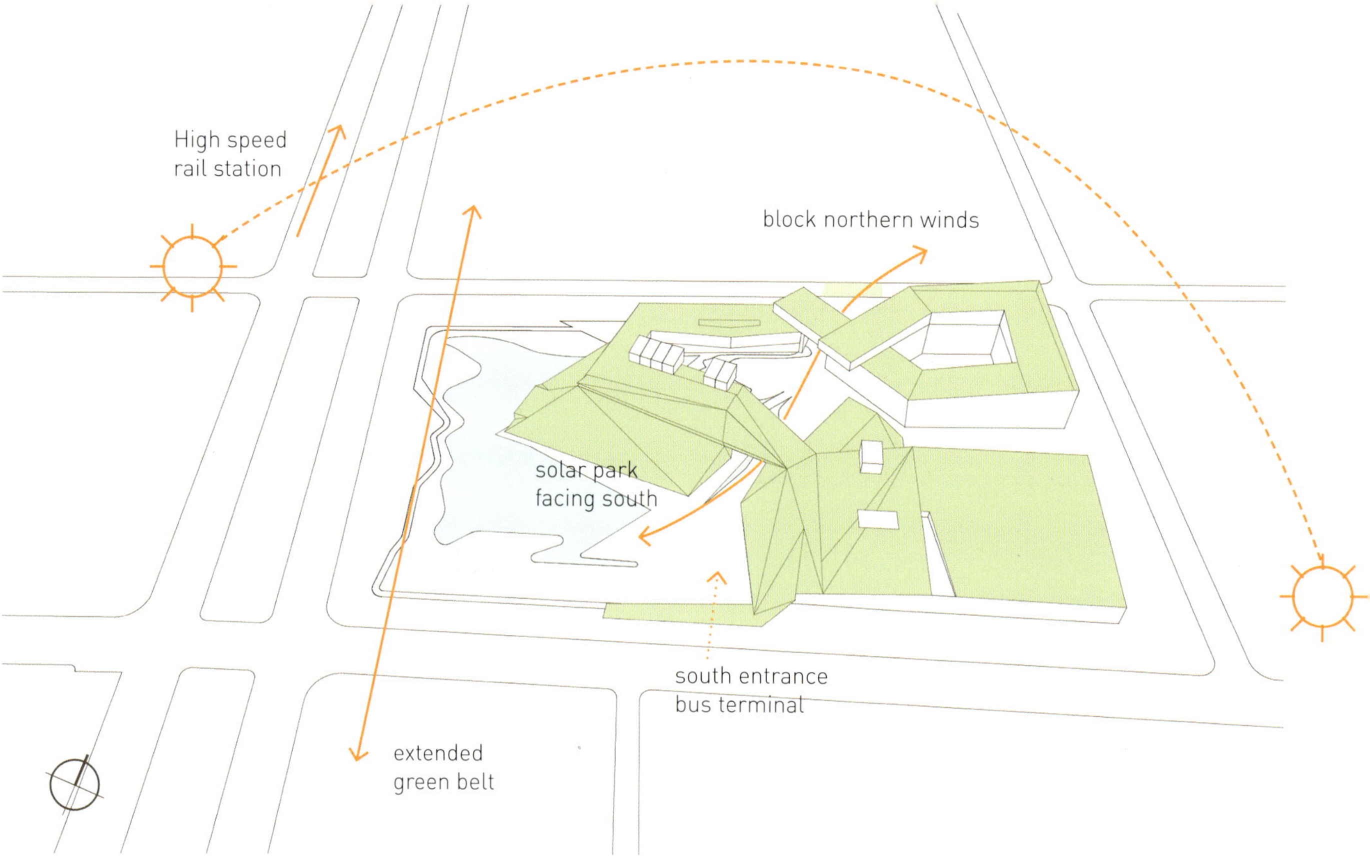

Above: Sloped roofs directed towards the south maximize efficiency of the PV panels and act as an extension of the park.

Right: Solar Garden diagram showing the different uses of PV panels as a demonstration for educational purpose.
Below: Section through the site showing the relationship between the building and landscape.

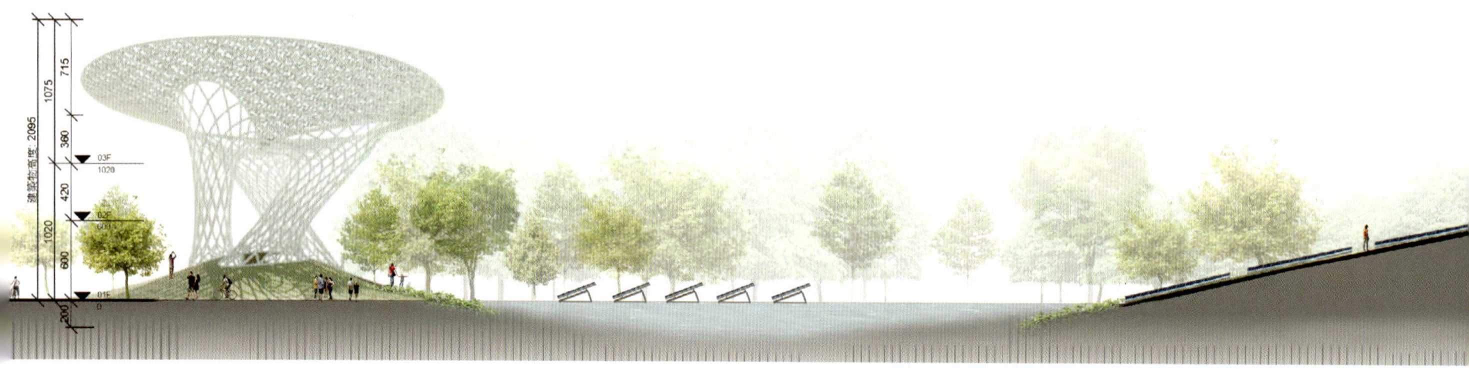

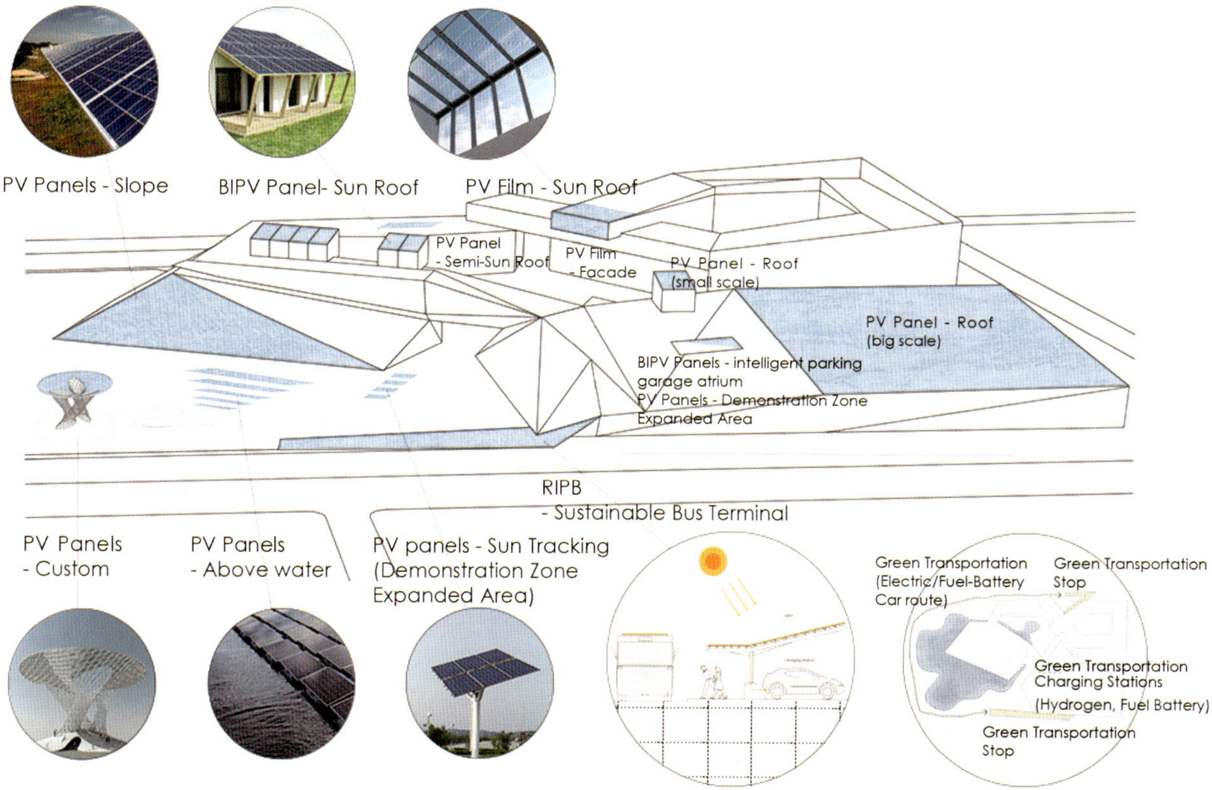
PV Panels - Slope
BIPV Panel- Sun Roof
PV Film - Sun Roof
PV Panel
- Semi-Sun Roof
PV Film
- Facade
PV Panel - Roof
(small scale)
PV Panel - Roof
(big scale)
BIPV Panels - intelligent parking
garage atrium
PV Panels - Demonstration Zone
Expanded Area
RIPB
- Sustainable Bus Terminal
PV Panels
- Custom
PV Panels
- Above water
PV panels - Sun Tracking
(Demonstration Zone
Expanded Area)
Green Transportation
(Electric/Fuel-Battery
Car route)
Green Transportation
Stop
Green Transportation
Charging Stations
(Hydrogen, Fuel Battery)
Green Transportation
Stop

展示交流
招待所
招待所
餐廳(200人座位)及廚房
04F
1440
03F
1020
02F
600
01F
0
420
420
600
200
建築物高度: 1440

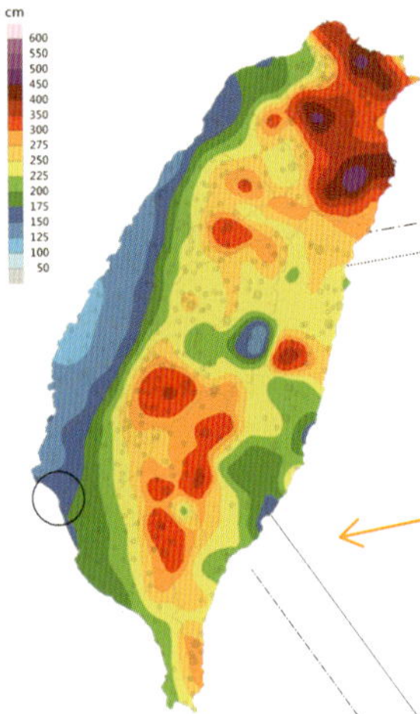

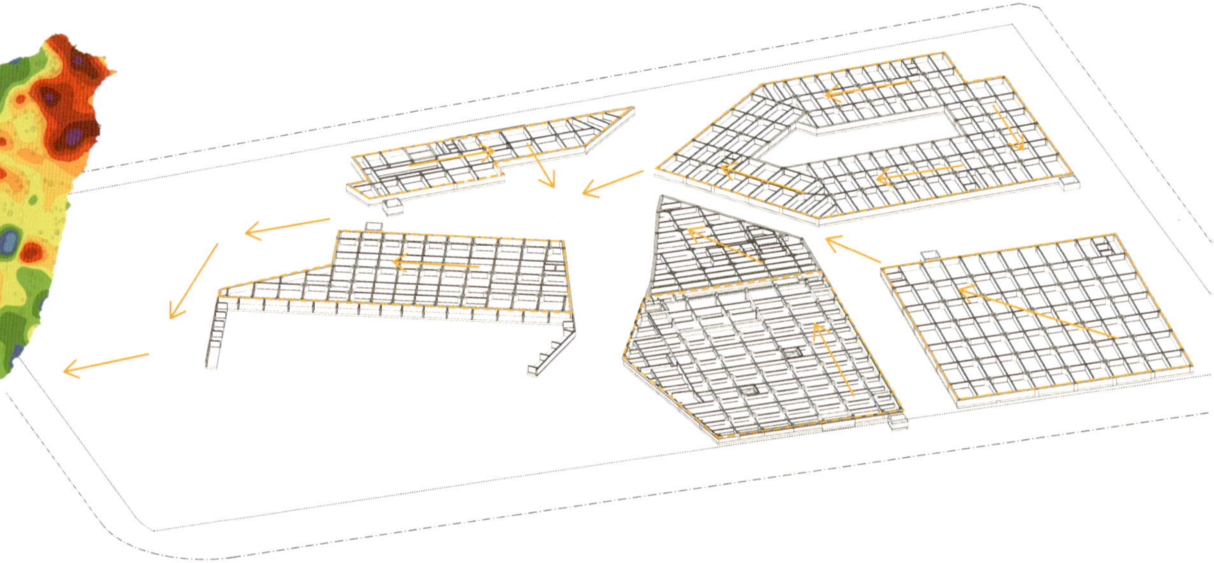

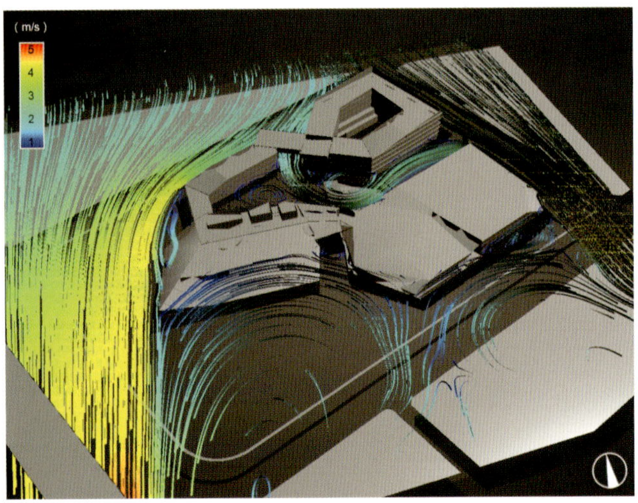

Wind simulation winter – northern wind

Wind simulation summer – southern wind

Above (bottom): Wind simulation graphics. Source: Building and Climate Lab, NCKU.
Above (top left): Map of Taiwan with analysis of the annual rainfall distribution from 1989 to 2010. the purple color corresponds to the greatest amount of rainfall and the blue color corresponds to the least amount. Source: Taiwan Typhoon Flood Research Center, National Research Institute.
Above (top right): Due to highly even rainfall throughout the year, the "raft" foundation also functions as a reservoir which can store 10,000m^3 of rain water for irrigation and feed the eco-pond.

Right (above): Double-skin, green façade provides shading for the research center building.
Right (below): The perforated metal panels and the green strings together filter the fierce sun-light before they enter the buildings.

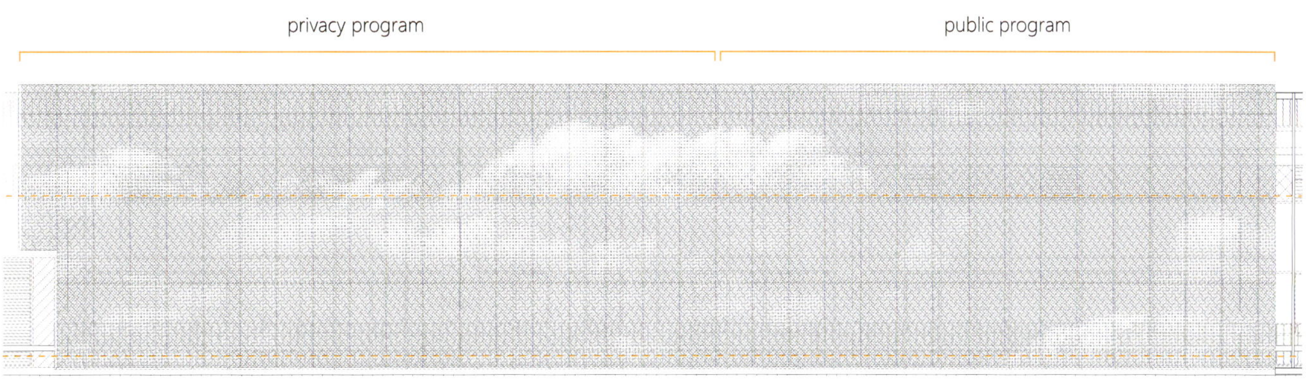
privacy program
public program

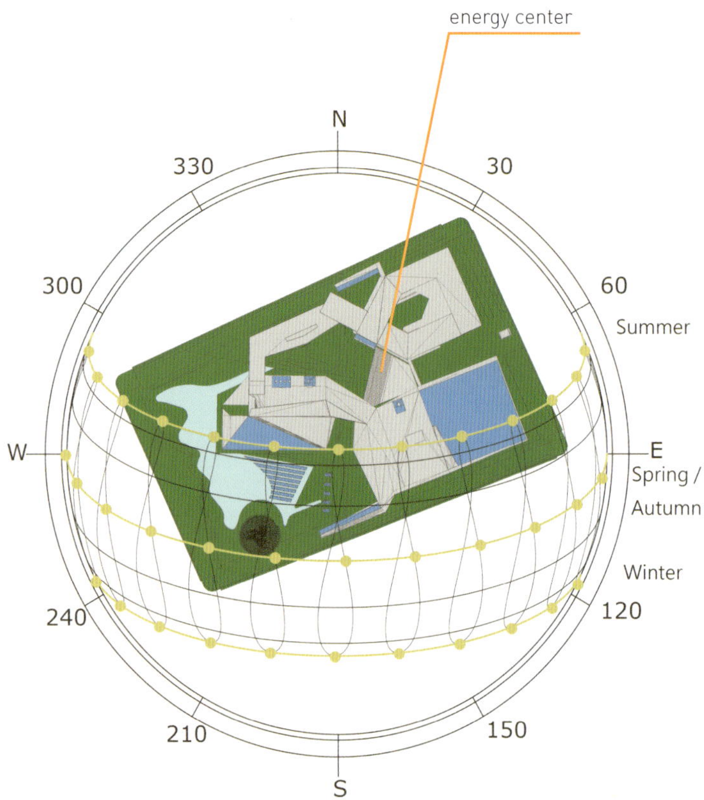

The Energy Center is positioned in the center of the campus to distribute electricity, water, and chilled water for HVAC for the whole campus.

Above: Sun path diagram.

Right: The green courtyard is the center of the complex.

energy center

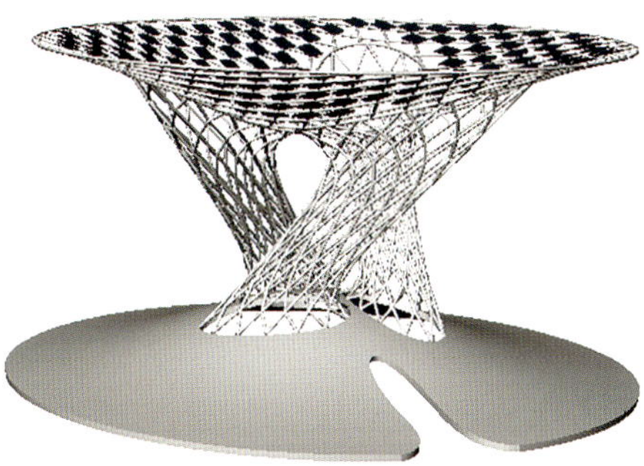

Left: The solar tree symbolizes the new era of renewable energy; its tree trunks represent Environment, Education, and Economy – E^3, the mission of this project.

Right: Solar tree under construction.

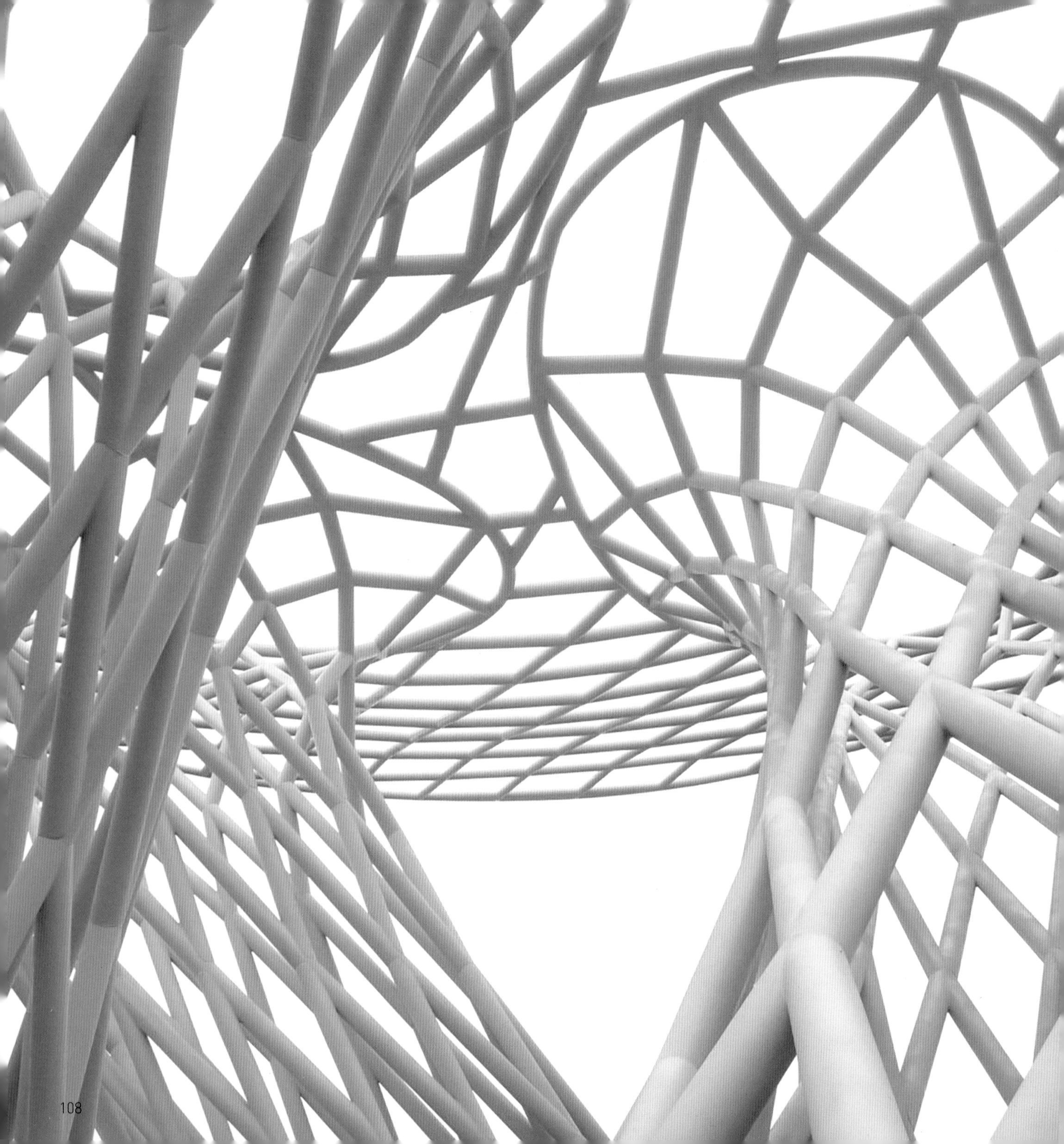

The solar tree, in order to allow for a wider energy-collecting surface, uses not one but three trunks to support its crown. Its hollow structure, composed of a network of tubes that runs between its "root" and its "leaves," conveys a light-weight feeling to a massive structure.

SHIMEN CIRCULAR VILLAGE
NORTH COAST TAIWAN, 2018

Located amid beautiful mountain scenery, with an outstanding view of the Pacific Ocean, this project aspires to build with the greatest respect for nature and its environment. This future park plan is for an environmental education center with accommodation facilities. The proposal embraces the charming forest with a strategy for low-maintenance and a minimal footprint.

The site condition is peculiar as it has the topography of cliffs, ridges, plains, valleys, and the geographical conditions of the adjacent sea areas. The rich environmental changes create diversified habitat conditions, thus enriching the wealthy ecosystem. In order to enhance the connection with nature the concept of "bare necessity" is developed. The living facilities are designed with the minimum of unit space, which accommodates only the most basic needs for its tenants. The main-activity area separates spaces for each different need and also uses a modular pre-fabricated construction system. The boundary between inside and outside, man-made and natural is no longer so absolute. The overall plan aims to reduce man-made materials and relatively enlarge the natural environment.

ORIGIN natural force

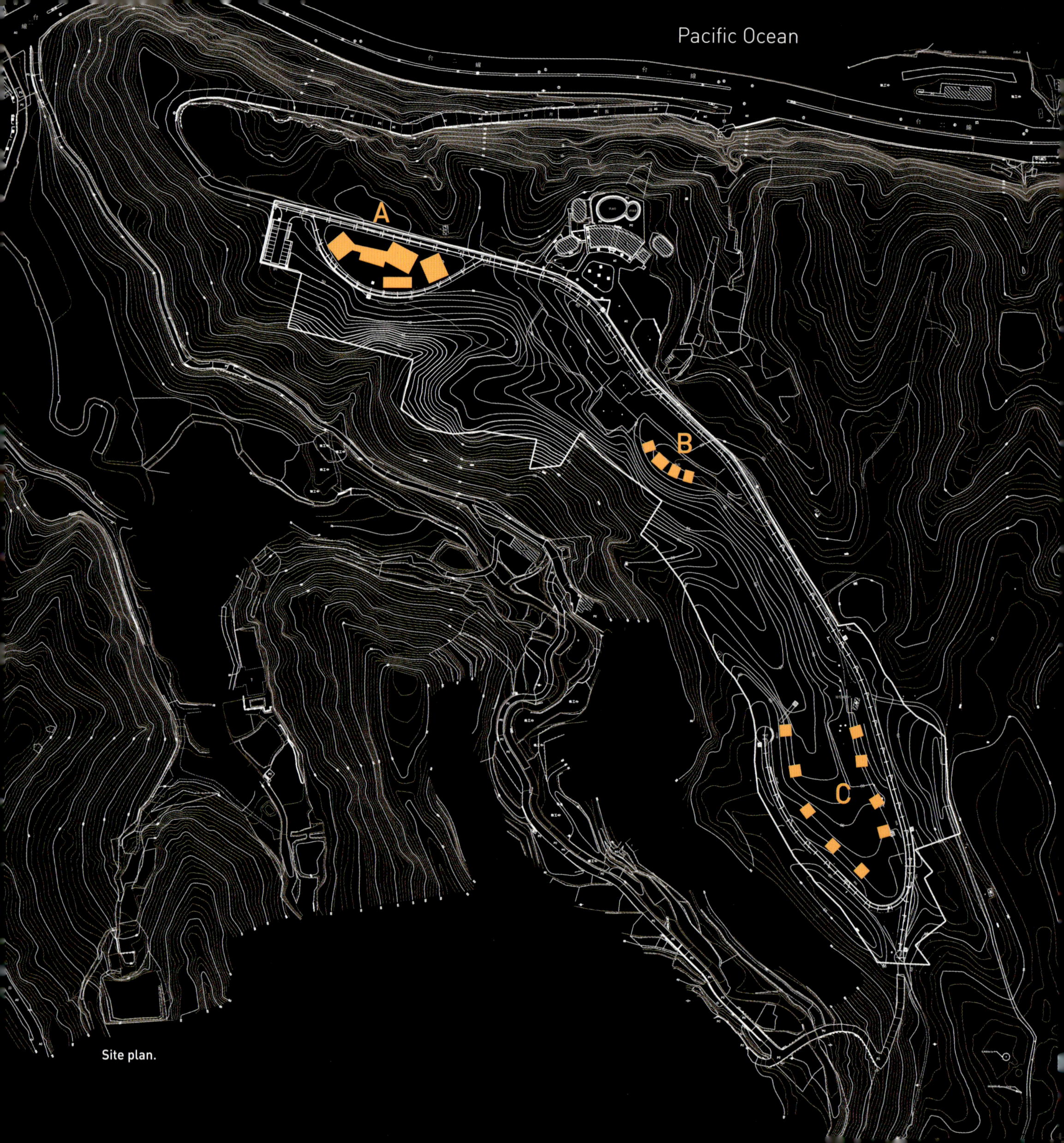

Site plan.

Schematic sections explaining the design approach to the three different shapes of the terrain.

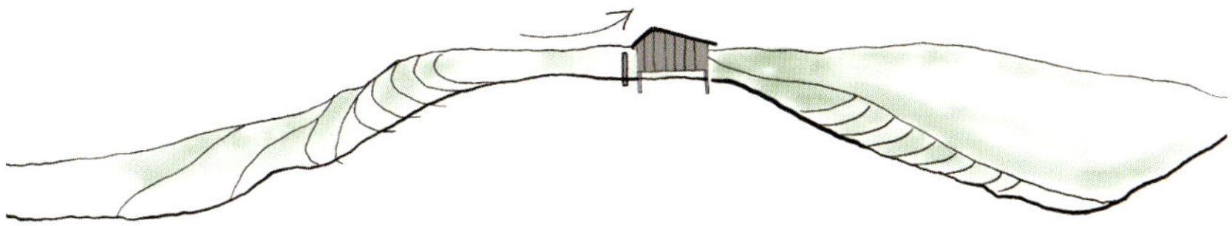

AREA A – Located at the northwest part of the site exposed to the ocean's breeze and winds.

AREA B – Site partially exposed to the winds.

AREA C – Southeastern-site valley protected by the mountain and forest.

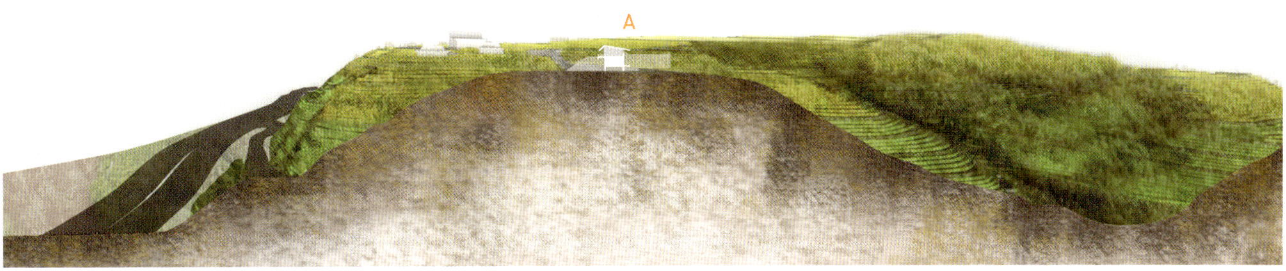

Section through the terrain, zone A.

Inspired by the indigenous architecture on Orchid Island, an island in the Pacific off Taiwan's east coast, the "wind wall" (using local stacked rock) was placed to the north of the building to guide the northern gust winds over the roof.

Above: The interior space protected by the wall.
Right: Orchid Island wall that inspired the design.

Left (above): The buildings closed towards north winds.
Left (below): Orchid Island houses protected against harsh weather.

Above: The complex opens towards south and hides towards north.
Right: Early sketch of the composition.

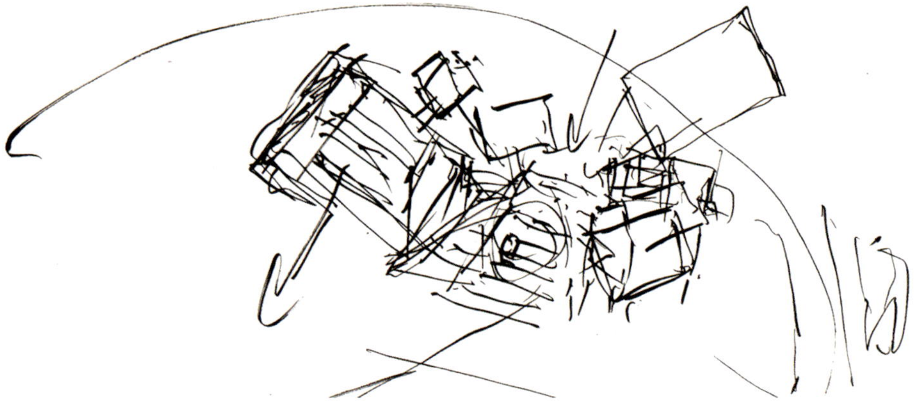

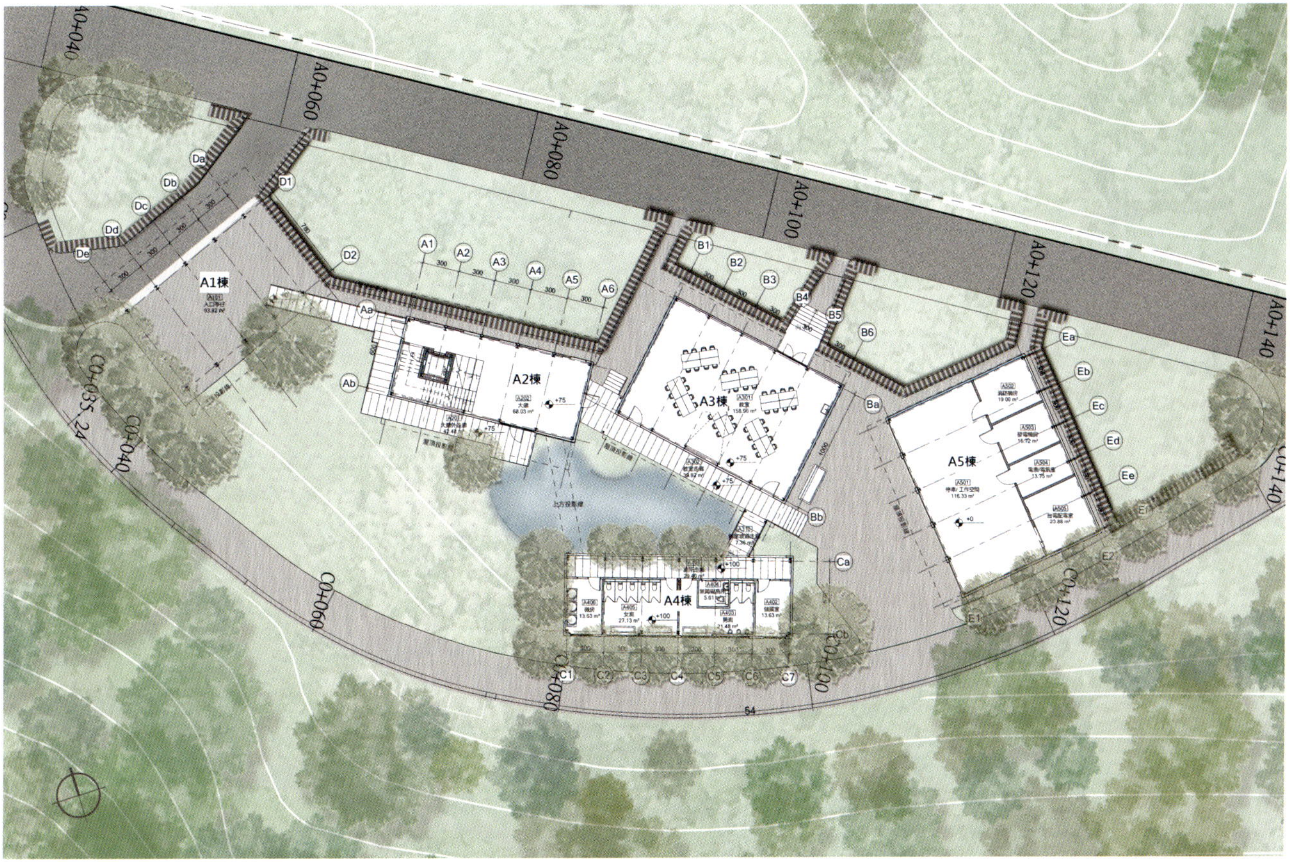

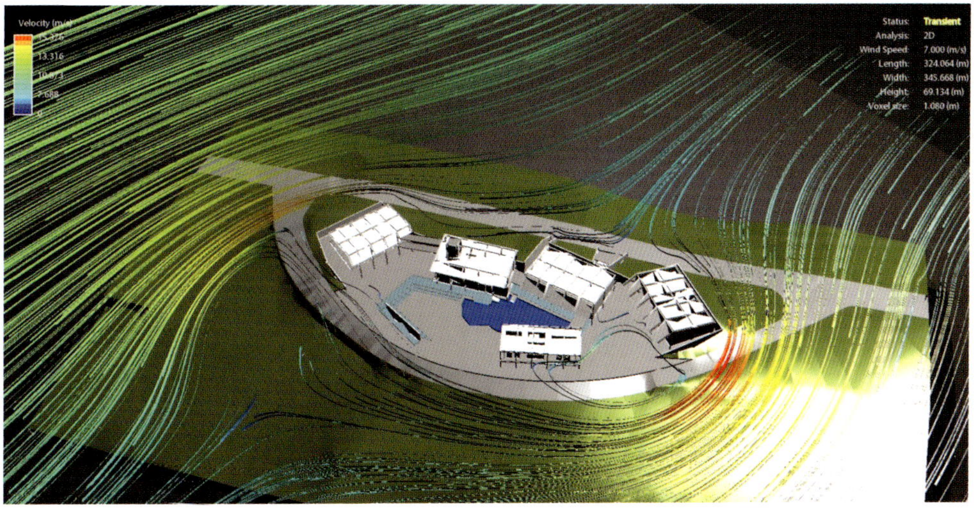

Above: Ground-floor plan. Right: Wind simulation graphics. Source: Building and Climate Lab, NCKU.

Sectional perspective

Interior view

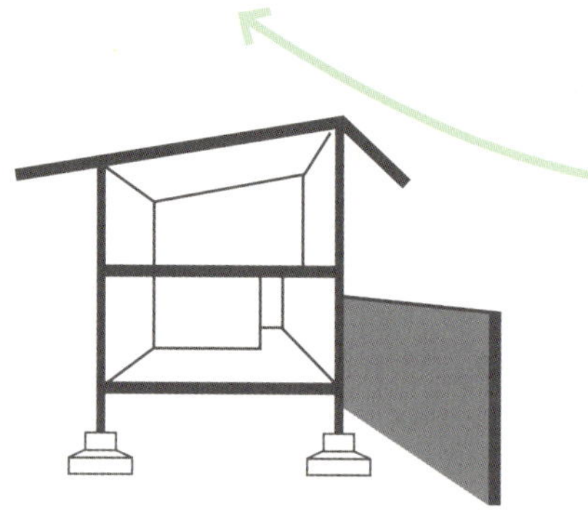

A2 Hall and semi-outdoor platform

The appearance of the A2 building is completely different from that of the A1 building. Most of the solid walls respond to the internal space and external environmental conditions. However, the 1F north is ventilated by the landscape stone wall, and the open-floor sliding door is designed to meet the needs of ventilation and landscape.

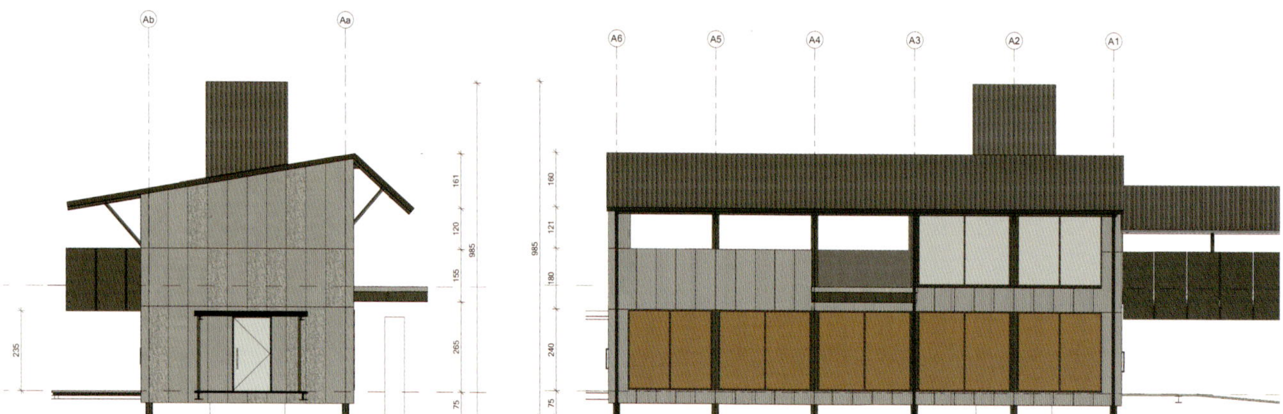

Elevations

Sectional perspective

Interior view

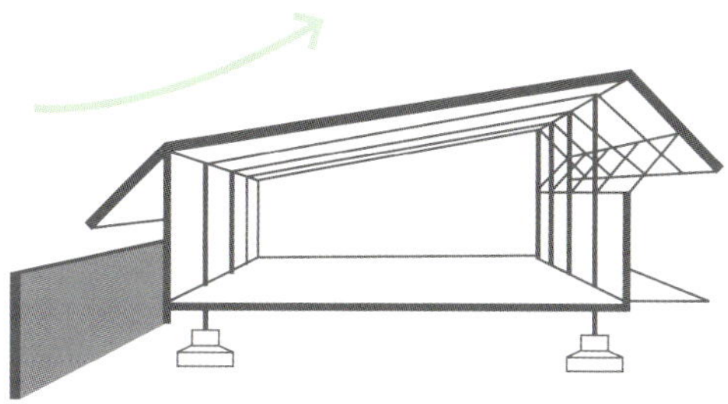

A3 Classroom space

This building is a single-story building with a sloping roof. The short façade is a solid wall, and the long wall is only open at a high place. With the height of the roof flap, it can also introduce sufficient natural light while controlling the north wind.

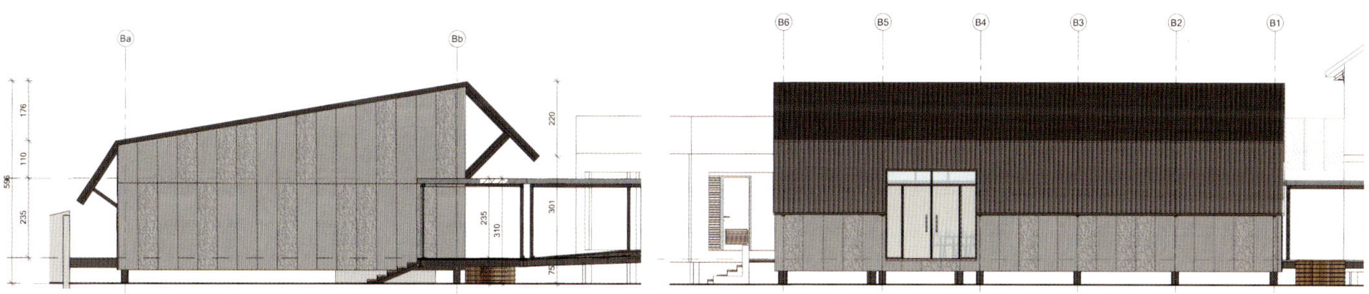

Elevations

Life composes a symphony with just a few notes; with only four nucleobases (A, T, G, and C) a long string of DNA, which carries the reproduction instructions of a species, is composed. Different life forms are created just through the variation in the line-up of the nucleobases. Therefore, despite their diverse appearances, they share similar internal systems. In the process of architecture design, there is only a limited amount of materials and construction systems that can be used.

Regardless, infinite possibilities are still achieved through the technological improvement and hybridization of different materials and construction systems. In the midst of all these possibilities, the circulatory system plays a crucial role in the development of architectural space. The circulatory system, like an organism's life sustaining system, circulates people, resources, and energy throughout the building; bringing non-organic materials and construction systems to life.

FORM

circulation
FORM
structural system
building material

circulation

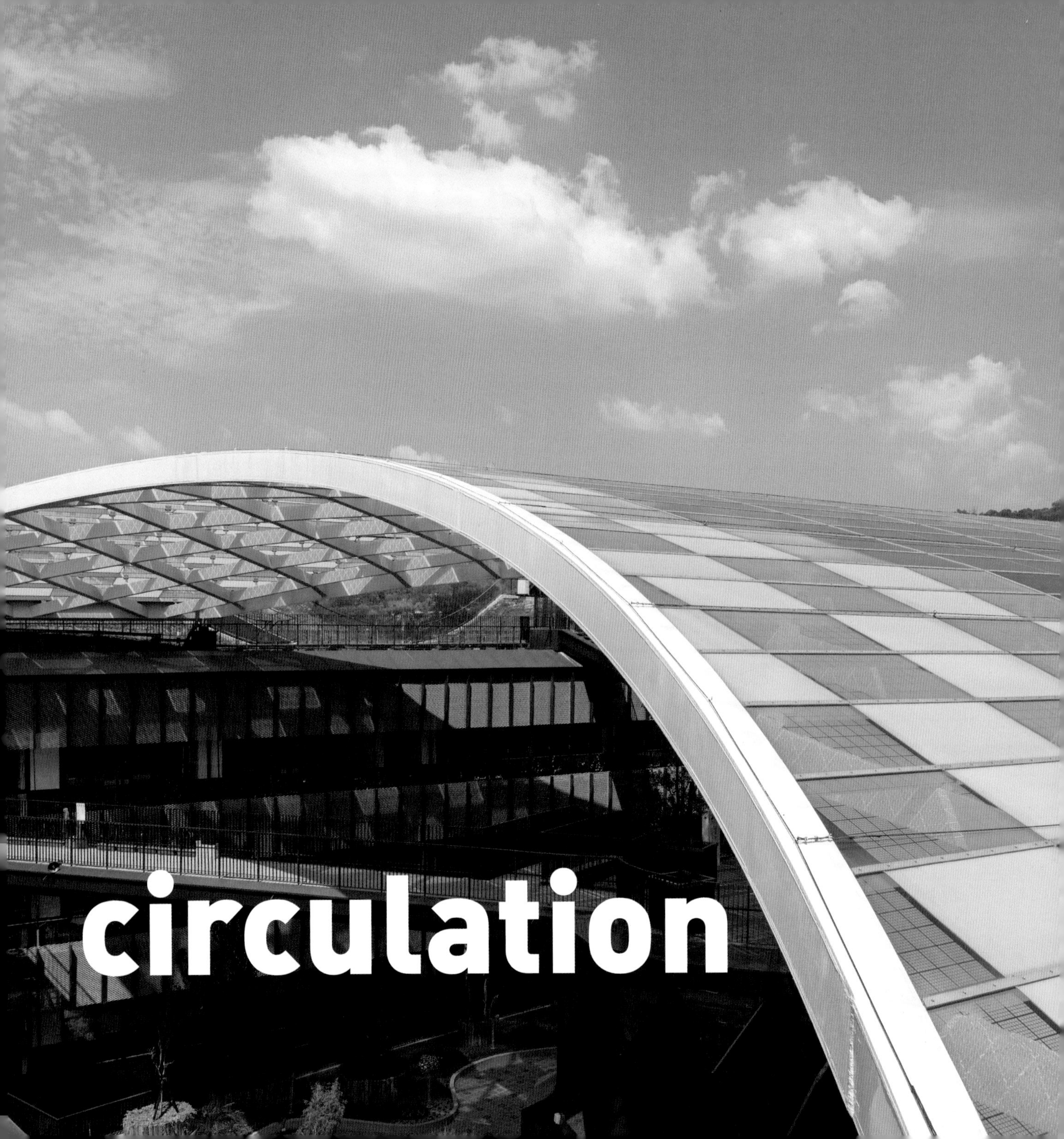

The circulatory system is the life-sustaining system of a building, the bridge that connects the different parts of a building and its site to the surroundings. More specifically, it can be imagined as a framework that organizes different parts of the architecture, horizontally by pathways, hallways, corridors, as well as vertically by elevators, occupants, and vehicles. The Circulatory system is a deciding factor on the efficiency of the design, because as people and goods move along through the system, telecommunication cables and electricity, HVAC systems are all arranged in accordance with it.

We can imagine the circulatory system as a dynamic network of energy flow, and through it, the energy of the surrounding environment is guided into the site and the interior of the architecture. Vice versa, the energy of the interior and the site can also be distributed outwards. The energy referred to includes solar, wind, biosphere, occupants and activities, noise and sometimes pollutants. Imagine the wind as a guide that directs the crafting of the main circulation, and all the corresponding activities are developing along that path and finally are gathered around the areas where one can be immersed in the rays of sunlight. As for the main vertical circulation, the views can create a sense of community by linking together essential functions and activities. Since the network of nature will always form into a loop, therefore architecture can share that similarity by effectively creating a guiding network for energies that can also become a loop that connects the interior with the exterior, and the ground level with the roof; providing an invisible energy to the form of the complementary architecture.

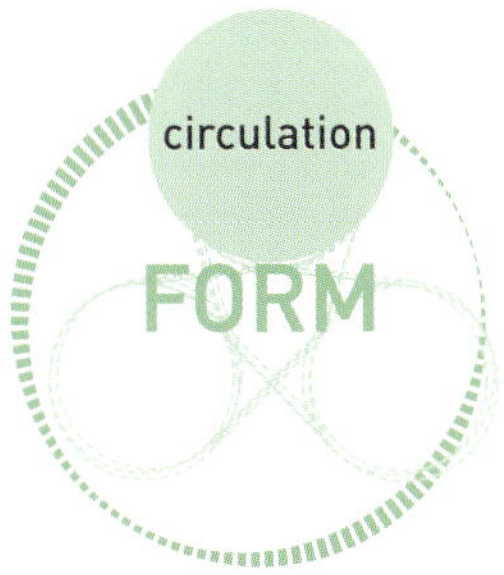

CENTRAL TAIWAN INNOVATION CAMPUS

NANTOU, 2014

CTIC is a research hub which also welcomes the community to use its canteen, lecture hall, exhibition space, and multilevel gardens, so two circulation loops are required, one for the public, the other restricted for internal use only.

The journey of these researchers starts from the entrance plaza on the ground level containing an eco-pond, continues through the lobby, then to the employees dining area, and proceeds to the lobby in the restricted zone. The three different courtyards connect different levels of the building allowing for this journey to be diverse and sensorially rich. The exhibition space and the library located at the core area connect with the laboratories and offices through the footbridges, which as a whole serve as a common space for the researchers to exchange their creative ideas.

The general public can begin their visit by passing through the lobby and going up the steps at the central atrium. Natural light and the ambience of greenness are introduced into the interior through the full-height glass panels which also allows indoor activities to be extended to the outdoor platform. The semi-outdoor platform on the rooftop houses trees and vegetation, as well as a canopy formed by solar panels, these spaces are intended for the public to stay and take a rest. The general public can therefore enjoy overlooking the spectacular view of Bagua Plateau without any obstruction.

The façade is composed entirely of metal-framed curtain walls and aluminum-louver panels; 3,358 pieces of architectural exterior sunshades, designed by Noiz Architects (Keisuke Toyoda and Chia-Hsuan Tsai), were manually installed by the construction team.

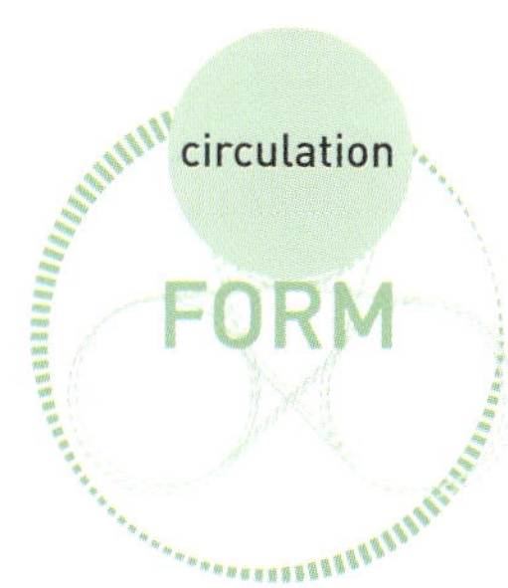

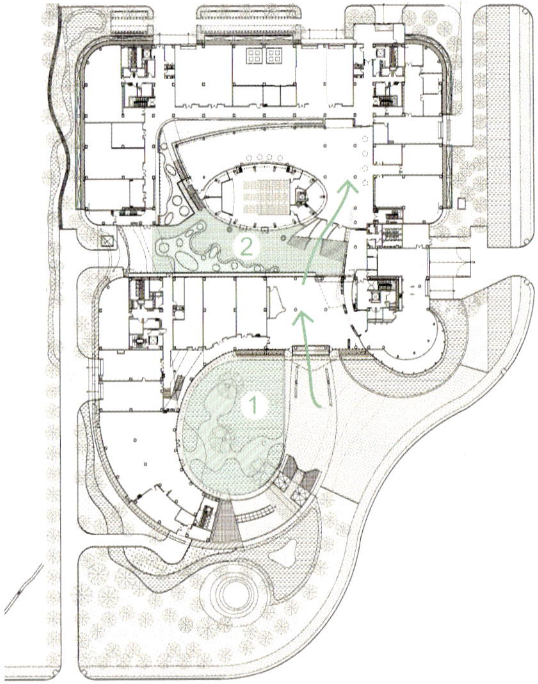

Ground-floor plan.

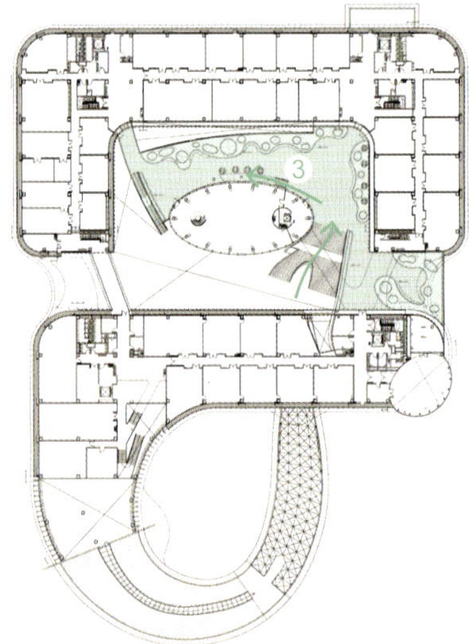

First-floor plan.

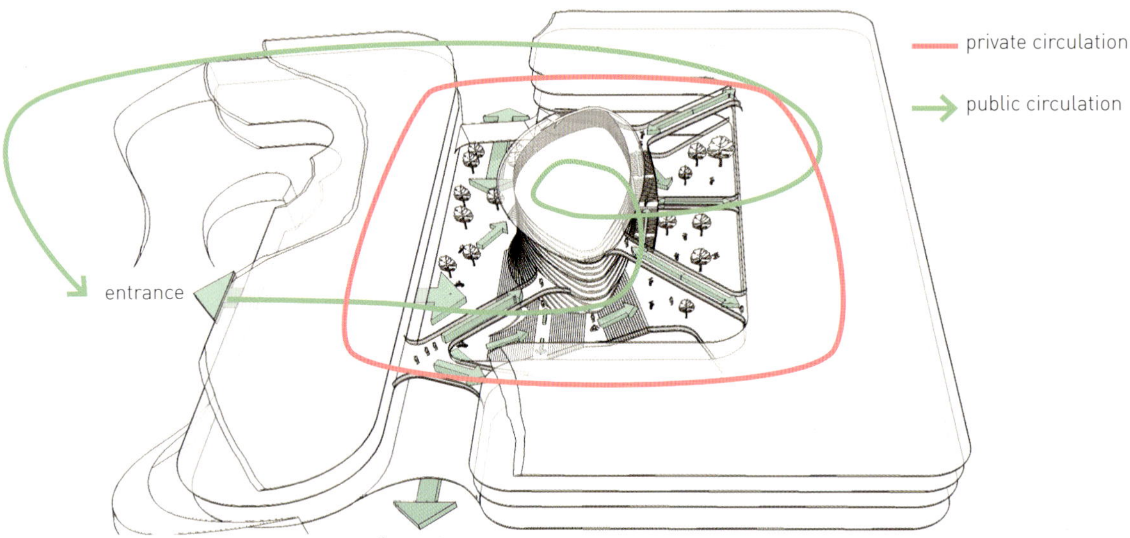

Above: Schematic diagram of the circulatory system throughout the building.

Right: Aerial view of the building's entrance eco-pond.

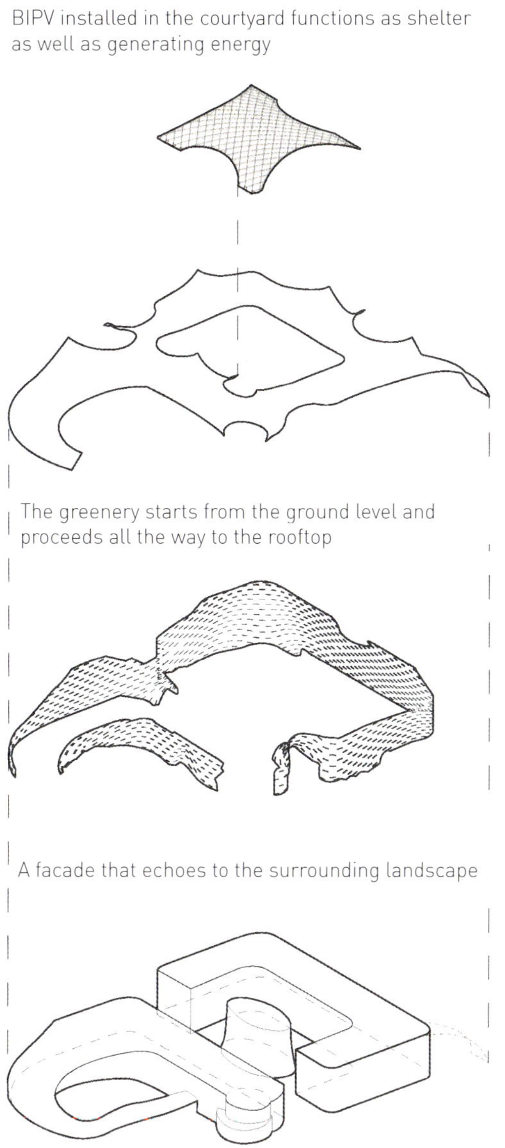

Above: Diagram describing the building's skin.
Right: Different outdoor spaces/atmospheres.

Left: Aerial view of the building from the entrance side.

MOXA

MOXA HEADQUARTERS
TAOYUAN, 2016

MOXA headquarters houses three different functions: office, factory, and warehouse. The first goal of this project was to integrate the three parts as a whole so that the workers can move between different parts efficiently.

The second goal was to create a sense of community and wellness for the workers in the building, so that the quality of life can be translated to quality of work. In order to satisfy both goals, we facilitated a "we tube" that spirals up the center of the building.

Elements such as large-scale stairs, atriums, and ramps, utilized as a means for connecting each floor spatially, allows a natural flow of circulation while at the same time breaks the boundary of a stereotypical work environment. The XinYuan Foundation of Education, founded by MOXA, is also headquartered inside the factory. The foundation has a long history of sponsoring butterfly gardens throughout Taiwan in hope of reminding people of Taiwan's historical nickname of "The Butterfly Kingdom." Therefore, it is the foundation's intention that the employees of MOXA, take the time to observe and appreciate the growth cycle of a butterfly. The 6th floor of the MOXA factory is a co-habitat environment for both the employees and the butterflies. Through daily routines, the employees can observe the seasonal change of the butterfly garden as well as the natural ecology of the butterflies.

circulation
FORM

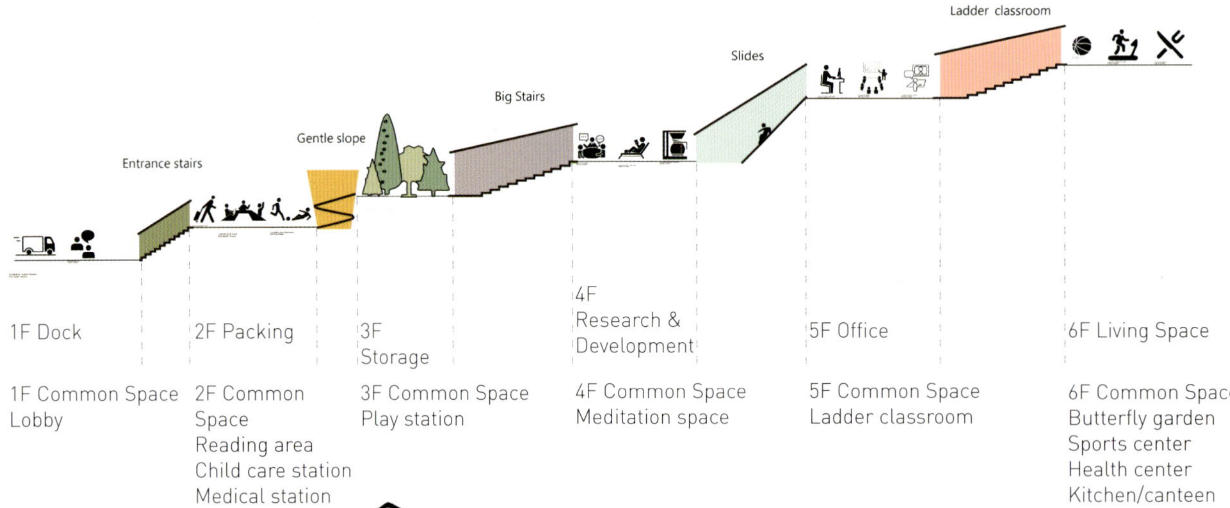

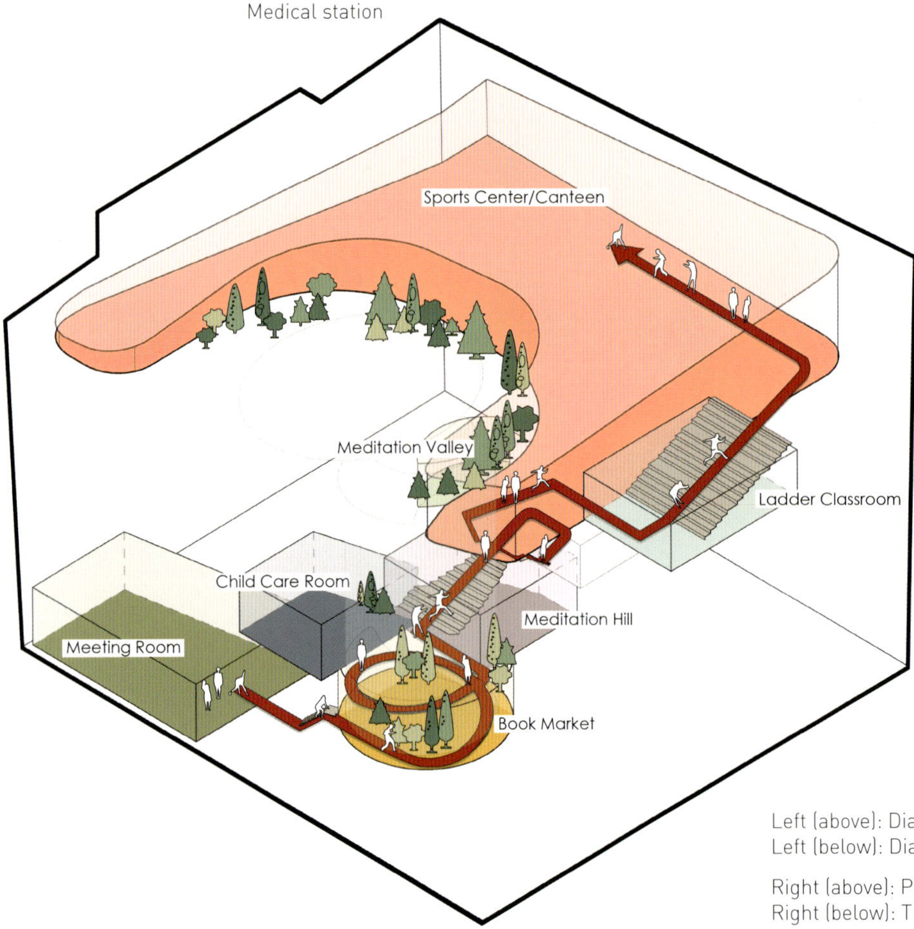

Left (above): Diagram representing the program by floor.
Left (below): Diagram of the circulatory system.

Right (above): Private meeting rooms.
Right (below): The stairs are transformed into a social space.

CONVERGENCE
INDUSTRY 4.0

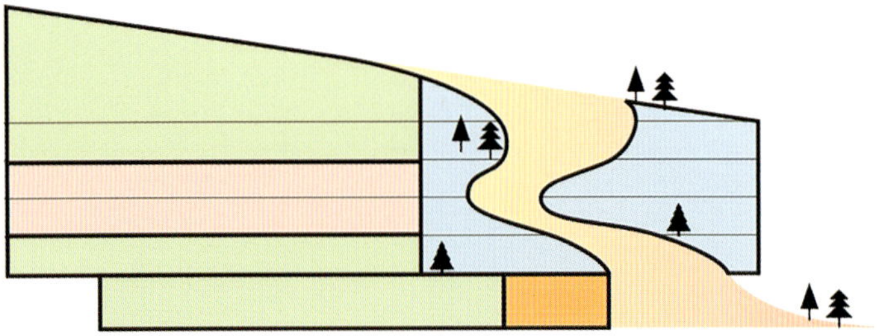

Space	Manufacture	Logistics	Office	Living	Services
Fl area	3070	1440	2160	1620	2790
%	28%	13%	19%	15%	25%

Above: Opened space dining hall on the 6th floor.
Left: Diagram of floor program and area.

Right (above): The 6th floor living garden.
Right (below): Diagram of the concept design.

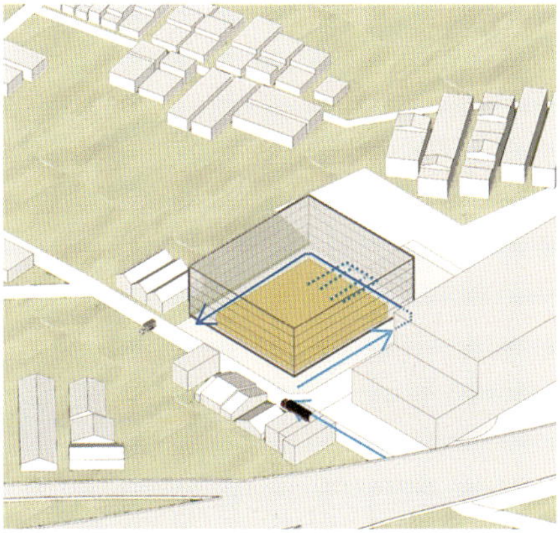

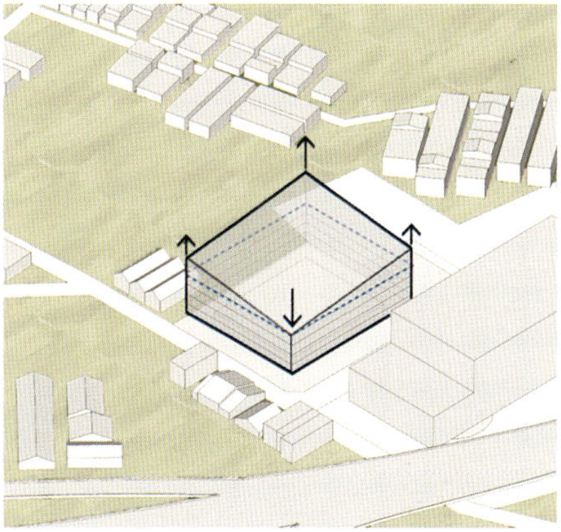

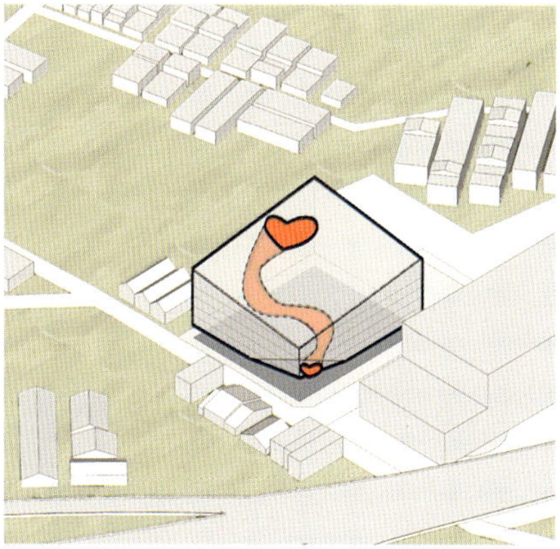

NATIONAL CENTRAL LIBRARY AND NATIONAL REPOSITORY LIBRARY: SOUTHERN BRANCH

TAINAN, 2018

This project has been an opportunity to investigate the role of the library in future use; instead of re-creating yet another monumental library, we proposed an open and transparent new learning environment with "rooms of knowledge" that define the contemporary use of a library as a less formal but interactive hub. To navigate people effectively between the outside and inside, and through different functional zones of the library, a circulatory system, with a main artery that connects many small loops, is employed. The main programs of the library, event hall, museum and depository, are linked through the main axis connecting the N-S sides of the site bringing people in smoothly.

As a response to the new-age learning environment such as co-learning, open source data sharing, and digital networking, we propose the future library be a hub for open learning that promotes collaboration. The main lobby, also known as the "salon," will be an interactive flexible space for learning and events which will redefine the traditional "see-the-books reading room" idea.

This project calls for a book museum in the library. From our point-of-view, we feel there is a need to redefine the entire museum rather than just the book museum. The curatorial of this museum embodies the theme of "Life of a Book." The path through the museum begins in the public main axis, showcasing the Book-bot (ASRS - automated storage and retrieval system), and then slowly arrives at the museum quarter surrounded by trees. The museum loop includes peeping into the "behind-the-scenes" of book restoration, preservation, and digitalization.

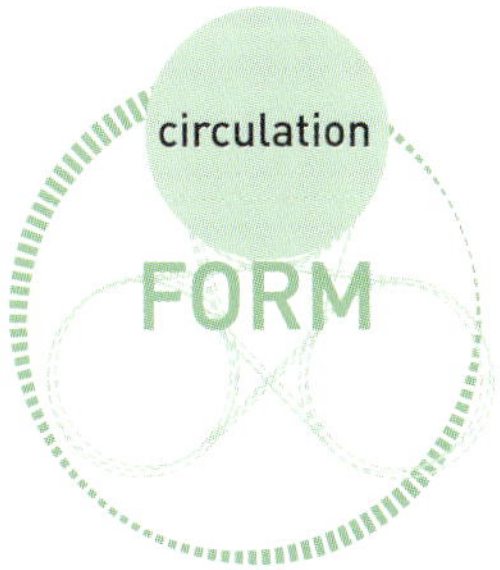

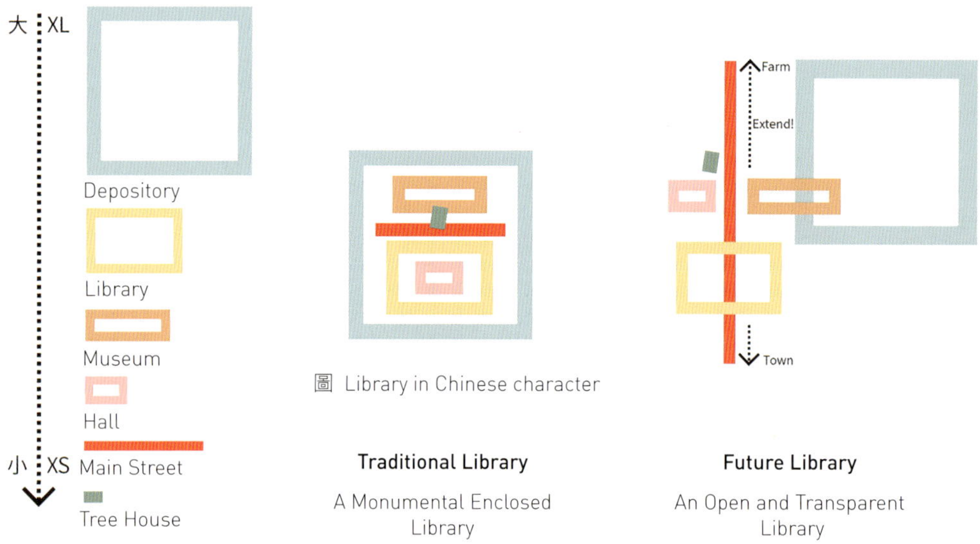

Above: The design concept inspired by the Chinese character "圖" meaning library, is decomposed in a circulatory system with the main artery that connects different loops.
Below: South entrance to the library with a boulevard that leads to different buildings and functions.

Right: The design strategy.

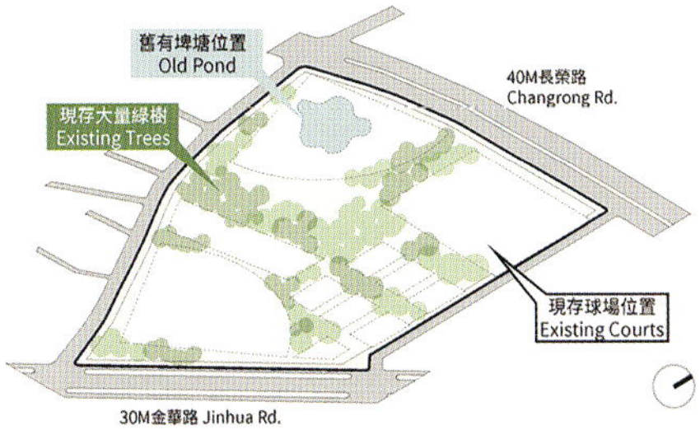

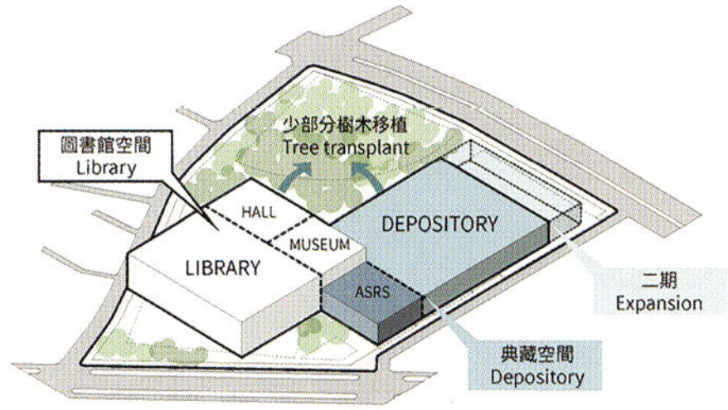

1. Site condition

The main roads are: 30M Jinhua road on the south side and 40M Changrong road on the north side. There are existing courts and a lot of trees, and the old pond is not conducive for excavation.

2. Massing strategy

Build on the existing sports courts, retain close to 90% of the trees, and transplant a few. The massing is mainly divided into a library and a one-floor depository to shorten the construction period. The second phase expansion space is reserved on the north side.

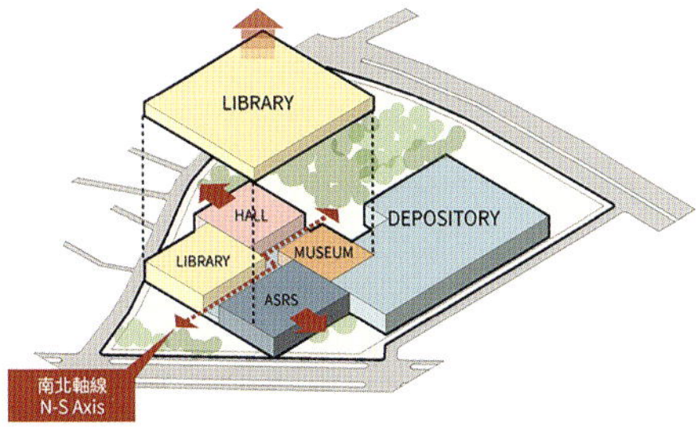

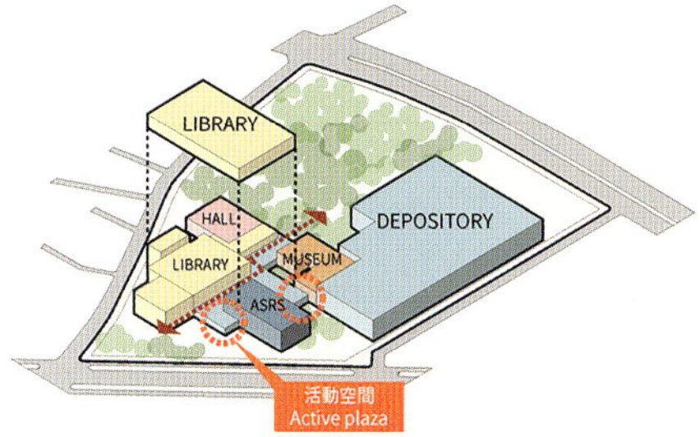

3. Program configuration strategy

The north-south axis in the middle connect the north and south green to create the activity and display space. The ASRS (automation depository)is near the axis to become part of the display.

4. Keep green and create activity space

The massing becomes smaller to avoid the displacement of trees, and the second floor terrace is built to create multi-level activity spaces.

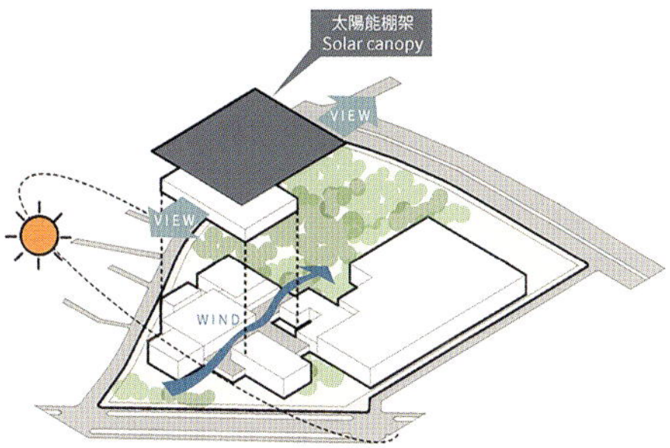

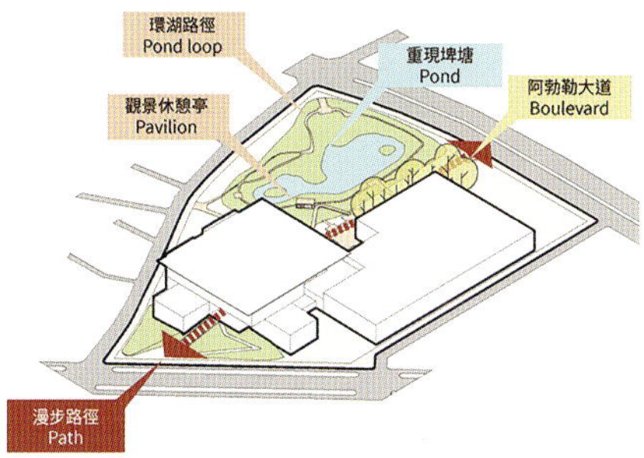

5. Response to physical environment

The north-south axis welcomes the south wind and the northern green space. The windows face north and south for soft reading light, and the solar canopy creates both energy and shade.

6. Landscape extend to town

Reinterpret the original pond with surrounding hills, and create a path and cabin around the pond.Take a stroll along the slope to the second terrace and down to the boulevard, blending the building with the landscape.

Book mountain – salon and main circulation of the library connecting all floors.

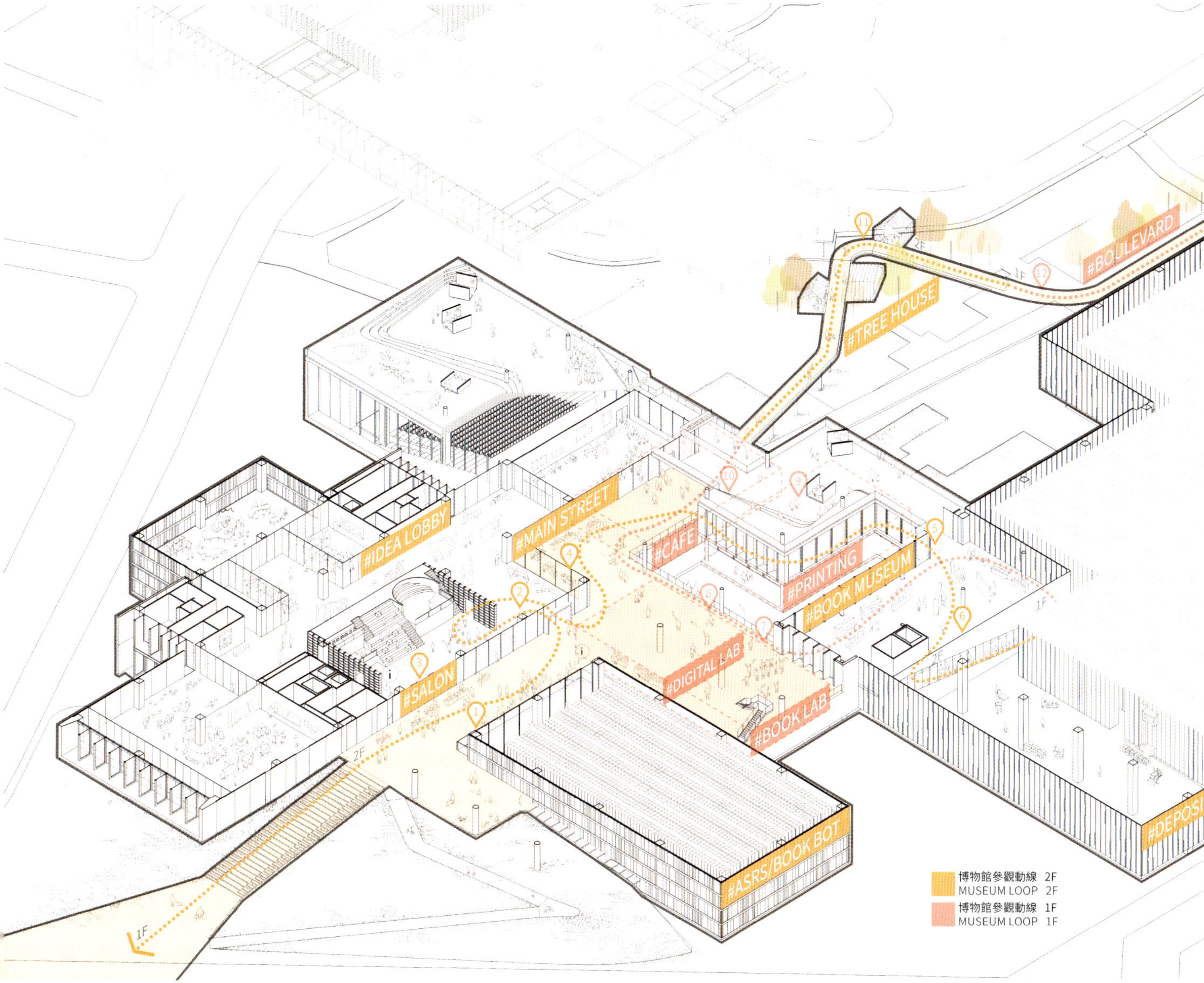

The library as a living museum—showcasing the journey of books. Lightness, transparency, and automation allow visitors the process to see behind the scenes, engaging them in an immersive experience of "edutainment" (education + entertainment). The entire chain of preparing the books, restoring them, and digitizing them becomes completely transparent, bringing about new possibilities for new visitor experiences.

Allowing visitors to walk by the transparent labs and letting them take a sneak peek at the process will engage them in a new learning experience: the "museum of books" is enlarged to the whole structure and shows visitors its lively activity.

辦公室
Office
學習共享區
ing & Sharing
多媒體
Multi Media
影音室
Video Room
市集
rket Place
合典藏館
ork Room
自動典藏
ASRS

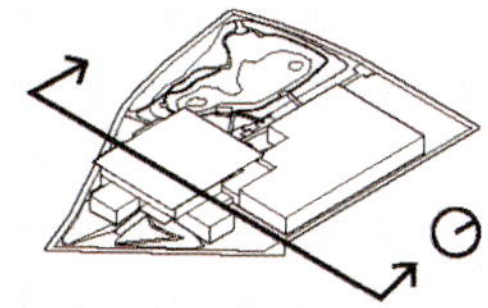

structural system

The form and material of a supporting system of a building often dictates the characteristic of its architecture; much like the supporting system in biology defines the form of most creatures: membrane of bacteria, skeleton of mammals, shell of crustaceans.

In modern days, several supporting systems, with their unique structural and sensual qualities are widely used: concrete, with its strength in heat, sound insulation, fire resistance, has long been a great structural material since the Roman Era.

Not only can concrete, due to its similarity with sedimentary rock, be a vessel to sensually express eternity and fluidity, but likewise steel is efficient in transferring tension and pressure. Aside from its quality of elasticity and malleability, steel can also bring out sensual aspects of openness and lightness. Timber behaves like steel structurally but is traditionally limited to smaller scale buildings. Thanks to the advancement of technology, timber has expanded its uses and sizes. Carbon, being the main primary element found in both timber and people, is able to stimulate a complementary sensation. Most importantly, many have considered the innovative use of composite timber (glulam, CLT) to be the last hope for zero carbon emissions in architecture.

MINQUAN ELEMENTARY SCHOOL
KAOHSIUNG, 2011

In 2009, Typhoon Morakot washed away many lives and homes in the mountain-side aboriginal village, including the scenic Minquan Elementary School. We wanted to not only reconstruct all that was lost as a result of this tremendous disaster, but additionally create new designs that add to the future needs of the site.

The first step was to relocate the school to higher ground, specifically where the old village was situated one hundred years ago; here the risk of landslide is minimized. The second step was to create a design that would maintain the cultivations and knowledge of local traditional Taiwanese Aborigines, through connecting with the practices and cultures which have guided the tribe people for hundreds of years, thus restoring the faith of the community.

The project is divided into three separate buildings: the library, the elementary school, and the dormitory.

Minquan Elementary School is influenced by Bunun and Cou's tribal community shelters. The library building, centrally located on the school campus, is inspired by the traditional Bunun male gathering pavillion, Kuba. Along with less cost needed for transportation and less of a carbon footprint, building with Taiwanese Sugi assists local forest management and also increases the quality of biodiversity.

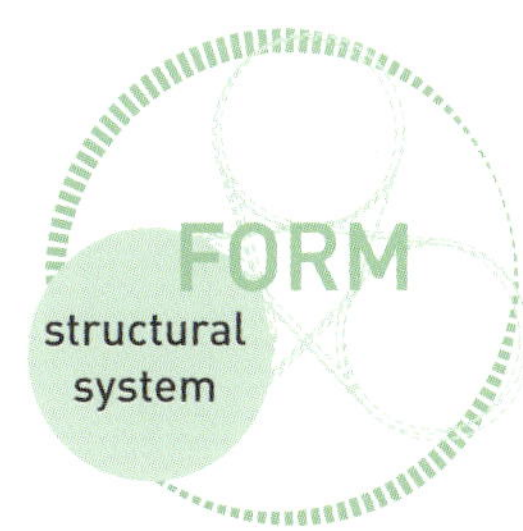

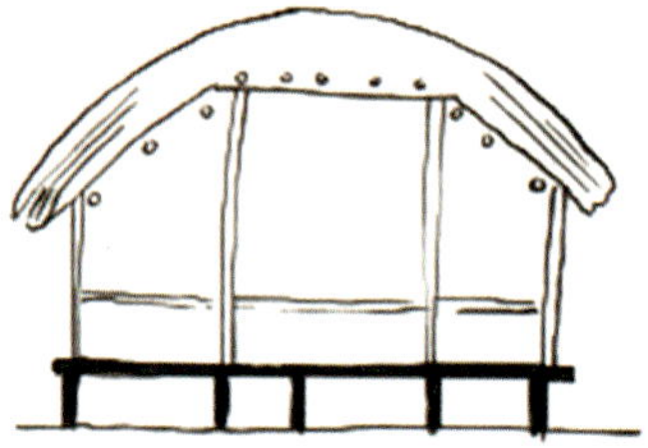

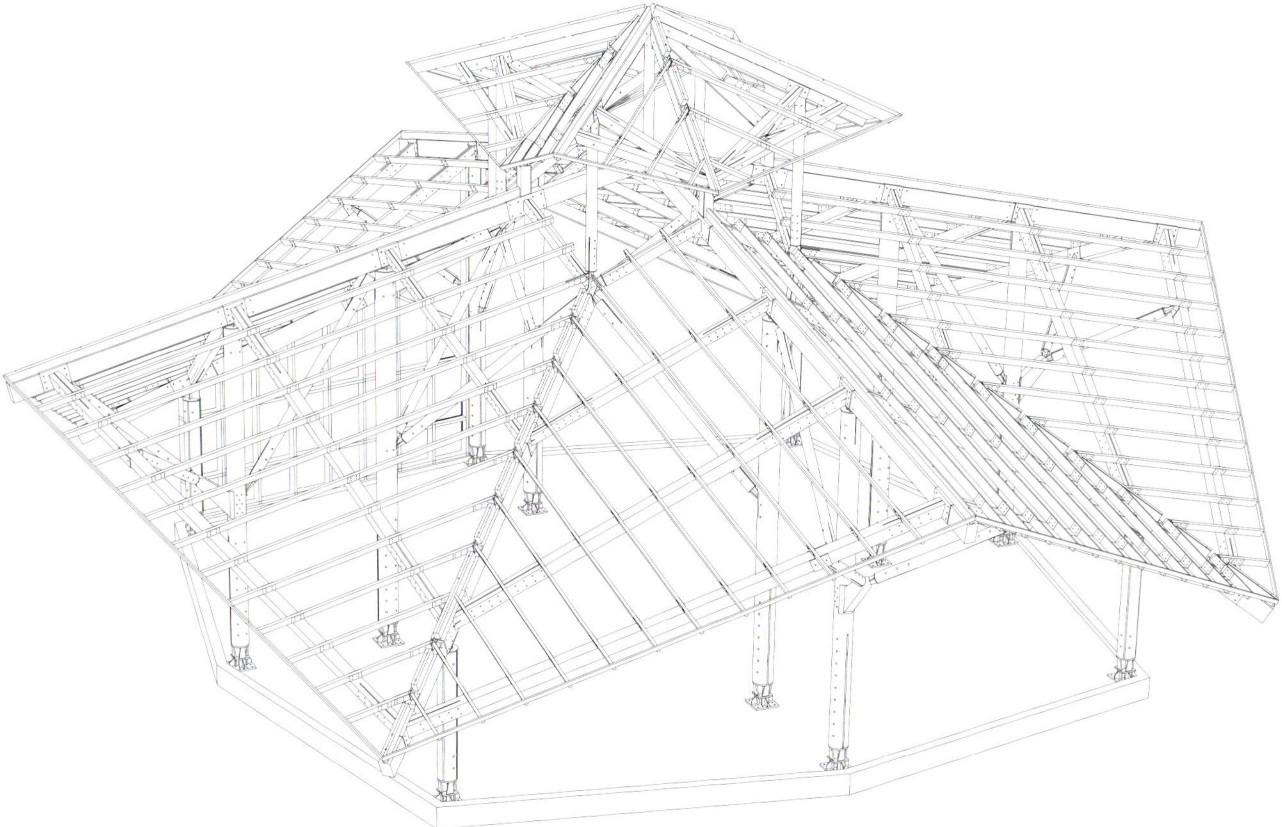

Above: 3D wooden structural system drawing.
Below: Construction site photos.

Left (above): View of the Library.
Left (below): Datura flower was the inspiration for the Library's roof shape.
Cakuru, an Austronesian indigenous house architecture type where the wisdom is passed to the younger by the elderly.

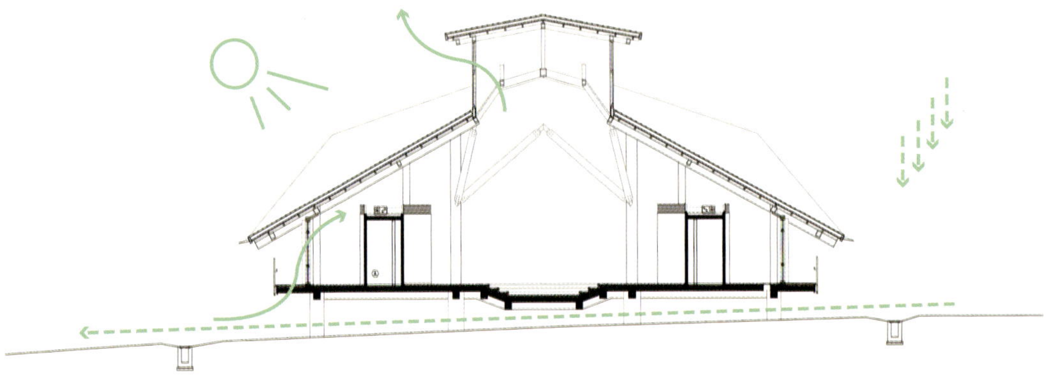

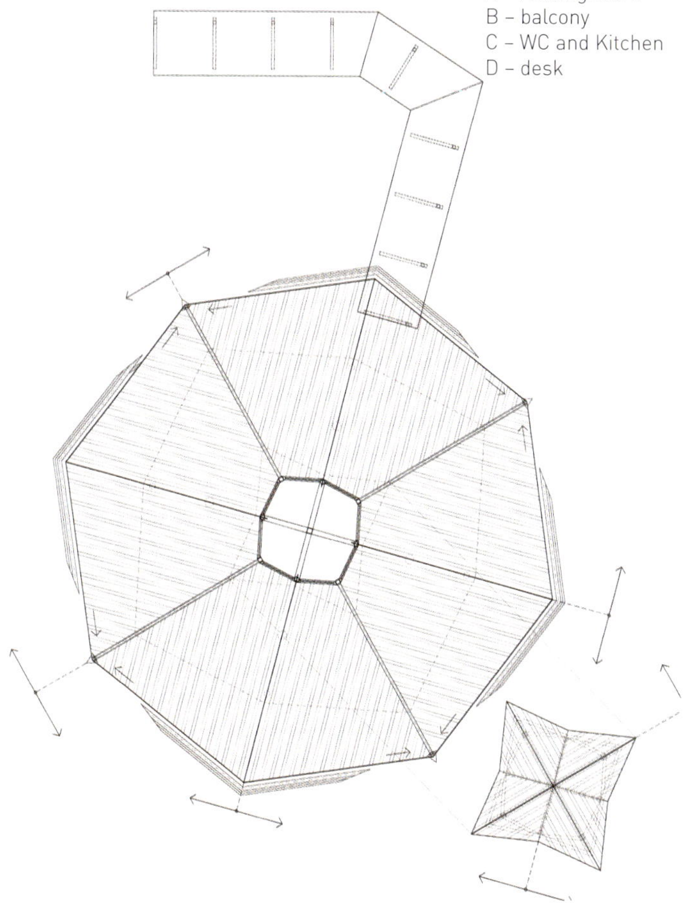

Above: Floor plan and roof plan.
Right: The library's interior during final construction phase.

Left (above): The Library building raised from the ground.
Left (below): Air circulation and ventilation strategy. Raised building to allow for the rain water to drain naturally.

ABORIGINAL GALLERY AND HANDICRAFT SHOPS

TAITUNG, 2016

Situated between the Pacific Ocean and the central mountain range of Taiwan, the fluctuating thin-shell structure, formed by steel tubes and spray concrete, best embodies the characteristics of Austronesian culture—that is the culture of ocean sailors and mountain hunters. The structure guides the wind through it like a sail, cools the space, and induces activities beneath it. The mosaic artwork, portraying a mother and a baby whale swimming in the Pacific Ocean, makes the fluctuating shell look like incoming waves you can surf.

The shell spans 20 meters by 50 meters to provide a free and opened market place. Its wooden ceiling holds the waterproof membrane and the spray concrete.

In Taiwan, there are approximately 10,000 containers retrieved from the ocean each year, providing about 15,000 square meters of recycled space. The aboriginal handcraft shops are housed in 40, 20, and 40 foot long recycled shipping containers, piled up four-story high and arranged in different directions to create terraces at different levels encouraging activities on the inside and outside of the containers and nourishing the vitality of the market place.

The container shops are cooled by small, individually-controlled air conditioning units, they are flexible and economical, while the walkway and terraces are naturally ventilated. In Taitung's tropical climate, this combined cooling strategy reduces the refrigeration use by 50% and the electricity use by 60%.

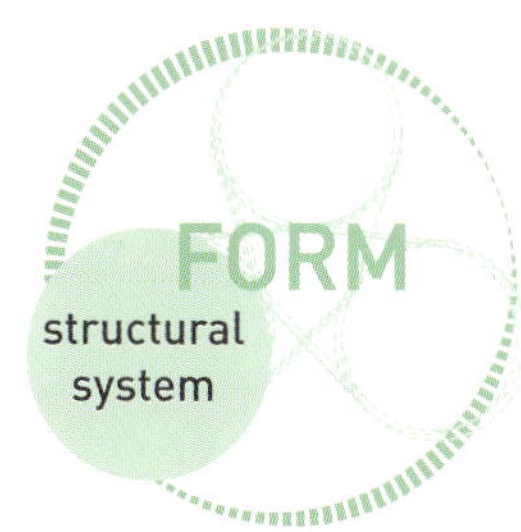

Above: Strip plan of the site up to the sea line. To the left is the galleria, to the right is the incubator center featured in "program."
Below: The building system diagram.

Right: Under the large roof there are two types of space, one is the interior commercial space formed by shipping containers, the other is the semi-outdoor corridor with natural ventilation.

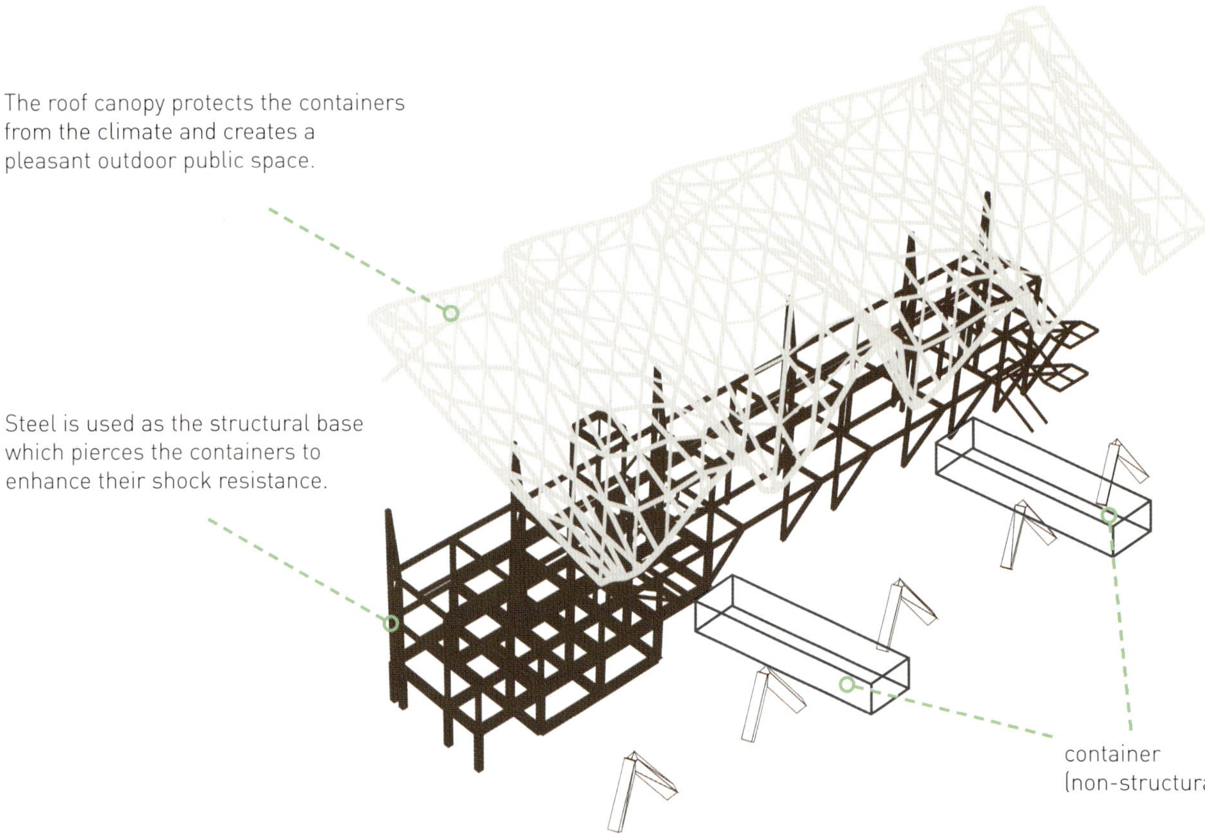

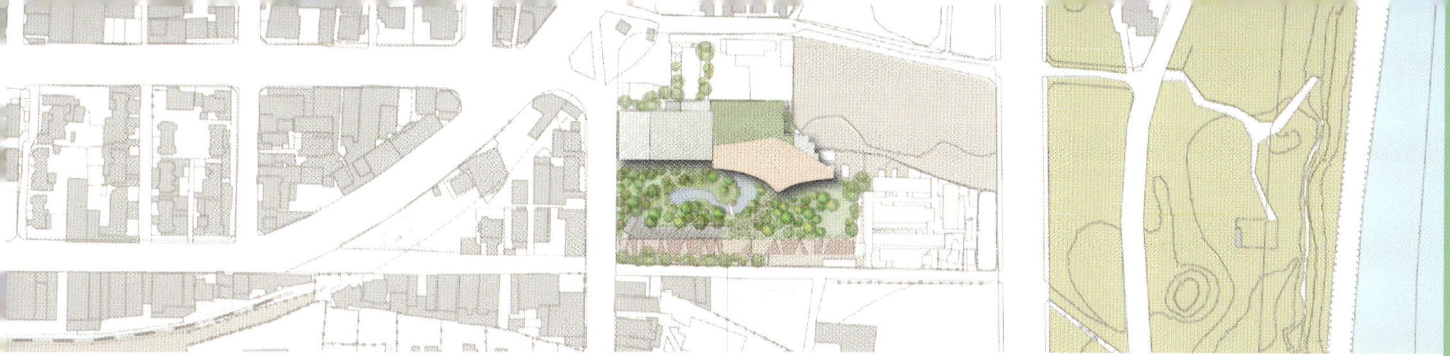

Above: Underneath the roof, a comfortable shade space suitable for all kinds of activities in the subtropical climate.
Below: Initial sketch of the undulating roof.

Left (above): The wavy roof resembles the ocean and mountain landscape in Taitung.
Left (below): Photos showing original Austronesian architecture style.

Above: Transversal section.
Below: The structural system diagram.

Left: Photos during the building construction.

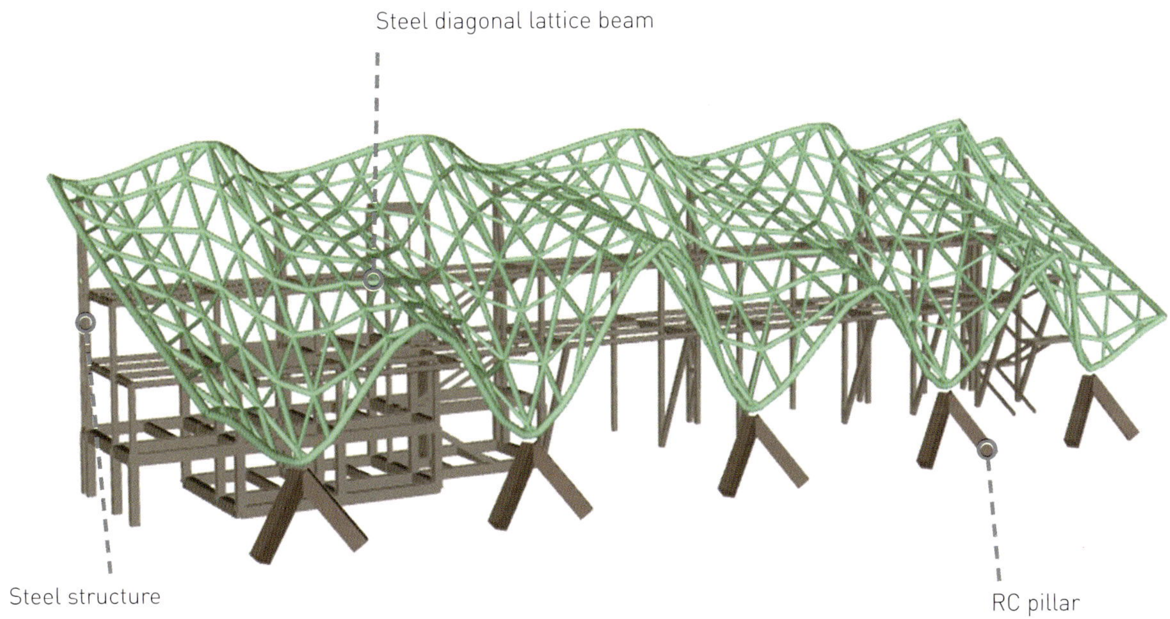

CHENGGONG MARKET RECONSTRUCTION

TAIPEI, 2013 (COMPETITION)

Even though convenient and vibrant, traditional markets still pose hygienic and aesthetic issues in communities. The reconstruction plan of this old market was intended to place the new market underground in order to clear out the lot for a community park solving these issues.

Natural light was still most desirable even though the market is underground, and apparent, visible entrances to the market were ever more essential for the business since it is not noticeable from the street. To, as the phrase goes, "kill two birds in one stone," we employed three consecutive hyperbolic paraboloid shells. The arch and the suspension mechanism generated by the hyperbolic shape were used to convert the load into an in-plane stress which is effectively transmitted to the four fulcrums of the age to form a span of about 40 meters. The lifted part of the shell lets the natural light in along the street and naturally forms dual entrances at two opposite street corners, while the lower ends of the shell provide the support for the structure and pedestrian access to the park.

The market is intended to be vibrant and active with a very rich sensorial experience. The hyperbolic paraboloid shell consists of reinforced-concrete-grid units to bear the load of soil from the park, and also be the main architectural feature of the underground space. The natural light allowed in gives the undulating-shell grid dramatic gradient of light and shade, corresponding to the vitality of the marketplace.

FORM
structural system

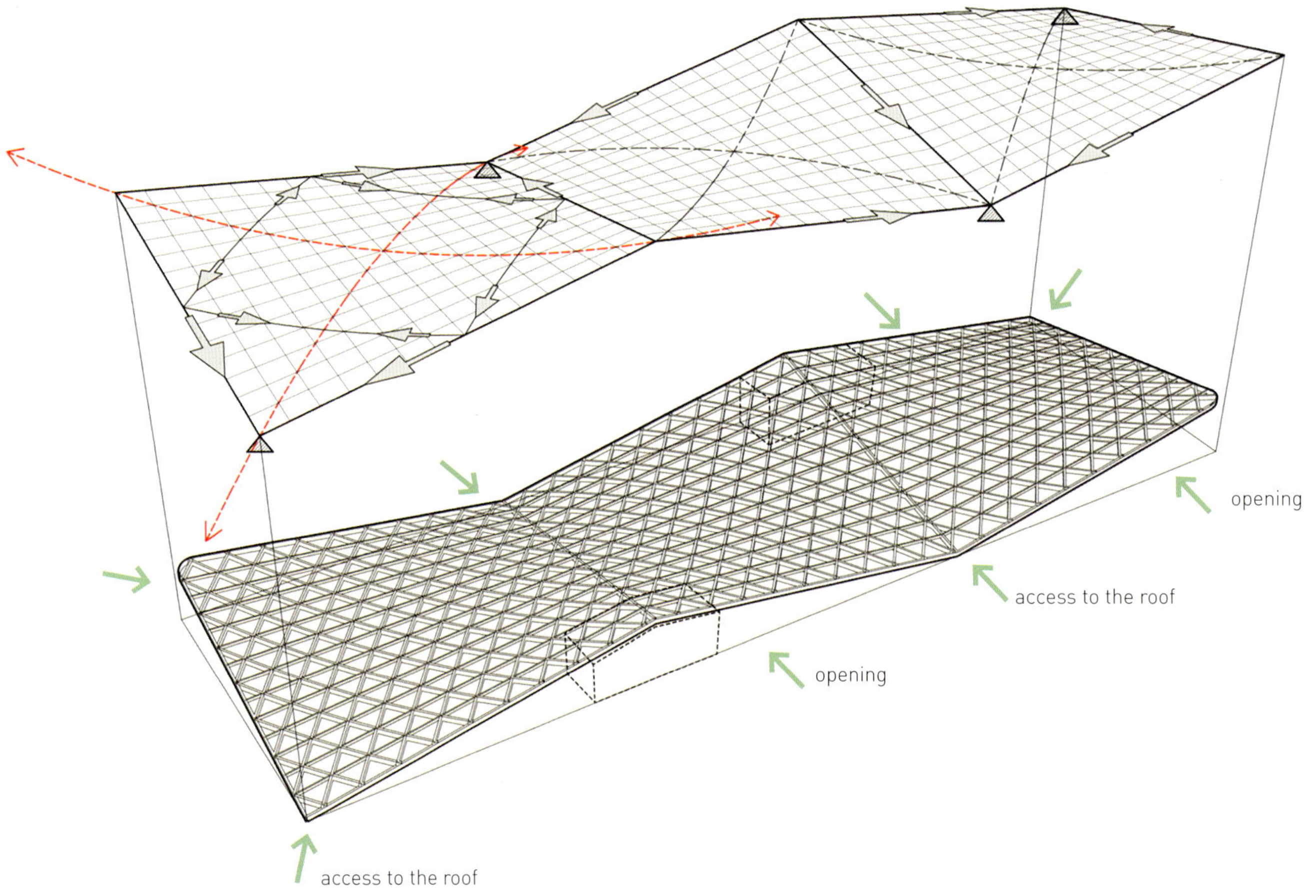

Above: The interconnection of the three consecutive hyperbolic paraboloid shapes creates openings and accesses from the ground to the roof alternatively.

Right (above): One of the market's entrances.
Right (below): The lively, fifth façade.

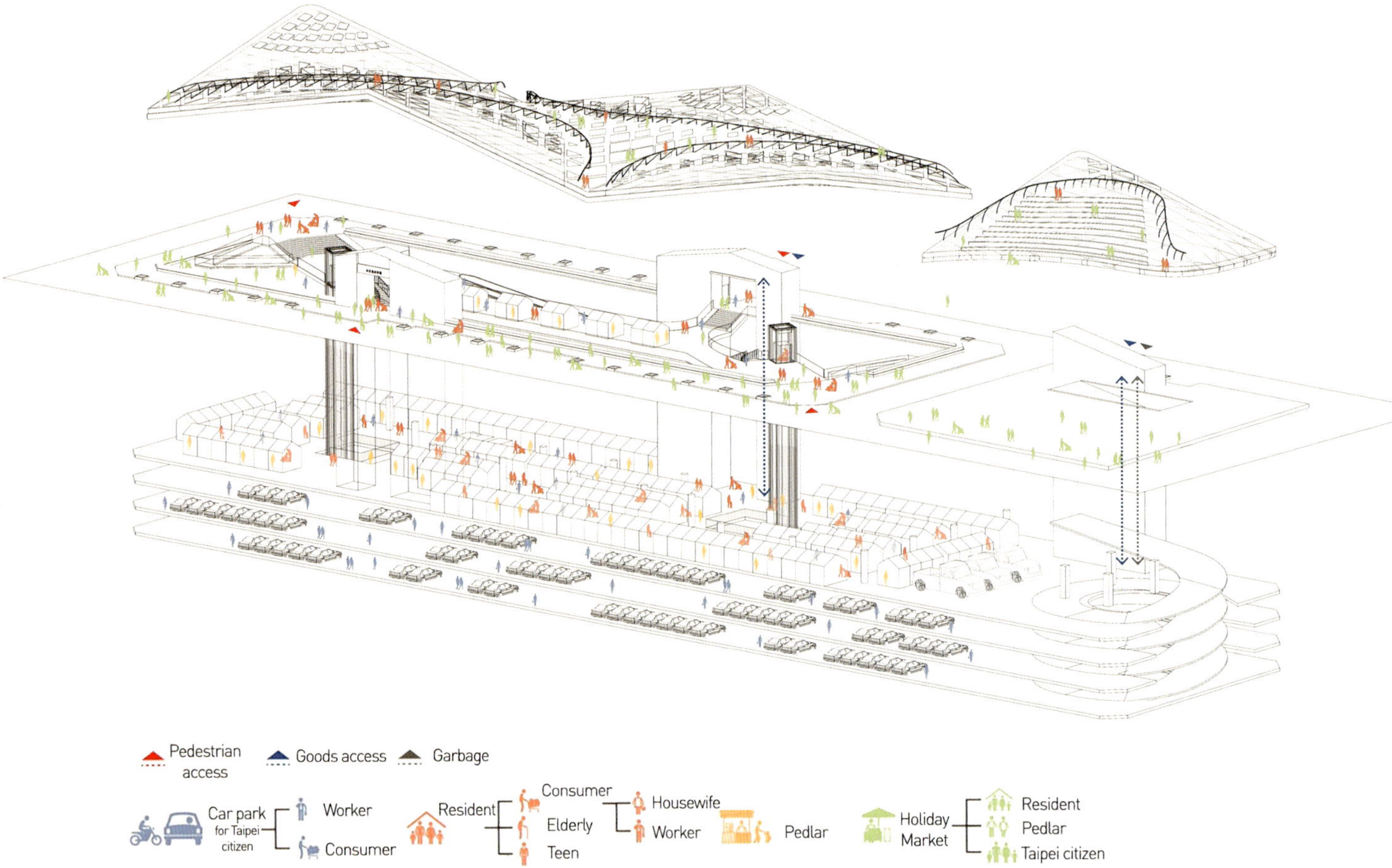

Above: Open diagram 3D view, showing the activity movement throughout the market.
Below: Elevation view showing the movement produced by the structural system.

Right (above): The structural form naturally provides the entrance canopy that leads to the underground market and the openings that let the natural light and fresh air in.
Right (below): Interior rendering of the vendors stalls illuminated from above.

公有成功市場

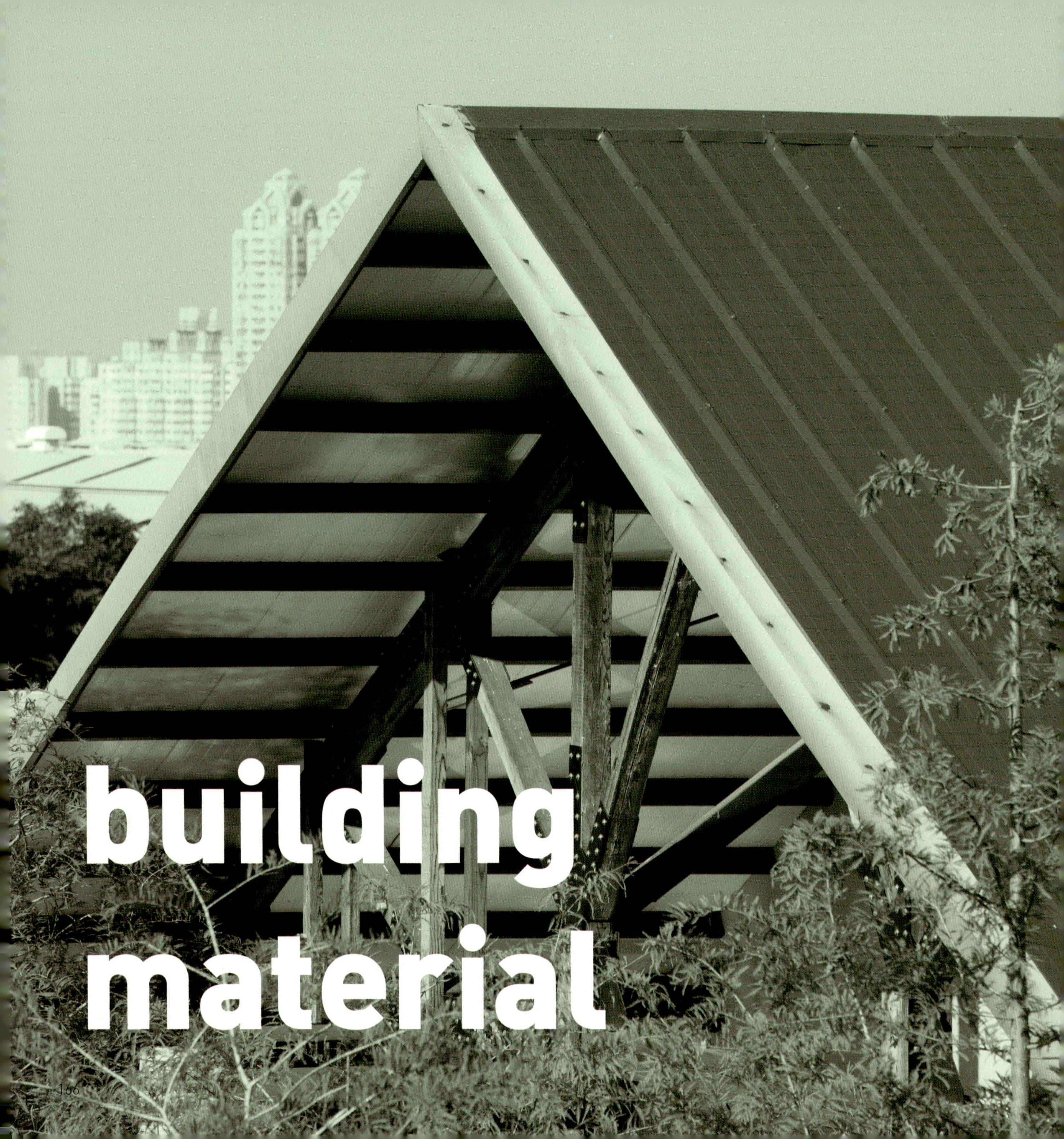

building material

Life is opportunistic, it takes whatever available resources are around it as building blocks to construct itself. That is one of the main reasons why life presents such great diversity across the ecosystem. Life constantly labors for its building materials; just as architects seemingly never cease searching for the availability of building materials. Intentionally or unintentionally, that contributes to the great diversity of architecture in different geological regions.

Buildings can serve both practical and spiritual purposes; building materials can satisfy construction purposes and convey sensuality, through its workability, weatherability, color, texture, smell, sound absorption, and reflective properties.

One element in a specific life can be recycled and become an element in another life; a building material with proper durability and sensual quality can also live many lives and serve multiple purposes.

FORM building material

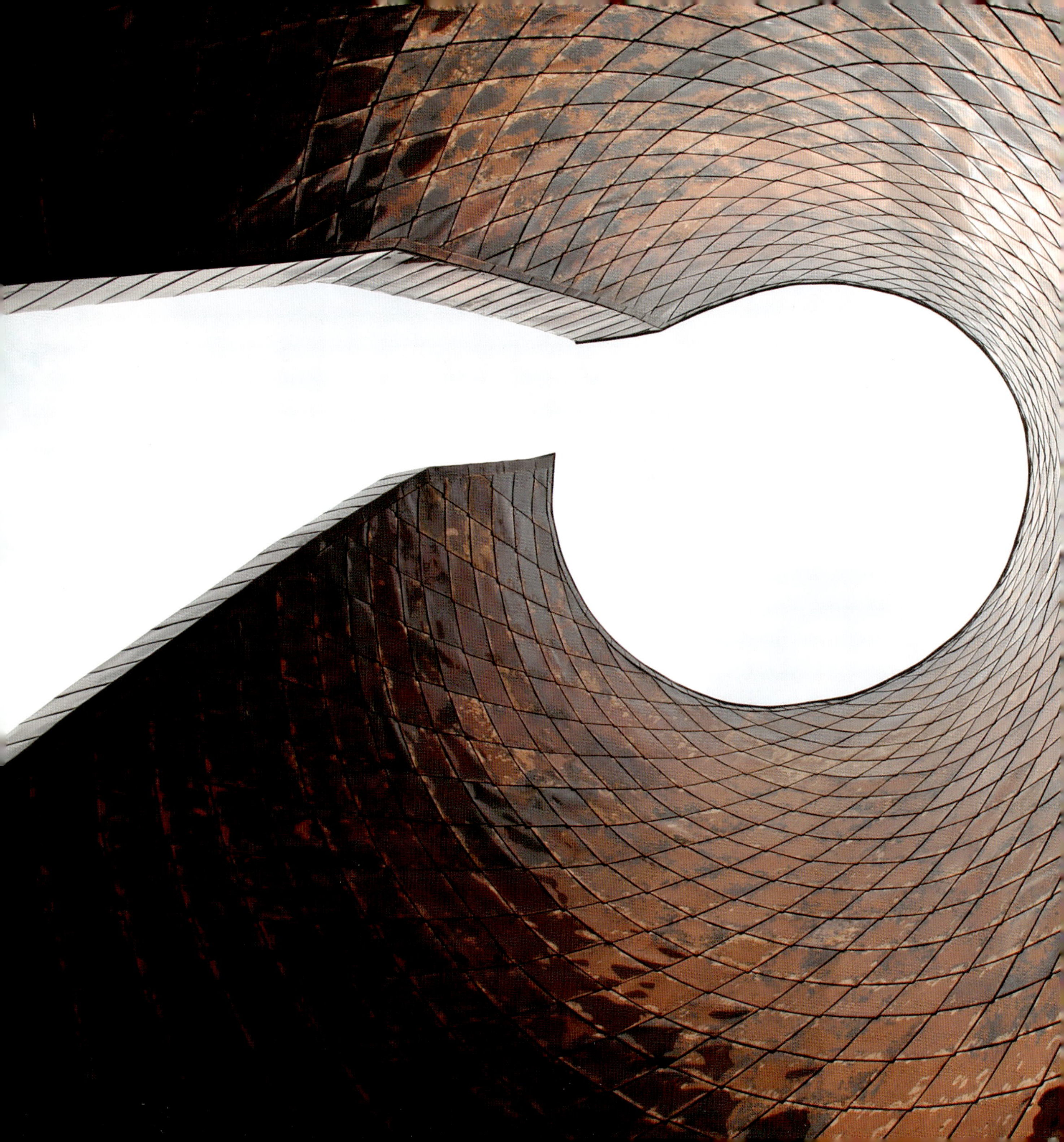

TAMSUI ART GALLERY
NEW TAIPEI CITY, 2007

Situated on the old main street of Tamsui, a historical port town, the new art gallery was built with the intention of activating new functions in the old town while prompting an interesting dialogue with its existing context. The historical buildings positioned on the main roads are largely made of stone, brick, lumber, and sometimes cladded with plaster. Over time, wear marks and corrosion manifest on these materials through weathering, depreciation, or simply mold accumulating on the surface. Therefore copper and titanium-alloy cladding and wood were selected as main façade materials because they also weather through time.

Besides that, the site had another particularity: it was the official residence for settlers during the Japanese occupation period. The intention was to create a dialogue between the surrounding context and the new building maintaining the spirit of this historical significance. Therefore, the tiles from the demolition of the original building were preserved and used for interior decoration in the new building.

In order to respect the surrounding environment, the building was intentionally set back to avoid blocking the rear view, and was meant to allow people in the square access to see the mountain view, creating a unique skyline and a new esthetic for the old street.

The multi-purpose interior space is suitable for hosting various activities by opening the building to the square. Plus, small lecture spaces and special art exhibitions can provide a platform for creators to express themselves freely.

FORM building material

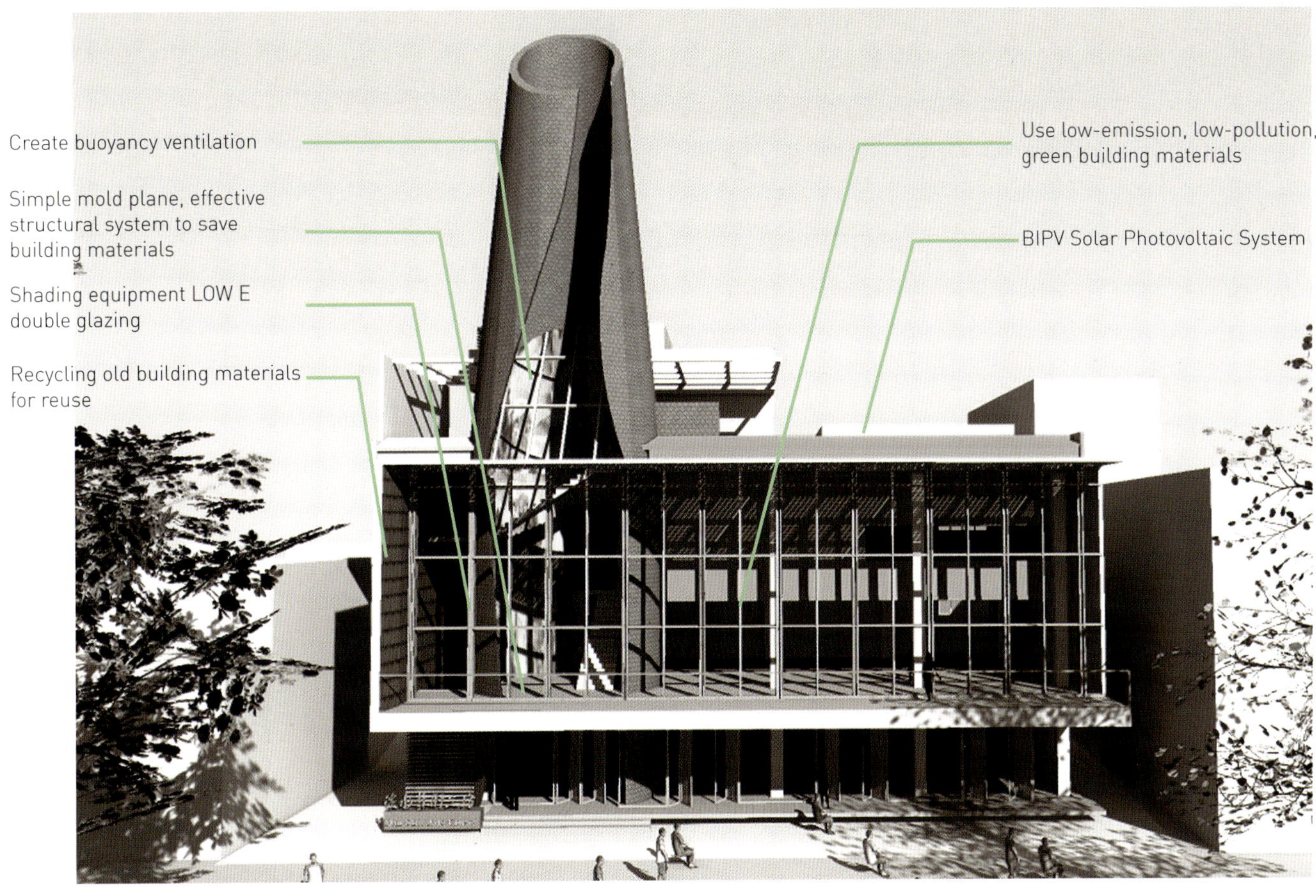

Above: 3D rendering describing the green building strategies.

Left: Street view of the building's main façade.
Light enters the interior space filtered by the PV panels.

Above: Tiles from the demolition of the existing building. These tiles were preserved and used for interior decoration in the new building.
Below: Photos showing the interior and exterior walls covered by the old building's roof tiles.

Right: Interior photo of the wall.

TAMING HIGH SCHOOL OF THE APPLIED ART

TAICHUNG, 2015

Creativity arises from giving new life to what is old, from this perspective the benefit of using old building materials generates a new usage, avoids discarding, and becomes an inspiration for the building's future users. In this project the wooden trusses and steel pipes were great examples of how well the life cycle of a material can be renewed and fit perfectly into a new context, an art school.

Therefore, the design for this art school project was mainly focused on creating a new campus for the purpose of nurturing esthetic art and craft-design education. Besides incorporating building materials this school was designed to be a low-carbon, ecological campus, exemplifying a comfort, energy-efficient lifestyle.

The structural system was divided into various types depending on their functions. The ordinary classrooms were built, with reinforced concrete (RC); the specialist classrooms were designed with the existing wooden trusses; and the gym was constructed with steel.

The rehabilitation of old materials for new structural use reversed the conventional process of design. The number and the size of the wooden trusses (33 all with a span of 14 meters) determined the number and size of the specialized classrooms and therefore had a significant impact on the site plan. The diameter and the thickness of the steel pipes limited the height of the entrance canopy. Before using, both the wooden trusses and the steel pipes needed to be examined by ultrasound machine to determine their structural properties since both were stored in a warehouse for more than a decade. Some steel pipes turned out to not be suitable due to erosion and all of the wooden trusses needed steel-plate reinforcement to meet the new structural codes.

FORM
building material

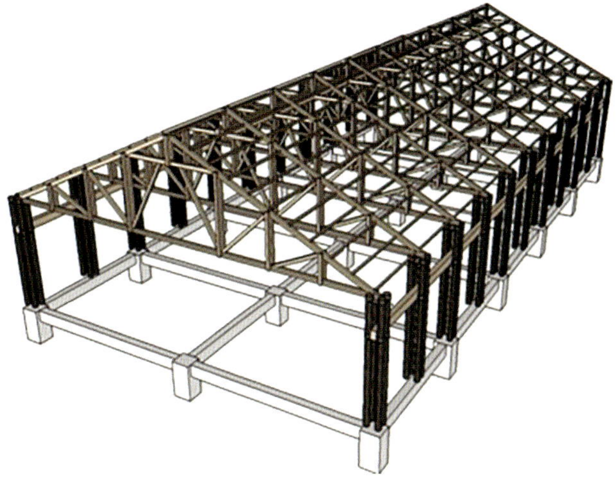

Above (left): The old wooden trusses in the warehouse.
Above (right): Each specialized art space consists of 11 trusses, three of its kind were erected.
Below: Section drawing of the pavilion showing the skylight to the north which minimizes direct sun light into the art space.

Left: The school pavilion with the recycled trusses.

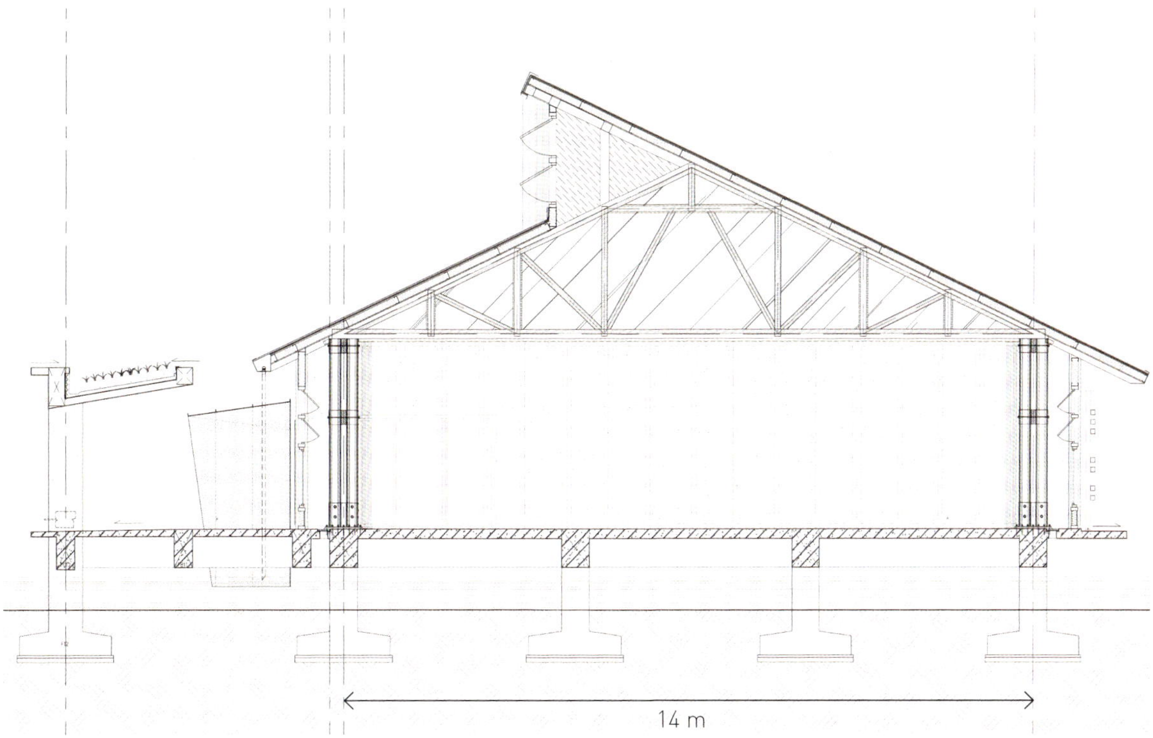

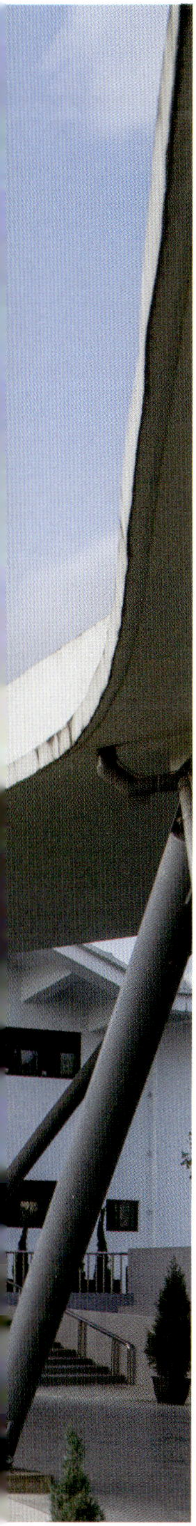

Left: The school entrance canopy which also serves as a multiple function space.

Right (above):The steel tubes for pumping sand from the reservoir before being recycled.
Right (below): The recycled steel column.

LCY INDUSTRIAL CENTER R&D
KAOHSIUNG, 2011

LCY Chemistry Corporation is a petrochemical company that has been making efforts to move from synthetic polymers, which are historically petrol-based, to bio-based polymers. TPE (thermal plastic), one of LCY's products—100% recyclable and decomposable, is an example of such a product.

The external façade of the R&D center is defined by the light verticality of the TPE pipes. They not only represent the company's identity but also help create an interior ambiance as well as a smooth urban perspective. By using these non-toxic "future building materials" in this project it clearly expresses a respectful attitude towards our planet.

The layout design of the R&D building considers embracing the summer's mild monsoons from the north-west and blocking the winter's prevailing winds from north east, whilst using TPE pipes as a sun shield on the east, north, and south sides to reduce sun radiation up to 56% while the interior diffusion-sunlight illumination is enhanced.

From third floor up, the open office and the laboratories, separated by a "canyon" are connected with bridge boxes with tinted glass (yellow, blue, and red). The BIPV which capes the canyon not only generates energy but also brings in natural light to brighten the tinted glass and bring energy into the center of the building.

FORM building material

Above: Photo and concept diagram of the pop out "boxes."

Left: LCY Chemistry Corporation developed recyclable building materials as experimental sunshade and promoted the innovative concept of green building.

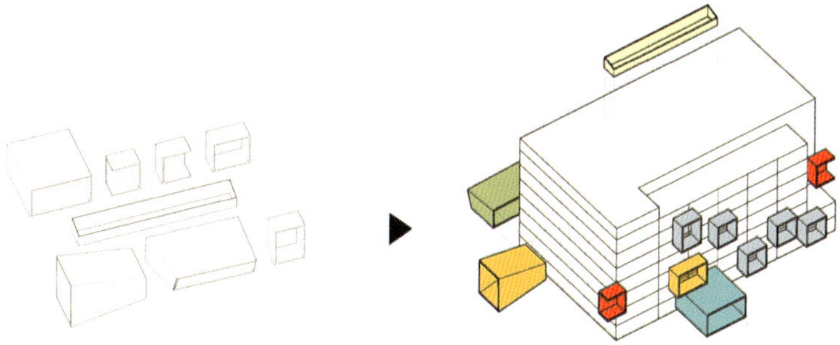

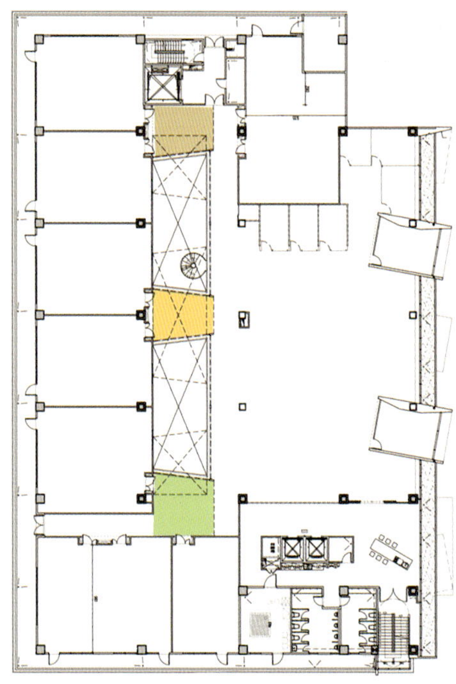

Above: Interior view of the office space with the colorful, lively bridges that link to the laboratory.

Left: Photo and floor plan showing the continuous informal meeting space through each floor enhancing the communication between its users.The PV panels not only harvest energy but also allow for filtered light to pass through.

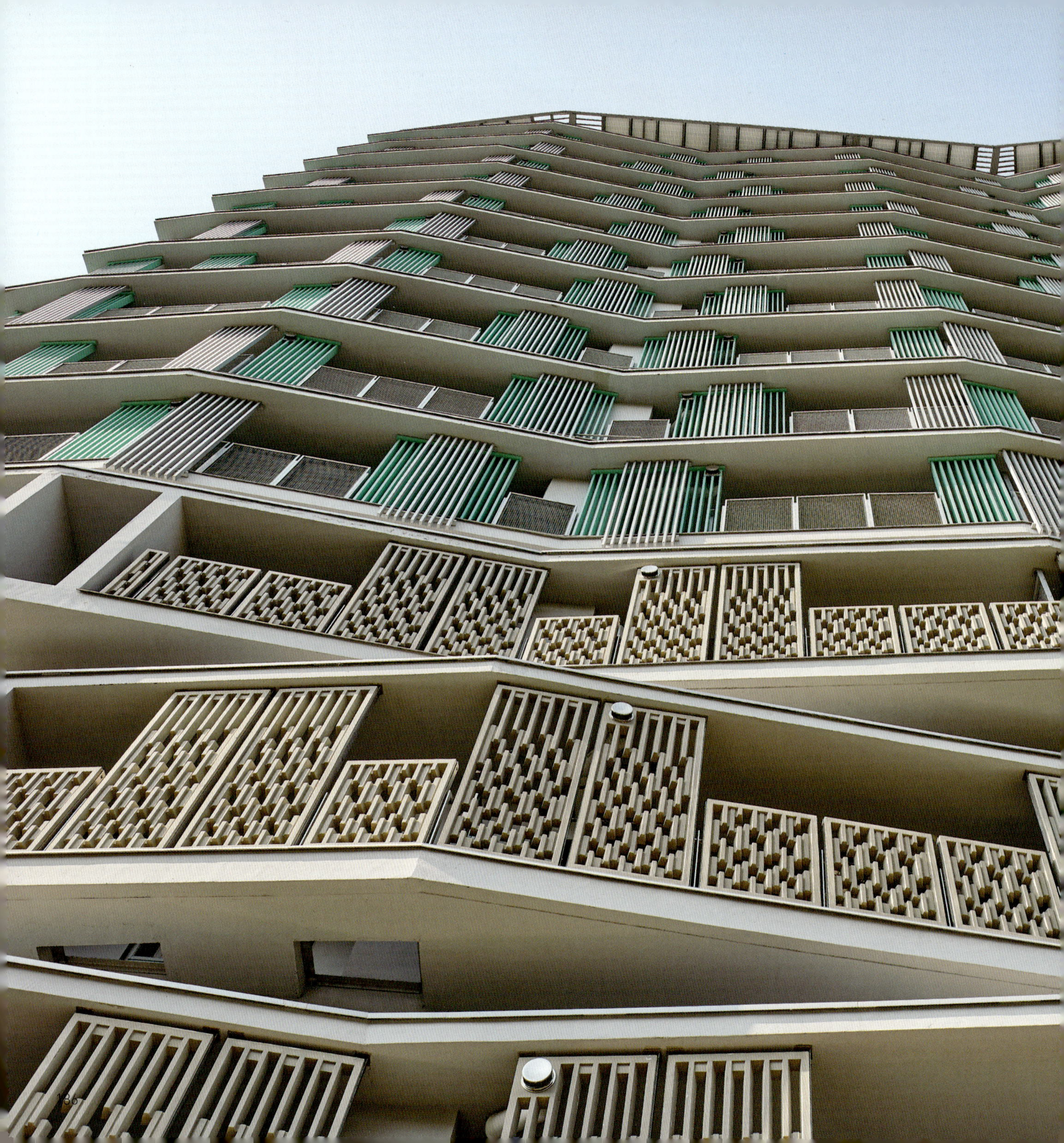

SONGSHAN PUBLIC HOUSING
TAIPEI, 2017

The building material selected for the podium balcony of the Songshan Housing Project was pre-casted GRC boards; which are manufactured and assembled in mass quantity; providing further meaning to the traditional tiles often presented in Taiwan's veteran's villages. Working together with the colorful aluminum louvers, from the upper portion of the building, the GRC panels represent the traditional veteran villages' unique characteristics, further harmonizing with the surrounding buildings' overall color scheme.

In order to satisfy the regulations for overall air permeability, as well as the structural strength, each GRC panel's opening pattern is carefully arranged into a diagonal formation in allowing stress to transfer freely. Integrated with the building itself, the sliding mechanism of the stainless-steel fixture helps to minimize the negative effects of the shifts in interlayer displacement.

During the process of fabrication, the construction company, collaborating with the designers, made numerous attempts to adjust the size and shape of the opening using wooden models. By adapting to a wedge style, the chance of demolding or corners cracking can be minimized, and at the same time it enhances the layering and lighting effects of the panel.

In order to accent the purity of the GRC, the panel will only be coated with protective coating; additional flashing is installed to prevent further erosion caused by water.

Left: The military village residence site before the intervention.
Left (below): The same decorative tiles applied in the new building.
Below: 3D drawing of the GRC panels.

Right (above): Close view of the main building podium façade.
Right (below): The drawing process for the GRC panels.

AMBA HOTEL RENOVATION

TAIPEI, 2013

The Amba Hotel Zhongshan branch was originally an eight-floor office building first established in the 1970s. It was renovated as Amba Hotel in 2015 with the platform of being "sustainable, cultural, and technological." The original office building was designed by renowned Taiwanese architect E.P. Kao, as a classic and contemporary piece of architecture. Continuous horizontal window openings and thick-steel concrete walls showcased a simplistic beauty with elegantly proportionate scales. The renovation aimed to preserve as much of the original exterior as possible, at the same time reinforcing the building's insulation and acoustic capability.

Through four phases (disassemble, reassemble, construction, application), we began to give new value to the discarded building materials such as the old aluminum window frames and grilles.

The disassembling of the aluminum frames was done through manual labor and light machinery; the process aimed not to damage the original size and shape of the frame. With the endless possibility of trimming, rearranging, reshaping, and re-constructing, determining how to transform and re-apply the disassembled frames proved to be a challenge. However, a discovery was made through the disassembly process that revealed four different frame section patterns from the top, bottom, left, and right frames. After numerous experiments, seven different sectional pattern arrangements were chosen to form an overall wall pattern at the front entrance.

In order to lower the complexity of the fabrication process and ease the onsite assembly difficulties, we created sheets after sheets of pre-assembled instruction drawings so the onsite operators could easily comprehend and accurately assemble each individual piece.

FORM
building material

A		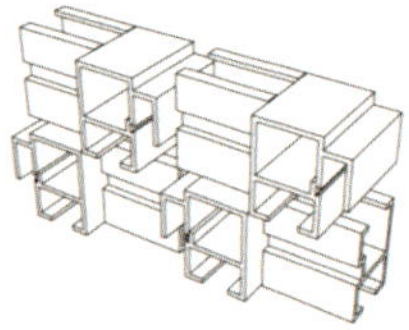	UNIT 4 x4, UNIT 3 x4
B		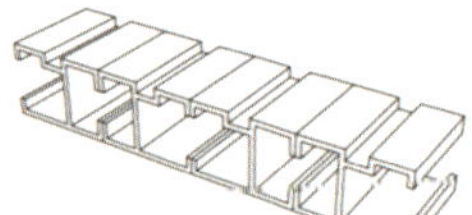	UNIT 4 x4
C		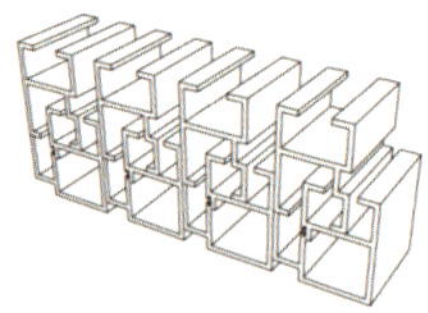	UNIT 4 x4, UNIT 3 x4
D		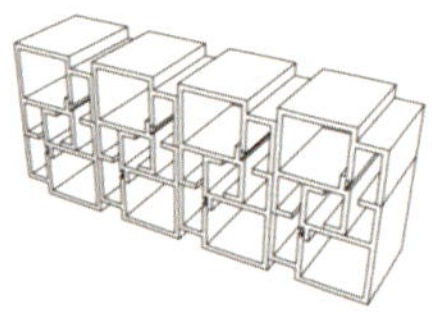	UNIT 4 x4, UNIT 3 x4
E		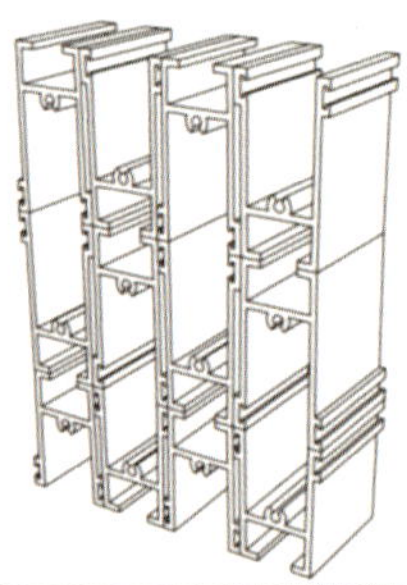	UNIT 1 x8, UNIT 2 x4
F		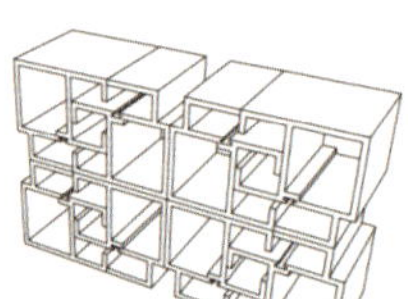	UNIT 3 x8
G	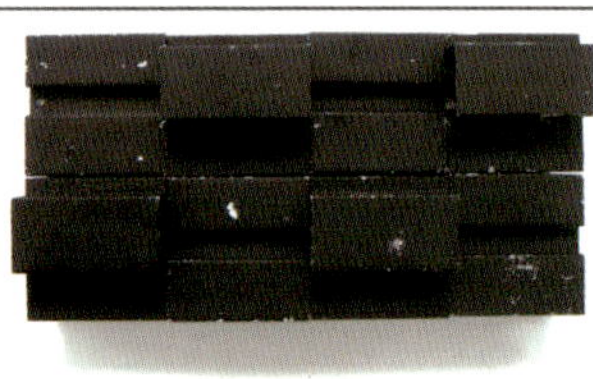	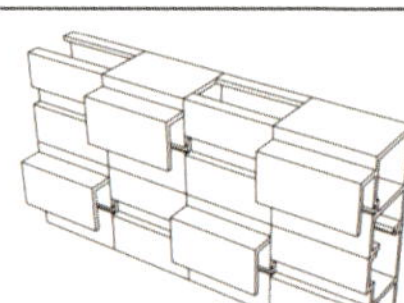	UNIT 4 x4, UNIT 3 x4

Above: Prototype of the wall's design.
Right: The prototype of the new wall.
Below: Different types of assembly options.

Left: Assembly options of the section cuts for the aluminum frames.

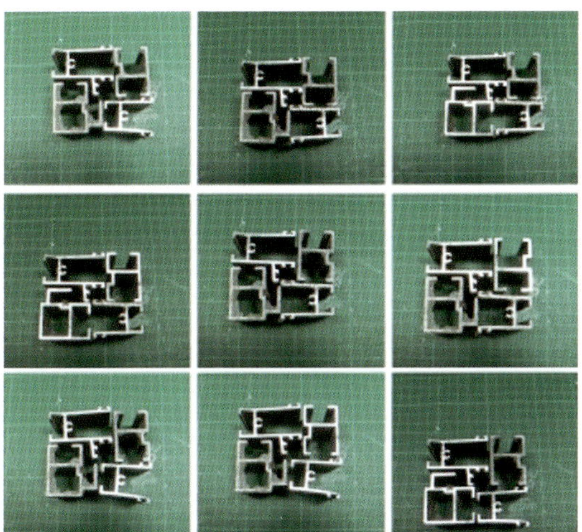

Left (above): The existing windows that would be dismantled, cut, and re-arranged in the new wall façade.
Below: The new decorative entrance wall and roof.

In order to save on-site assembly time, the assembling was made in a modular way. When the factory cuts the aluminum material, it assembles a certain size first, for example: 6x6 or 8x8, which can reduce time and quality. It is also easy to control, but it is still necessary to calculate the quantity beforehand to avoid miscalculation.

FENGTAY AGRICULTURE R&D CENTER

YUNLIN, 2016

Fengtay Foundation is a non-profit organization in southern Taiwan that is dedicated to promote organic agriculture. The park features office space for the foundation, laboratories for inspection and certification of organic products, and a logistical center for the cleaning and packaging of agricultural products.

Brick was considered one of the most essential building materials in Taiwan's rural villages in the 19th-century. Therefore, in an attempt to revitalize the spirit of Taiwan's 19th-century agriculture and coexistence with nature, the façade uses brick as its choice building material. The goal of this project was to reform agricultural regulations, which means the application of brick as a building material needed to likewise deviate from traditional mortar methods. A new construction method was established to provide the brick façade with a richer and more contemporary expression by linking each brick with a steel rod. Each brick was separated by a rubber padding to maximize the overall façade permeability and at the same time breakthrough the height limit set by traditional methods of bricklaying. In order to verify this new method the client, design team, and construction team co-commissioned the NTU Seismological Lab to run a seismic study on a five-meter-high and a ten-meter-high model. This study aided in understanding the behavior of this new brick wall under seismic activity, which serviced in modifying the design based on the results of the study.

Due to the high permeability of the brick wall, the west-side façade resembles layers of shading blinds. It provides quite a poetic lighting effect in the space behind when the afternoon sun penetrates through the blinds. Not only does the brick wall provide an energy saving benefit, but also communicates a new sense of contemporary rural village esthetics.

FORM
building material

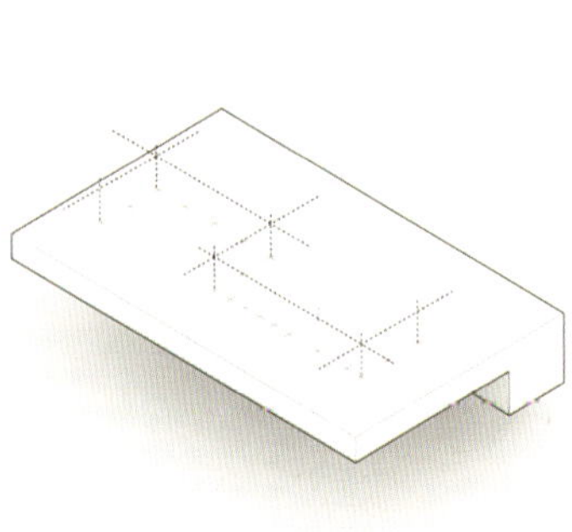

1 Monitor + fixed brick level + drilling

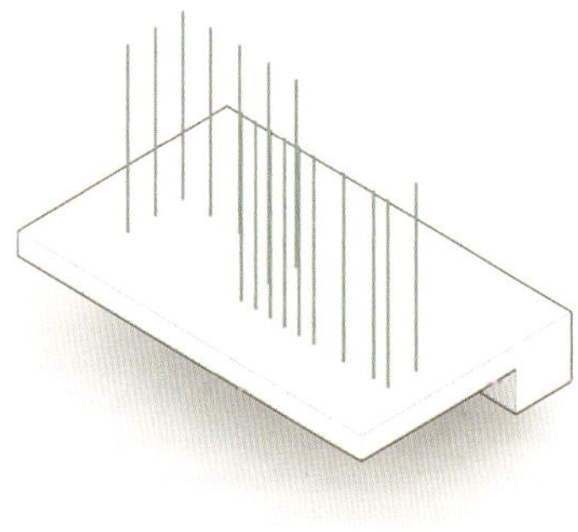

2 Stainless steel bar (H=120cm, D=16mm)

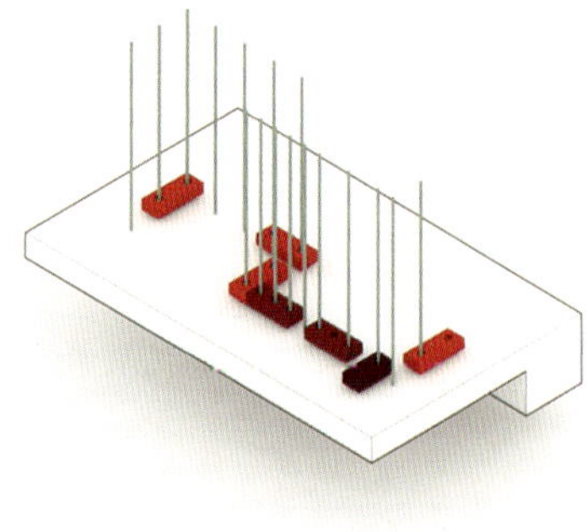

3 First layer

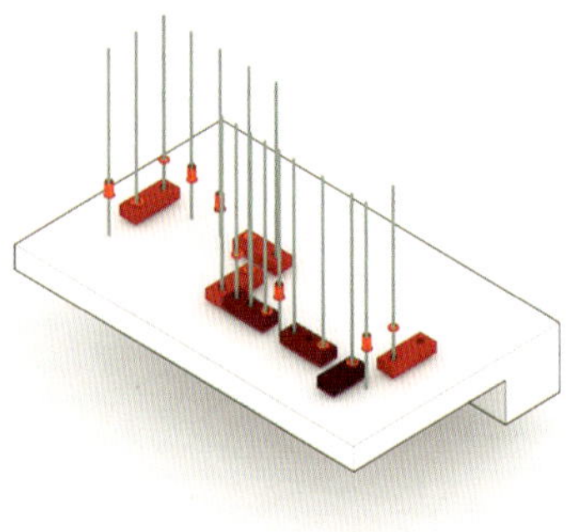

4 Place the gaskets – a total of three gaskets are used interchangeably

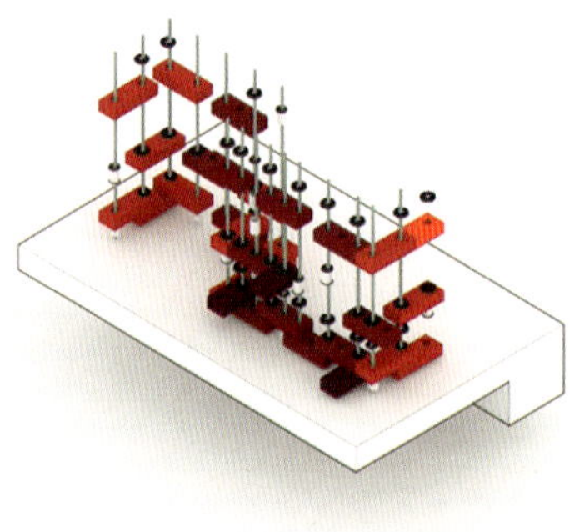

5 Monitor + building second layer + gasket (one set is four layers)

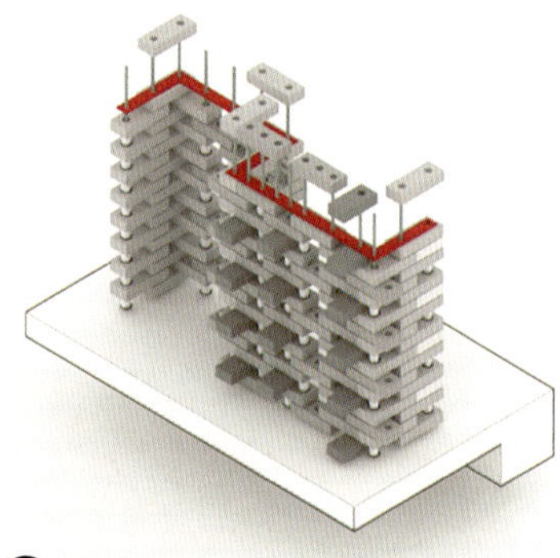

6 S-shaped stainless steel plate reinforcement placed every 13 layers. (three sets +1)

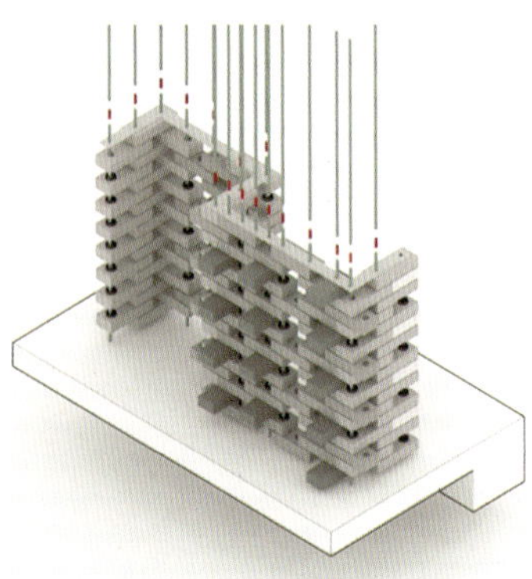

7 The stainless steel bar extends through the splicer each 120cm.

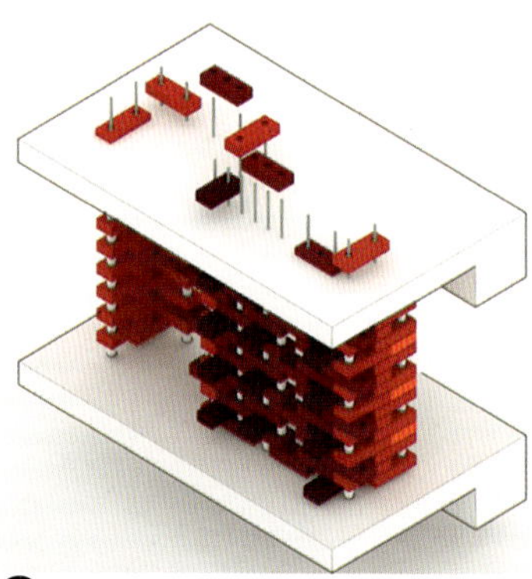

8 The bar is connected to the upper floor from the lock hole.

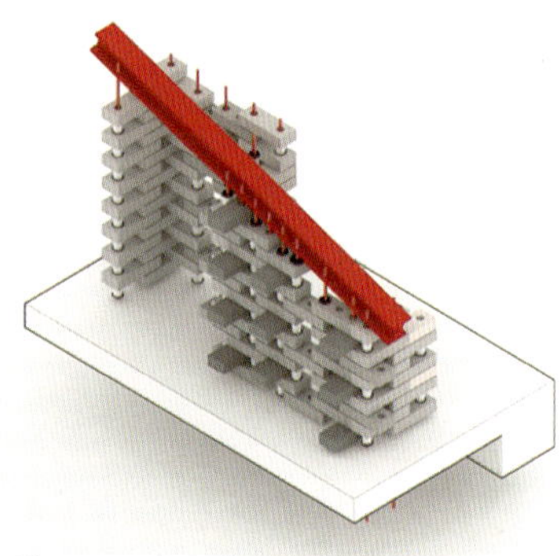

9 Welding and fixing with H-beam

1

2

3

4

5

6

7

8

9

Resistance tests of the brick wall in lab.

Above: Construction site photo showing the building's complex west brick façade.
Below: Construction site photo from the interior where the light is dynamically filtered by the brick.

All living beings have interface to regulate their relation with their external environment: cells have membrane to maintain suitable temperatures, pH value, and salinity; humans have skin to ward off bacteria, to perspire, and to sense cold, heat, and pain; birds have feathers to protect against wind and water, to control airflow while flying or landing and to regulate body temperature. Besides acting as a barrier, an interface also needs to have the ability to transmit various properties such as substance, energy, or genetic information in order to renew its elements of life.

For architecture, the interfaces accomplish almost exactly the same thing as those of organic beings. It's a barrier to withstand noise, fierce sunlight, rainwater, strong wind, cold air, and predators; it's a passage to let in gentle breeze, filtered sunlight, and occupants; it promotes mutual affinity to make connection with the surrounding neighborhoods and the city.

INTERFACE

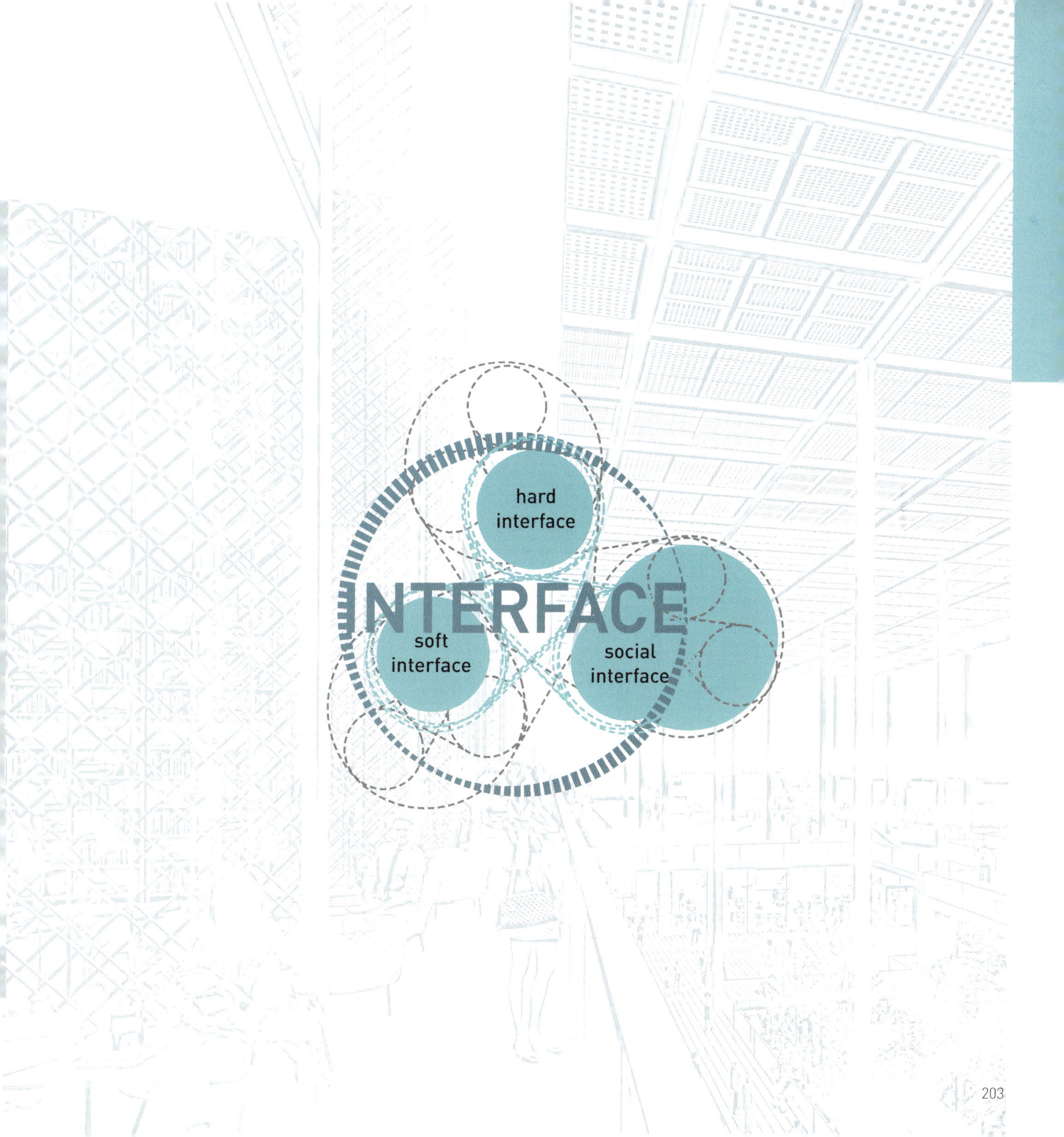
hard
interface
INTERFACE
soft
interface
social
interface

hard interface

Nature's esthetics are often bundled with functionality such as mating, hunting, shielding, warming, and cooling. The same principles should be applied to the outer shell of a building in response to the benefits and threats coming from the outside. The regulating mechanism of the outer shell, the hard interface, is designed to accommodate the needs of internal space through the adjustment of environmental properties such as temperature, light, radiation, ventilation, or acoustic.

Because the outer shell, often termed as the elevation, provides the main expression for the architectural intent and is often the main esthetics focus, it can be designed as a cultural symbol, a vessel to express social ideas, or even branding for the client. During this process the scale of the architecture will begin to shift from singular to a combination of small, medium, and large. As a result, the architecture will be amiable and further enrich the urban expression of the cityscape.

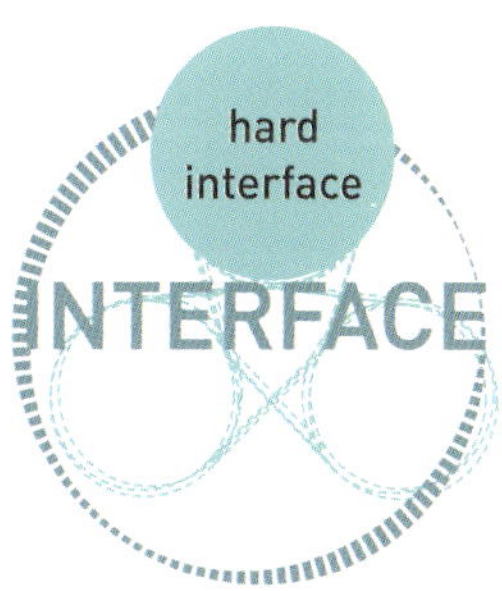

NATIONAL ARCHIVES
NEW TAIPEI CITY, 2018

The National Archives is the center for Taiwan's collective memory. Aside from its main function as a storage facility, another main objective of the National Archives is to facilitate the advancement and application of our memory as a nation. Therefore, the archives had to be able to provide both a creative and pleasant exhibition environment, with easy access and application of the information stored within the archives.

The site is located within the urban-development zone of Linkou District, a forest that naturally evolved over the span of two decades and features vast bio-diversity well suited for low altitude countries such as Taiwan. The building was placed at the northeastern corner, where younger trees are mostly concentrated in order to preserve the vast majority of the forest. A scenic route was designed to allow visitors to pace through the serene forest before arriving at the entrance plaza, which is at the same height as the surrounding tree crowns and acts as a buffer space between interior and exterior. The archive's façade is enveloped by a dynamic-looking double skin that allows for better control of its interior temperature.

The 50-meter-high archive building is a design inspired by Taiwan's active tectonic plates that have emerged, shaping the now Linkou platform. The pressurized plates are stacked on top of one another and extend upwards only to have their boundaries blurred by the sky—a symbolized gesture of how our memory as a nation is accumulated through time and, is pointing to a future that we can all hope for.

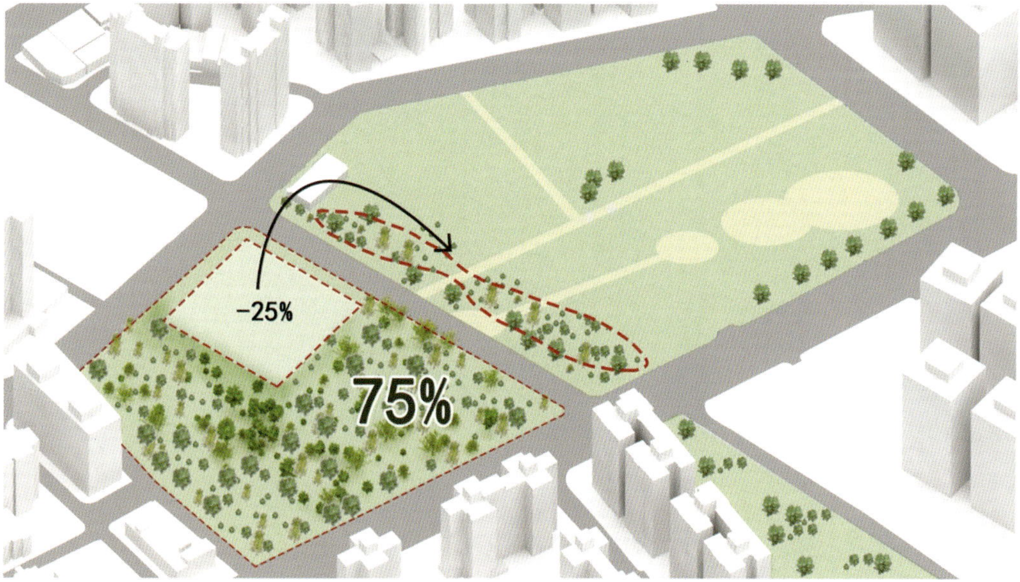

Above: The building is placed in the north eastern corner where the trees are largely younger and easier to move to the vicinity of the site.
Below: Concept diagram.

Left: Rendering view of the semi-outdoor space.

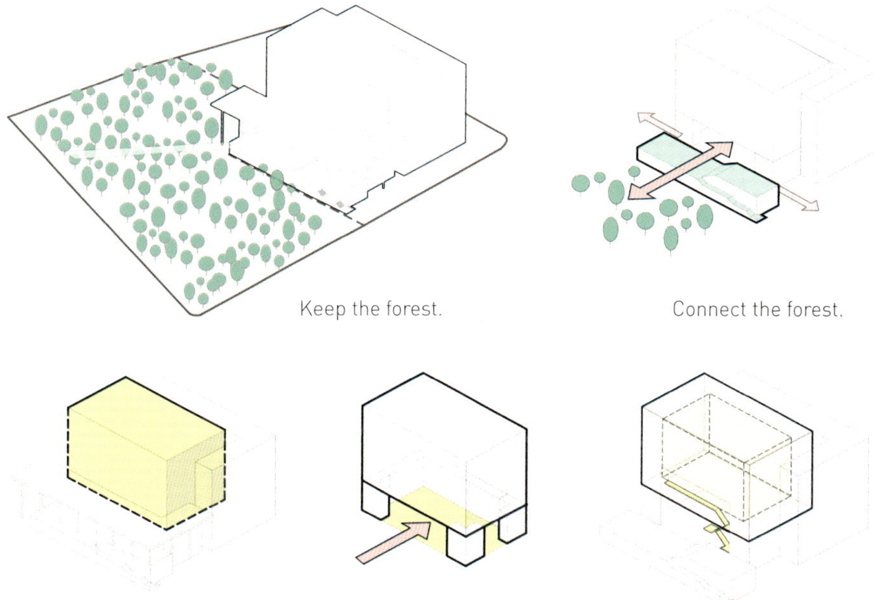

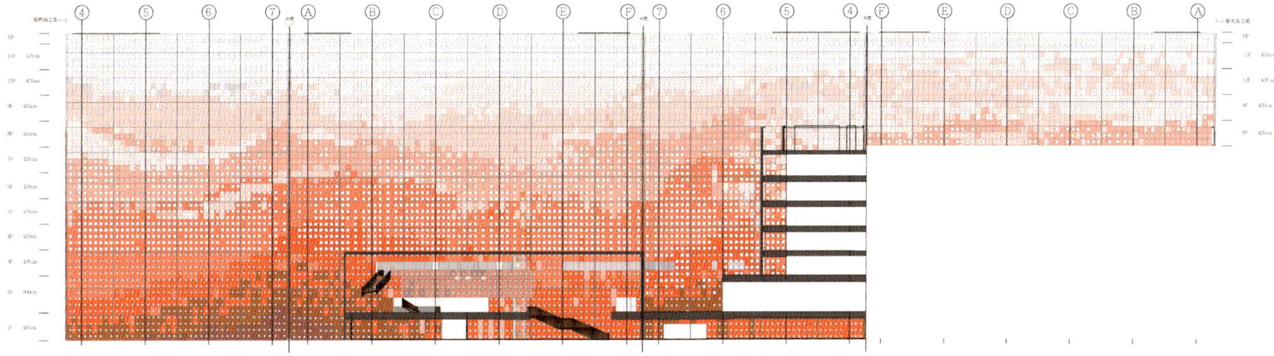

Above: Detailed drawing of the color-schemed façade which helps to reduce the visual impact of the building mass.
Below: Perspective section showing the protective hard interface surrounding the building's depository space.

Left: Rendering view of the entrance canopy and overall building.

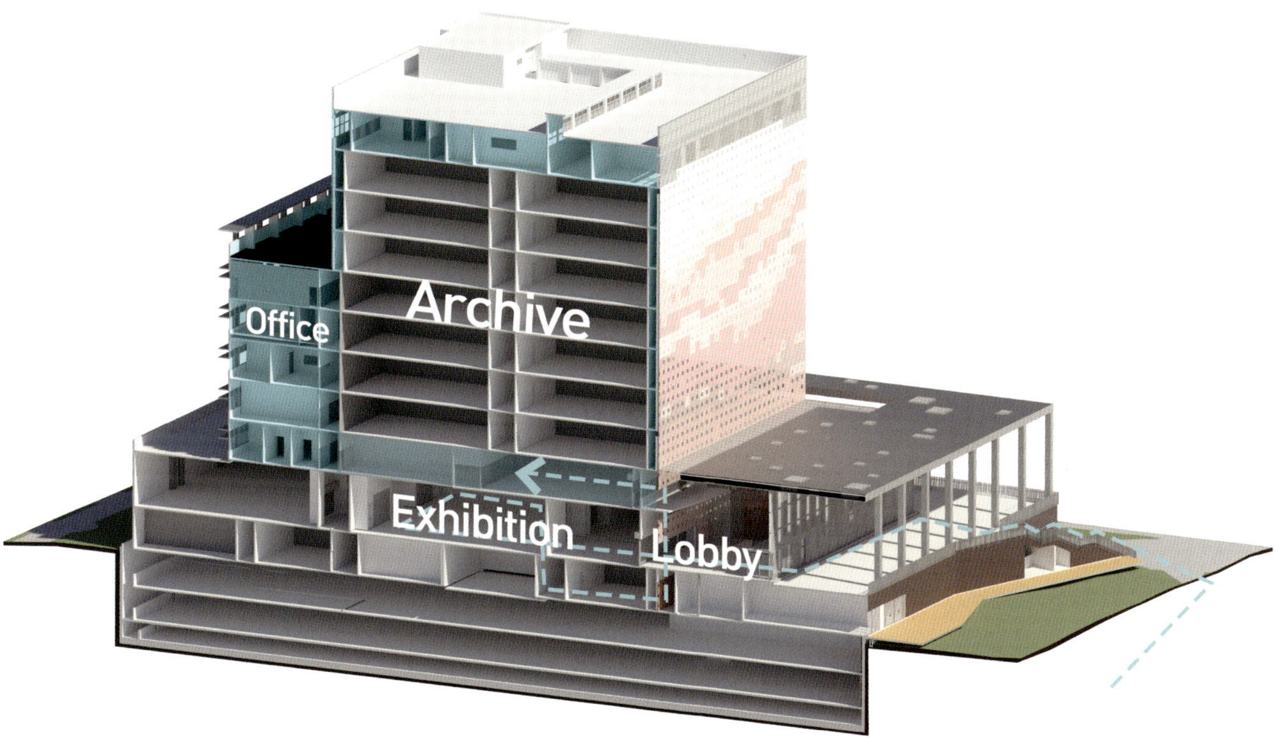

NTHU, GREEN ENERGY RESEARCH AND EDUCATION BUILDING

HSINCHU, 2016

This design aimed to promote an efficient environment for both students and teachers to work together by creating spaces that allow diverse outdoor and indoor campus activities. The introduction of public space in the interior of each floor such as the foyer, saloon, and exhibition hall were designed to be multi-functional spaces with flexibility intended to help elevate one's creative mindset.

The building shape is in a clear dialogue with its natural environment. Its strategic positioning blocks the northeast monsoon and creates a comfortable microclimate on the west-side lawn.

The building envelope is wrapped with an outer layer of perforated metal mesh panel that forms an insulated corridor (and maintenance walkway). This "second skin" is used to shield the direct sunlight and increase the indoor diffused light to provide an appropriate amount of illumination. Furthermore, the perforated panel can also effectively reduce the amount of solar radiation generated by the inner wall and contribute to a horizontal shading effect. The vertical pipe-lines for the laboratories are also benefited from the metal paneling by providing an extra layer of protection and enclosing the space for easier maintenance.

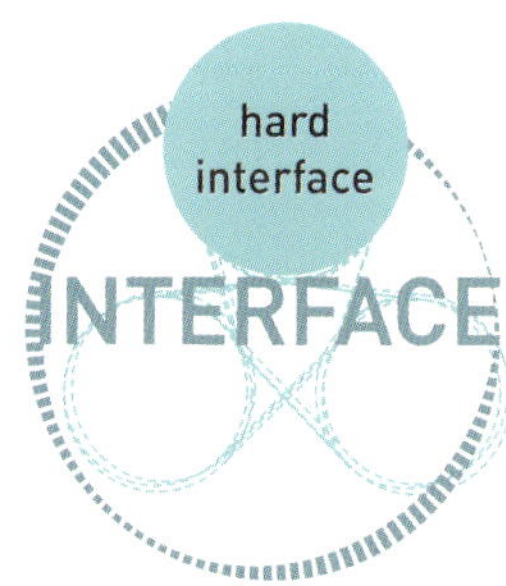

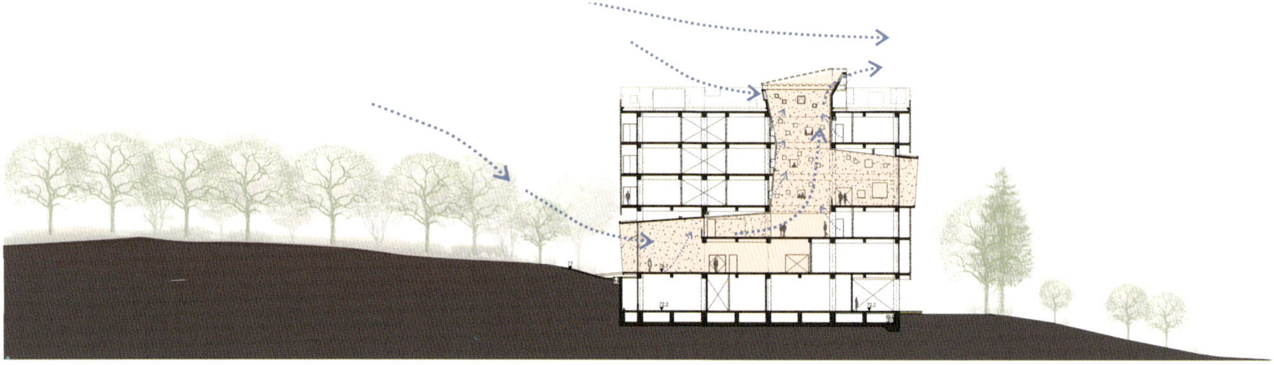

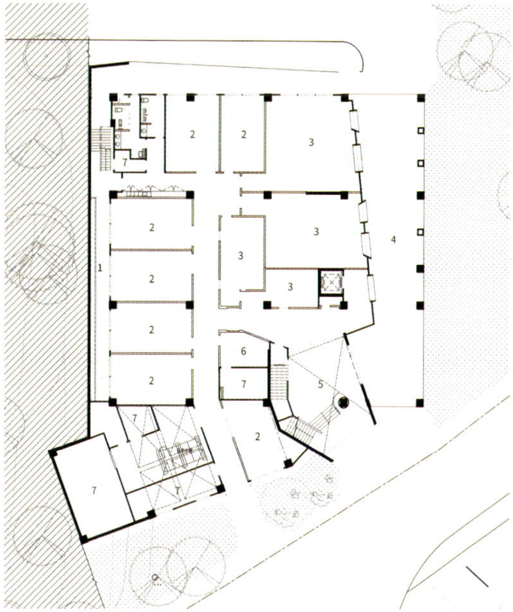

Ground Level Floor Plan

1. Light Well
2. Laboratory
3. Classroom
4. Semi-Outdoor Corridor
5. Lobby
6. Duty Room
7. Engine Room

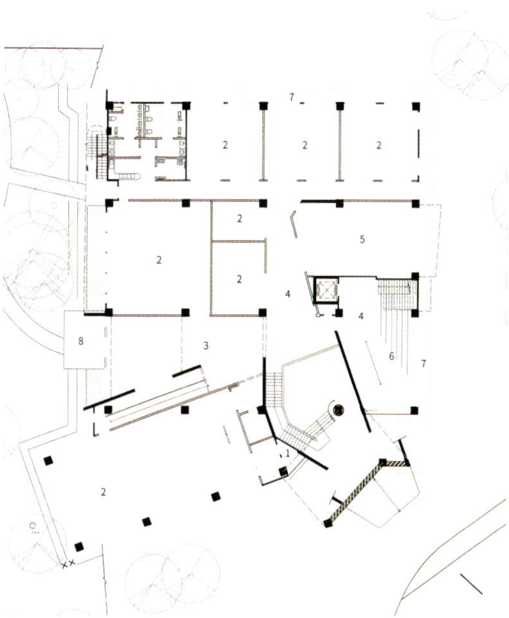

First Level Floor Plan

1. Balcony
2. Classroom
3. Lobby
4. Hall
5. Laboratory
6. Communicate Space
7. Repair Corridor
8. Foyer

Above: Aerial view of the building surrounded by greenery.
Right: Ground-floor and first-floor plan.

Left: Section diagram representing the ventilation through the building.

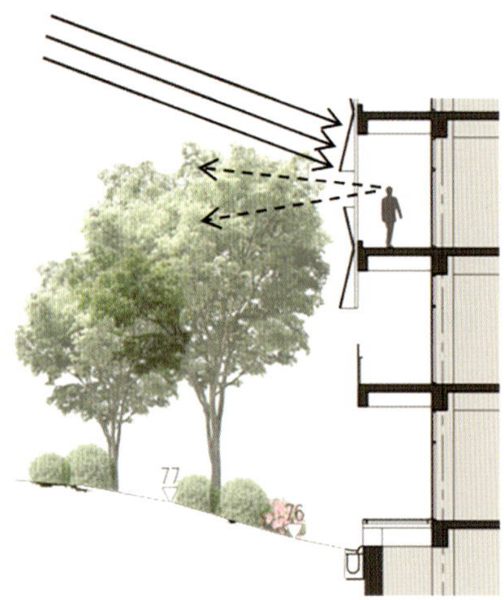
77
76

Left and Right: Photos of the outer expansion net which not only effectively reduces the amount of solar radiation, but also does not degrade the indoor illumination and, adds soft diffused light.

Left: Study of the building's façade.

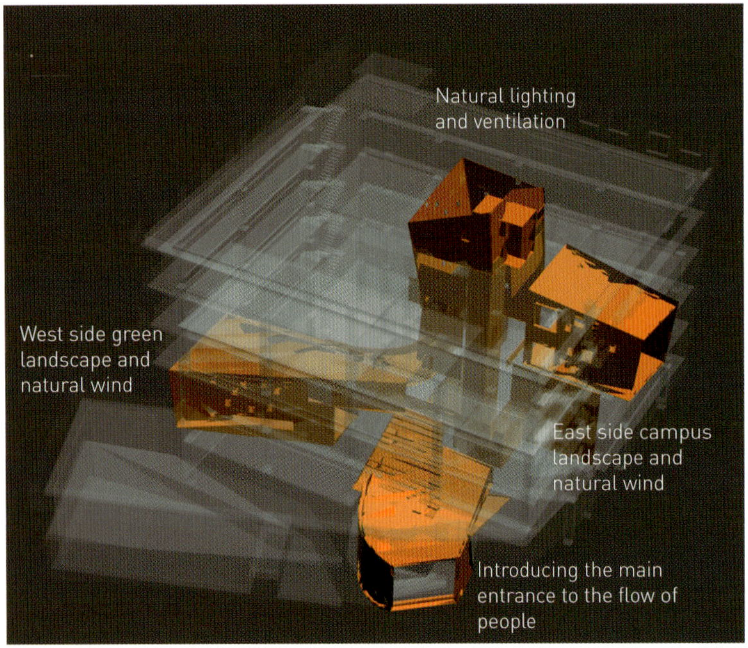

Above: The skylight illuminates the interior public space that pierces the volume.
Left: Diagram showing the multiple public spaces for natural ventilation and light.

Right: View of the building's façade.

GREEN ENERGY TECHNOLOGIES JOINT RESEARCH CENTER

TAINAN 2017

The Green Energy Technologies Joint Research Center is the central hub for Shalun Green Energy Science City. This center's purpose is to stimulate innovation within the sustainable-energy industry, bridge research outcomes from academia to industrialized technologies, and develop new products, systems, or services for green energy.

The building was designed to adapt to its natural environment and improve biodiversity. The design has a lower impact with the incorporation of ecological detention pools (rainwater gardens), collection wells, water-permeable pavements, turf grass belts, grass ditches, etc., in order to improve storm-runoff management, and reduce pollution on the surface directly into sewers into rivers and oceans. The rainwater or building's recycled water source can also improve the microclimate by stacking/flowing water generated by changes in topography.

The ground cooling channel was designed to pre-cool the external air so the air conditioner will consume less energy by utilizing the cool ambient temperate for the underground.

The design creates a comfortable R&D and incubation environment to increase interaction between people and energy. The open, semi-outdoor atrium creates visual continuity between the labs and offices on different floors allowing for discussion and communication spaces. The upper part of the atrium is covered by a solar panel scaffolding that provides good indoor lighting to reduce the amount of electricity used during the day. The light and shadow changes sprinkled through the gaps of the solar panels create a space atmosphere that bathes in the shade of the forest.

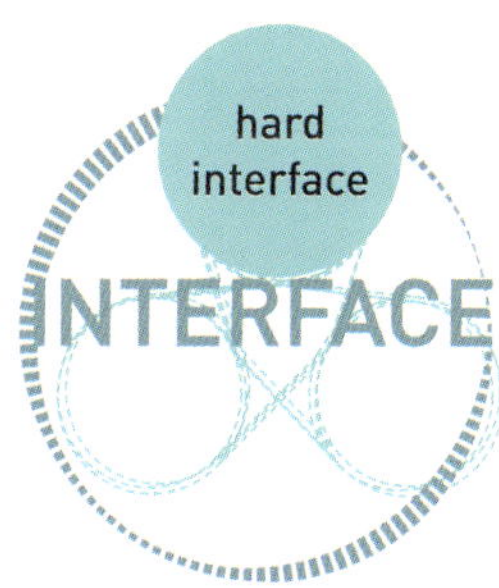

BUILDING STRATEGY

Day Light and Wind flow

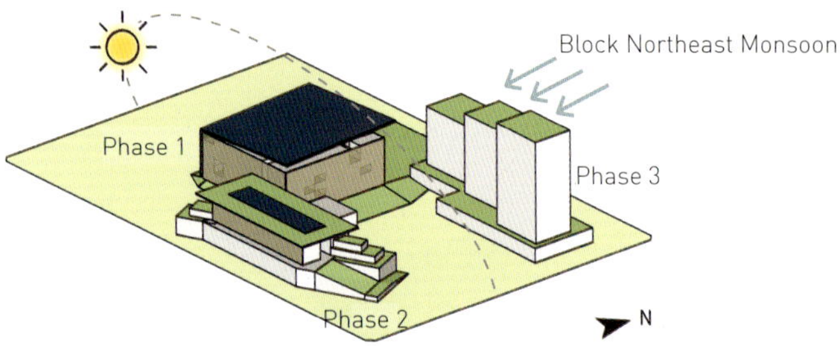

High Speed Rail and Greening

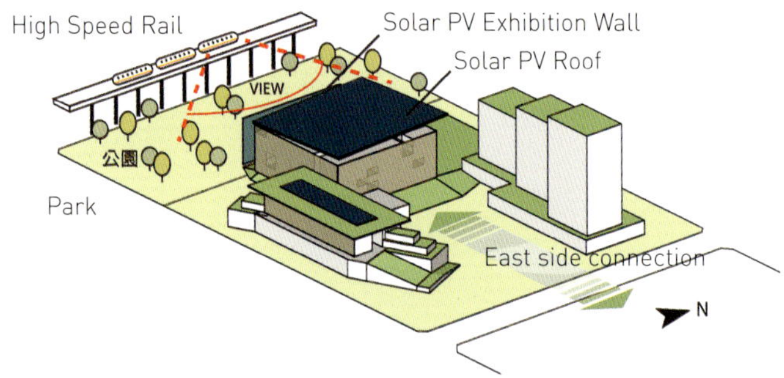

Excavation Balance and Ventilation

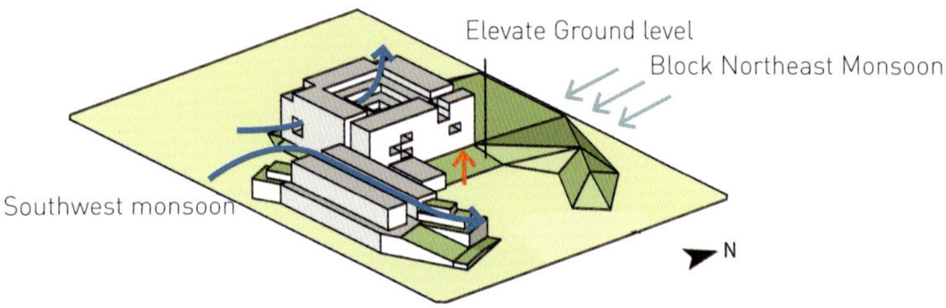

Heat Isolation, Energy Saving and Net Zero

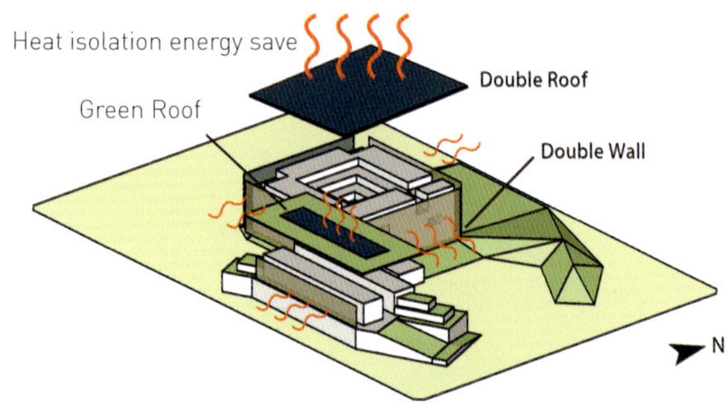

Ecology and Sharing

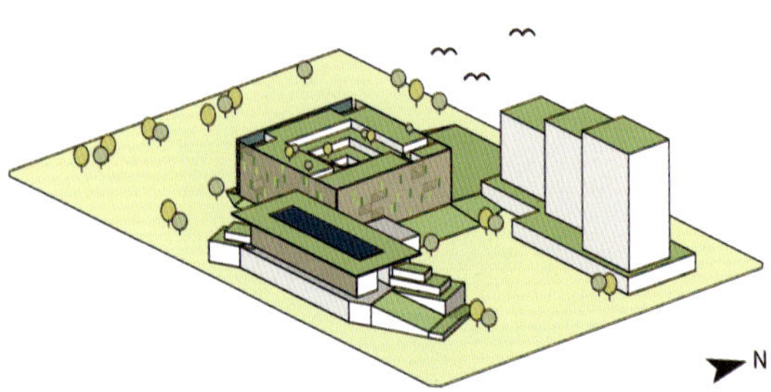

Maximum Natural Energy

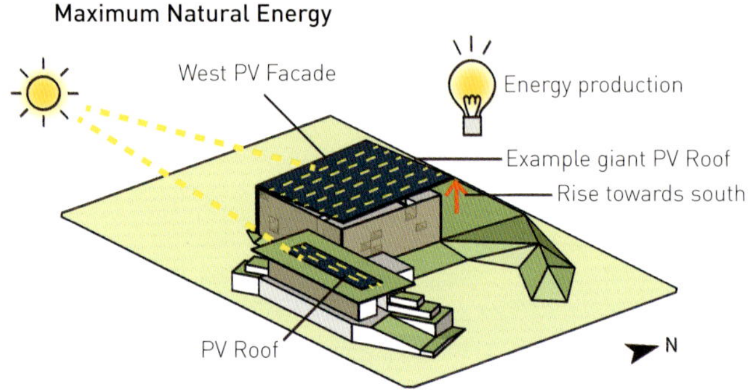

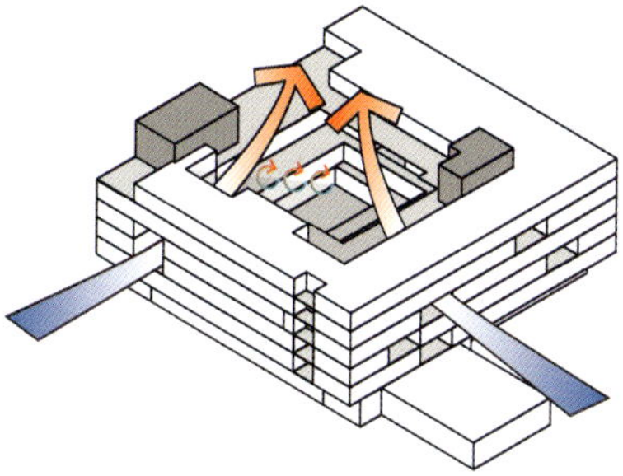

Circulation of Wind

The void of the façade and courtyard create natural ventilation to decrease overall temperature.

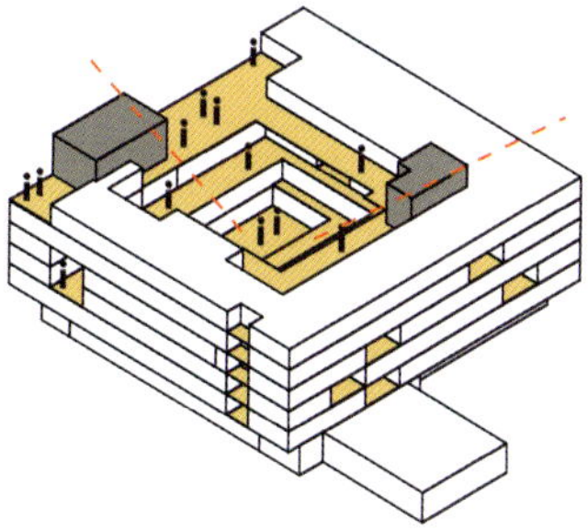

Communication of People

Creation of an exterior communication terrace to promote people from different department's interaction.

The layers of terrace provide great views for people to experience.

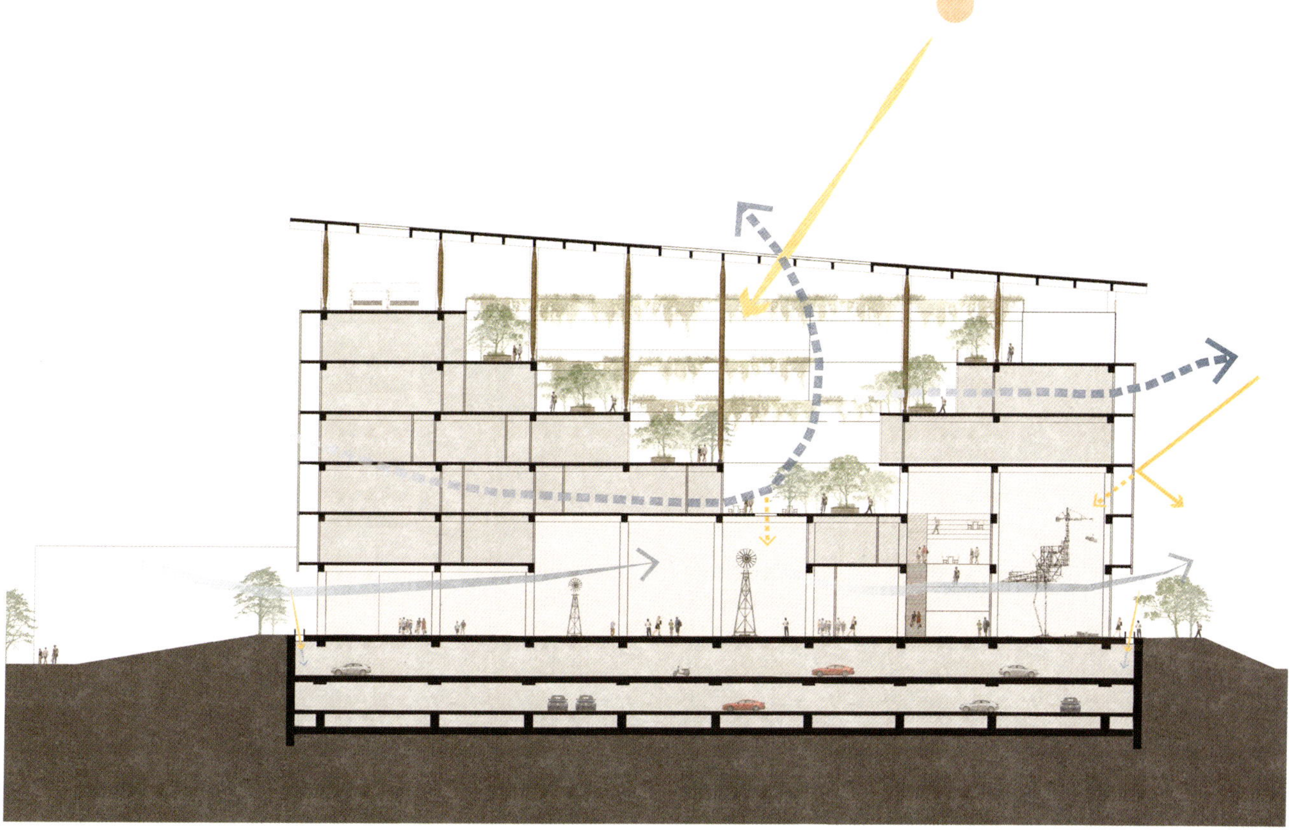

Section showing natural ventilation of the courtyard and its green terraces covered by PV roof.

Left: Rendering of the building's interior courtyard.

Below: Wind simulation graphics. Source: Building and Climate Lab, NCKU.

During the summer the main wind direction comes from the south. The vortex is formed on the east side of the site, and the outdoor space is cooled by the evapotranspiration of the eco-pond.

During the winter the main wind direction comes from the north. The cold wind is mostly shielded by the building volume.

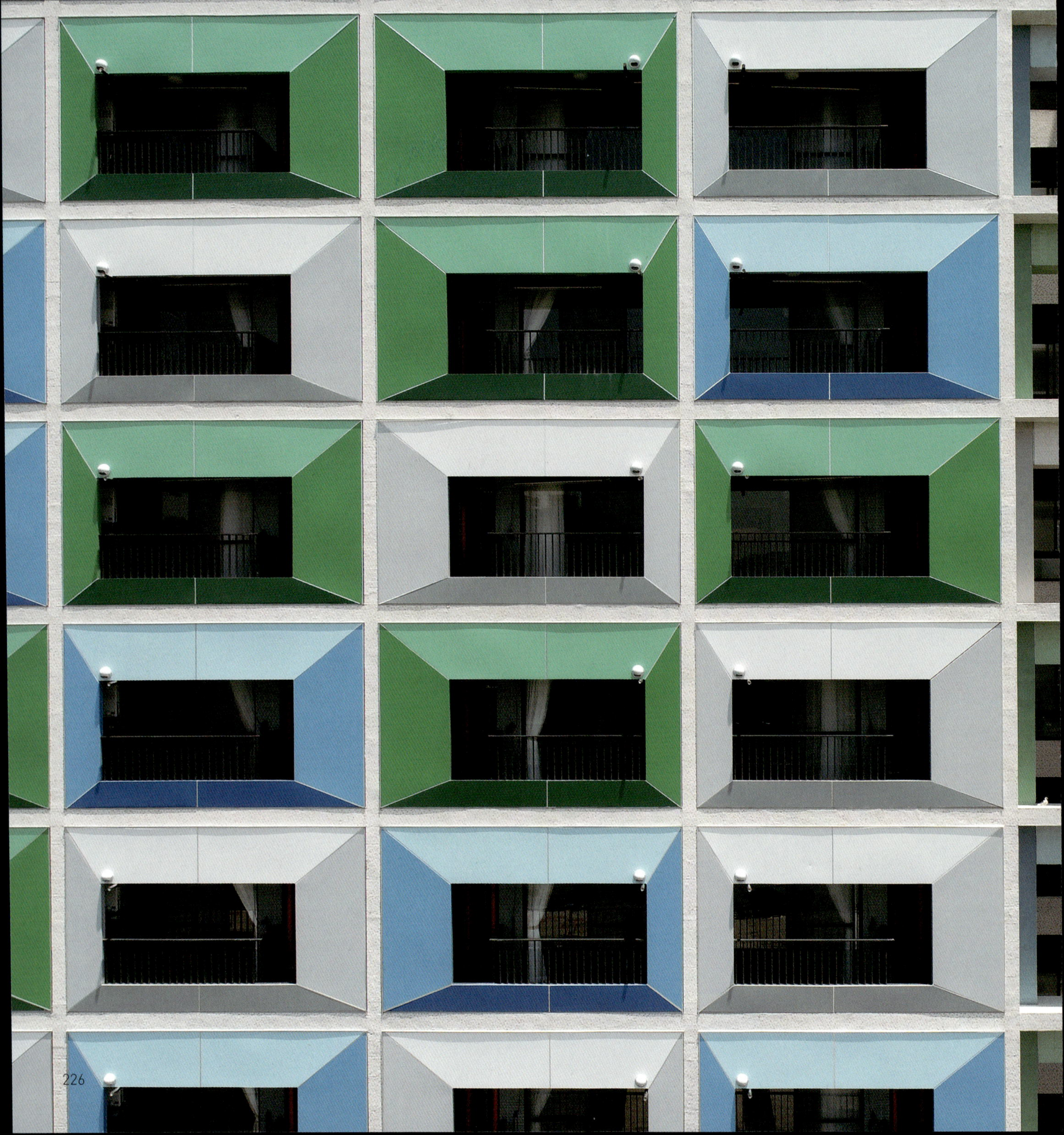

WANHUA PUBLIC HOUSING

TAIPEI, 2012

The high real-estate price in urban areas is a global issue; Taipei is no exception to this problem. Since urban-housing costs have far exceeded what most young adults can afford, the social housing project has become a priority for the City of Taipei. Qingnian Public Housing is situated in a neighborhood with a high population of elderly people, but with an abundance of open space and living conveniences. The introduction of social housing with young adults was intended to inject new energy into this neighborhood, the architectural design needed to achieve the same result. The main floor-plan configuration of Qingnian Public Housing was focused on one bedroom spaces, which meant the façade design could be a modular system, each one representing a single housing unit. As such, we designed each unit as a picture frame and each frame as a representation of a young adult or family, and the entire façade became a collage or photo album. The frame was not just for show, it was designed to minimize the visibility of water heaters, laundry machines, air condition units, and water pipes as to not interfere with the overall exterior appearance but add a touch of realness and livelihood to the surrounding area. The frame acts as a sun shade providing a comfortable interior and softer natural lighting. The building closest to the river front features blue and green as its main color scheme as a response to the river and mountain in the background, while the one closest to the city utilizes yellow and orange to complement the surrounding brick and wood historical buildings. The layering of colors is intended to help bring a fresh energy into the neighborhood.

hard interface

INTERFACE

Above: The façade represents a Facebook profile picture frame.
Right: The study of the façade's design in shape and color.

Left: Aerial view of the residential towers.

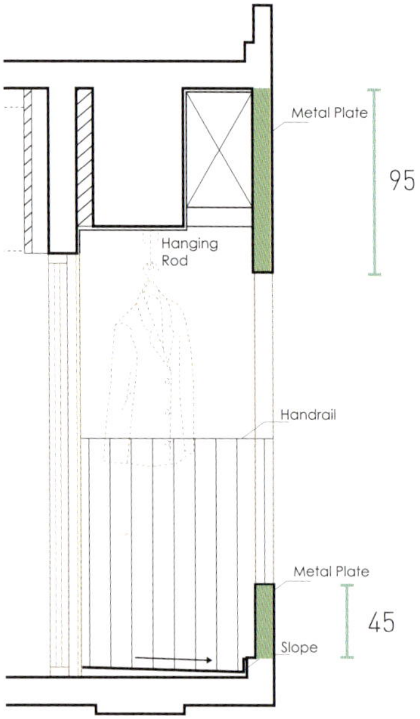

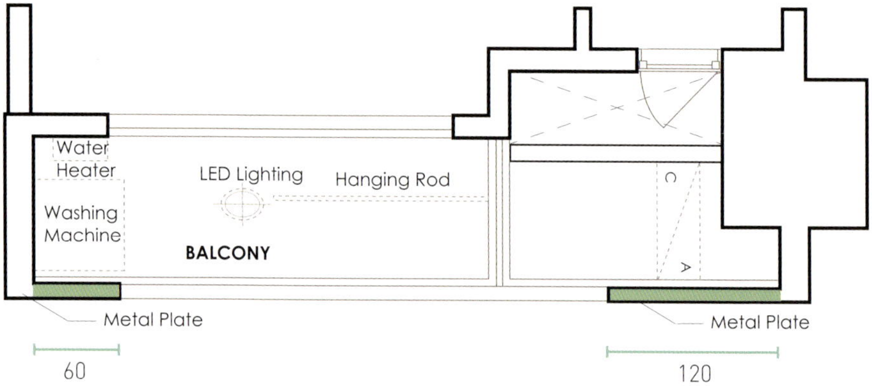

Above: Section and plan of the balcony's façade.
Right: The "frames" veil all the living utilities like air conditionings, washing machines, water heaters, and pipes.
Below: Shading simulation, conceptualizing the façade to create a double wall as a strategy for insulation of the exterior wall (average heat radiation simulation from May to October).
The outer peripheral area of the façade unit can reduce radiation heating by 50–70% and can reduce the heat of the RC exterior wall construction. The open surface portion can reduce the heat by 30%–50%, which can reduce the heating from the window.
1. No sunshade heating simulation.
2. Radiant-heat simulation of external shading.
3. Structural exterior wall heating condition.

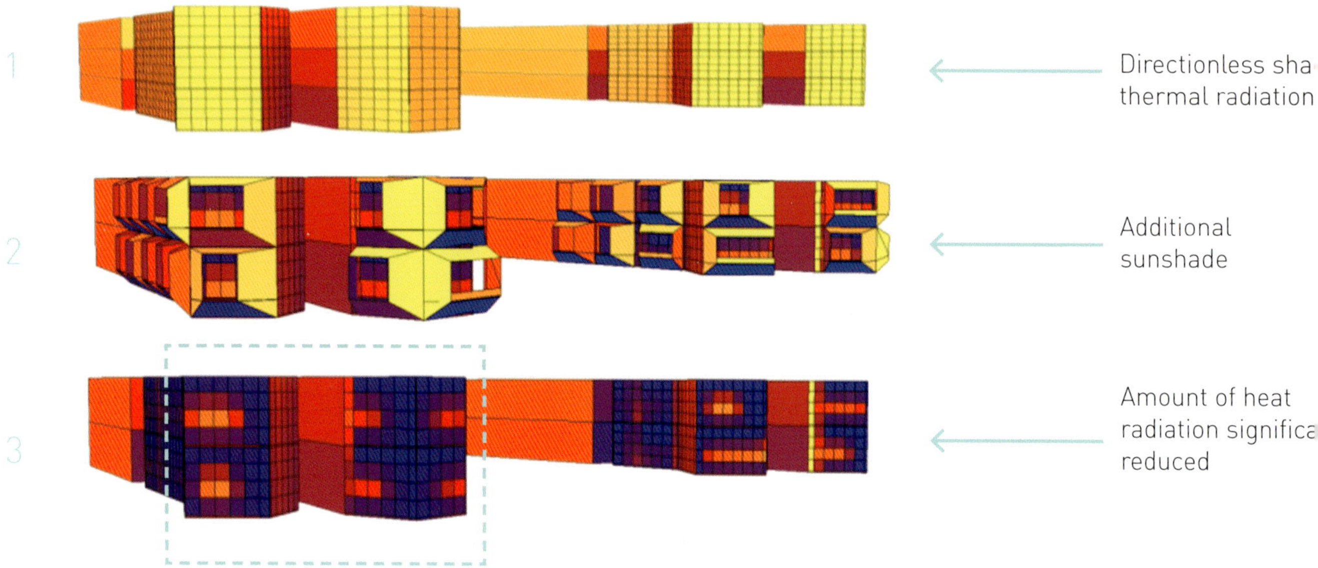

West-side elevation radiation

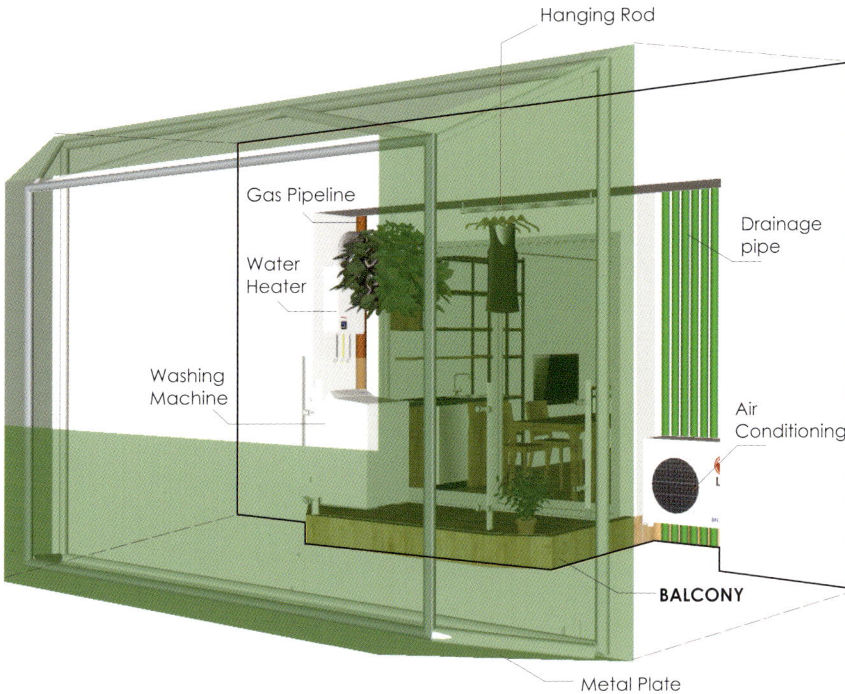

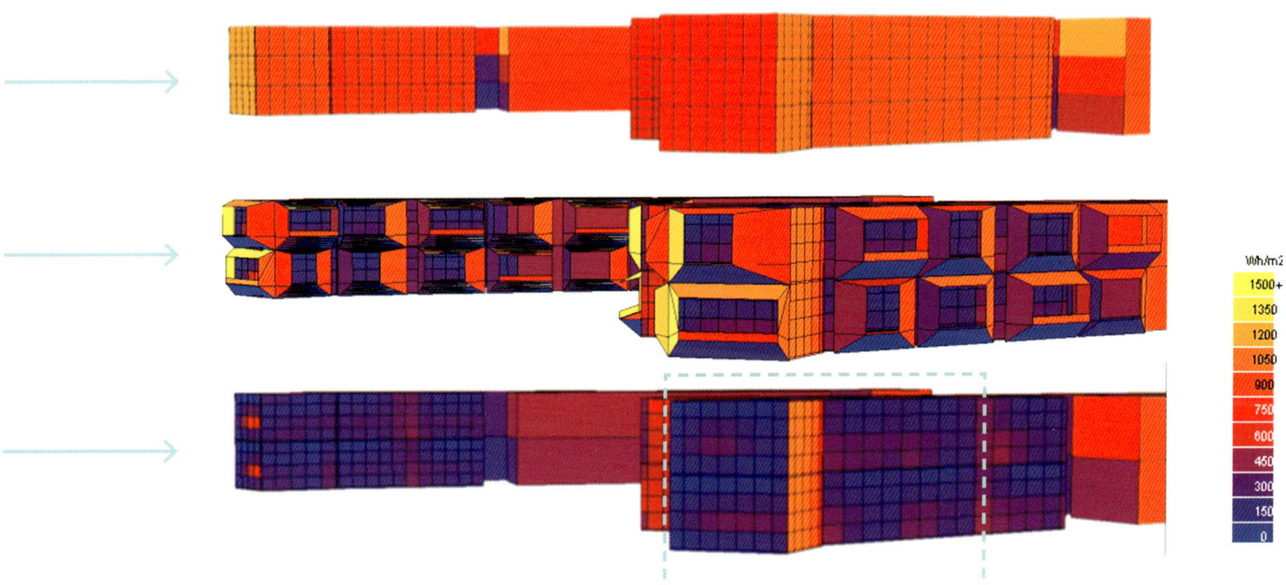

East-side elevation radiation

TAOYUAN WASTE TO ENERGY PLANT

TAOYUAN, 2018

The design of this waste incineration plant was to transform the building from a NIMBY (Not in my Backyard) to a YINMB (Yes in my backyard), using three design principles: landmark, green, and circular.

Through the organic undulating shape, greenery and circular energy façade and landscape environment, the occupants will have more knowledge of its eco-environment for their bio-energy center, and likewise the plant is to convert passive energy consumption into active production capacity.

The shape of the roof emerged from both the movement of water ripples and the abstract flow of energy. It depicts the natural landscape of the local ripples of water from the neighboring pond, the Qiangtang.

When the form matches the surrounding environment the amount of industrialization that a power plant possesses is transformed and reduced. The volume shape was generated from the undulating roof. This movement allowed for the roof area to be reduced, therefore building materials and costs also diminished.

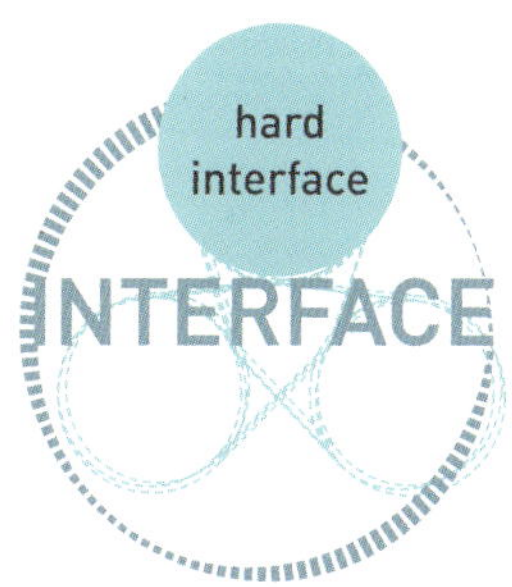

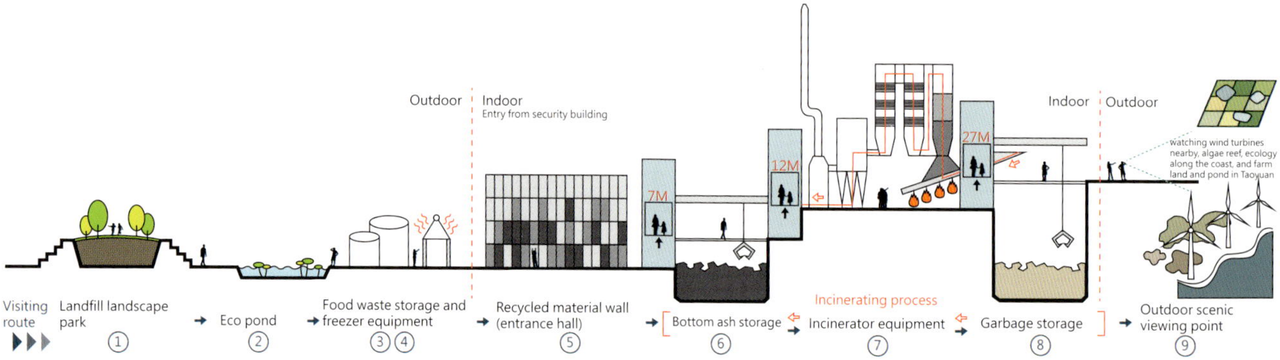

Above: Section diagram explaining the route taken by a visitor through the energy plant.
Below: Undulating roof inspired by the surrounding landscape.

Right: Strategy diagrams.

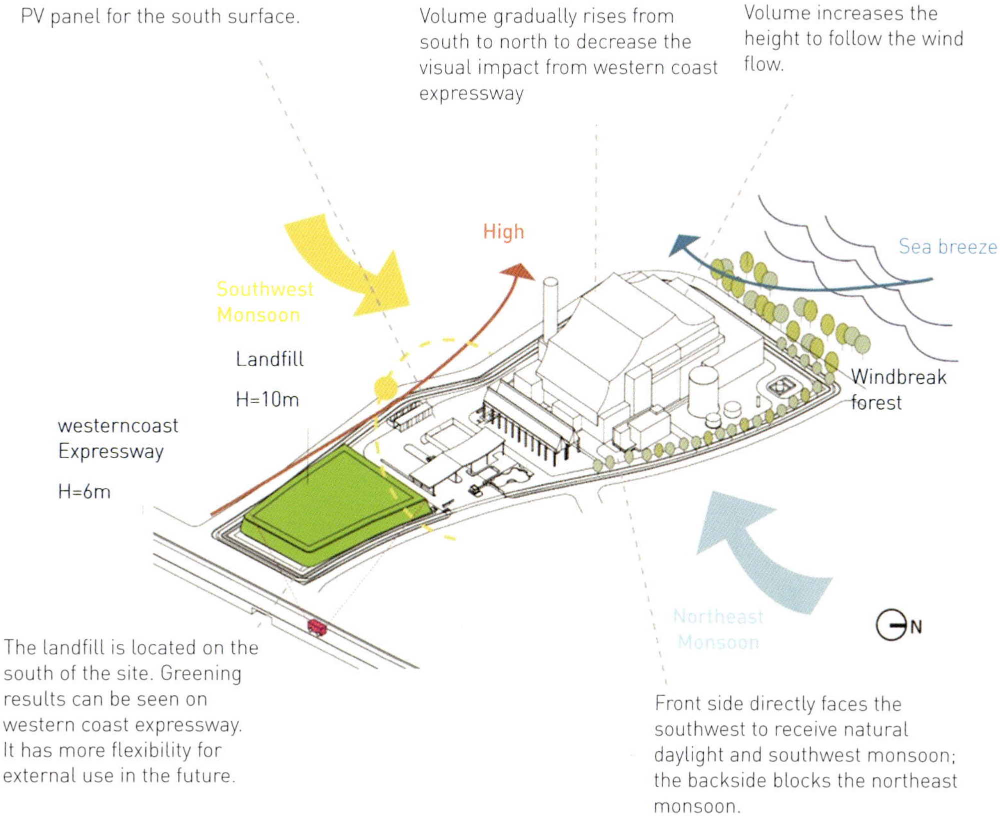
PV panel for the south surface.
Volume gradually rises from south to north to decrease the visual impact from western coast expressway
Volume increases the height to follow the wind flow.
High
Sea breeze
Southwest Monsoon
Landfill
H=10m
westerncoast Expressway
H=6m
Windbreak forest
Northeast Monsoon
N
The landfill is located on the south of the site. Greening results can be seen on western coast expressway. It has more flexibility for external use in the future.
Front side directly faces the southwest to receive natural daylight and southwest monsoon; the backside blocks the northeast monsoon.

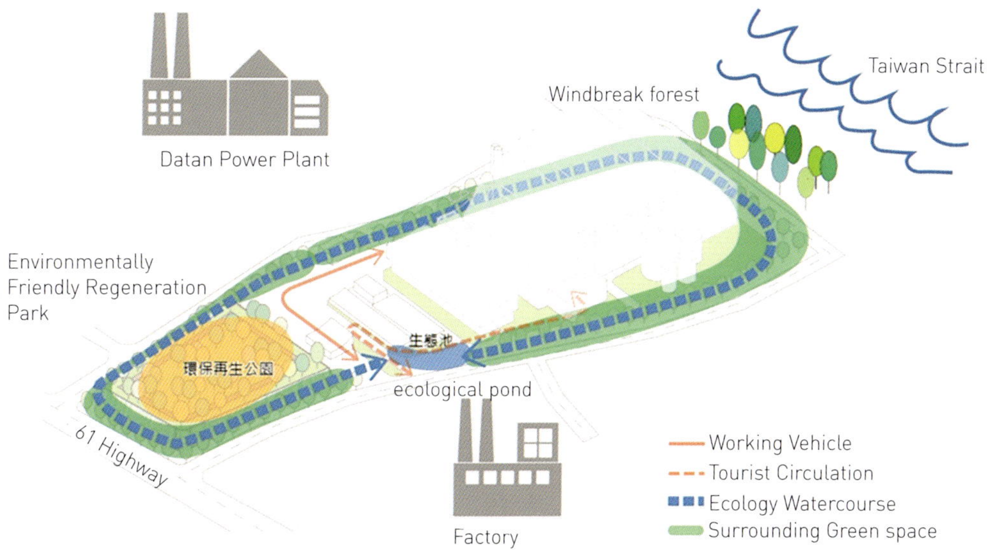
Taiwan Strait
Windbreak forest
Datan Power Plant
Environmentally Friendly Regeneration Park
環保再生公園
生態池
ecological pond
61 Highway
Factory
Working Vehicle
Tourist Circulation
Ecology Watercourse
Surrounding Green space

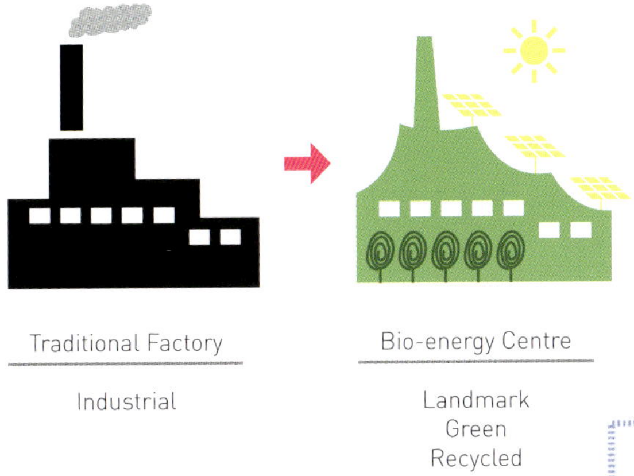

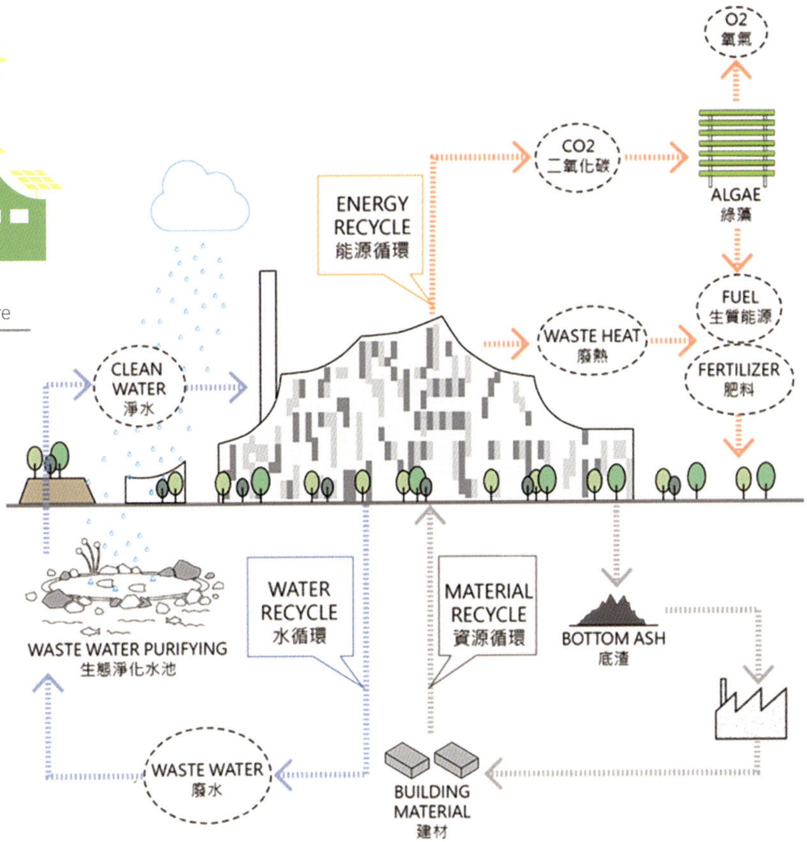

Left (above): Interior rendering showing the visitors experience from the power plant tour.
Left (below): Redefined energy plant image makes it an attractive landmark for visitors.

Right (above): Systems diagram.
Below: Elevation.

soft interface

The soft interface of nature can be best described as akin to the fur on mammals or feathers on birds. Their most essential function is to soften the impacts of harsh external conditions by acting as a buffer censoring direct contact with the skin itself. In architecture, external conditions such as wind, solar radiation, and rainfall will periodically become extreme, causing the regulatory mechanism of the hard interface—the exterior skin of the architecture—to withstand unbearable loads. At this point the soft interface becomes an accommodating mechanism to ease the load of the hard interface by creating an on-site microclimate as a buffer to the unpredictable external environments, making it more suitable for occupants.

Soft interface can include methods such as planting wind-resistant trees or using building mass configurations to block out winter's seasonal winds, while still allowing remaining walls to introduce accommodating fresh air into the building so open spaces can still be suitable for outdoor activities. The plants and artificial ponds in these open spaces can facilitate partial environmental ventilation by means of vaporization that reduces air temperatures and creates suitable conditions for natural ventilation. The trees planted on the east and west sides of the site help to minimize heat impact by acting as sources of shade to provide solar radiation relief for the exterior walls. The central courtyard was reserved as a suitable ground for plants that can promote bio-diversity and physical/spiritual wellness for the occupants.

ITRI SOUTHERN TAIWAN CAMPUS DORMITORY

TAINAN, 2007

The site is surrounded by valleys coming from three directions and fronted by lakes to the west. The layout of the design proposed to have the building cluster fit into the environment. The site, along with its networked landscape of the whole campus, was expected to be a great site for ecological observation. The building group was formed as part of the landscape vista working with the topography, and the roofs were designed as viewing platforms looking out onto the Chiayi plain.

The ecological pond in the center of the courtyard helped to adjust the micro-climate and works together with a nearby retention pool. With future efforts to cultivate the lake area in the vicinity of the construction site, the experience of strolling around the site and its neighborhoods is accentuated with the scenic body of water in stepped elevation and in varied scale, from manmade to natural.

Bamboo is constantly thriving within the campus area, and utilizing this local material helps to reduce the carbon footprint of the building. The application of bamboo ranges from planting to use for building materials like the exterior screening of the staircase, soft partition in the entrance area, or planted in the courtyard to complement the outdoor corridor. Further walking paths were implemented to center the bamboo forest around the site and the bamboo art area on the southern campus. Locally produced brick was chosen as the pavement for the semi-outdoor walkway.

INTERFACE
soft interface

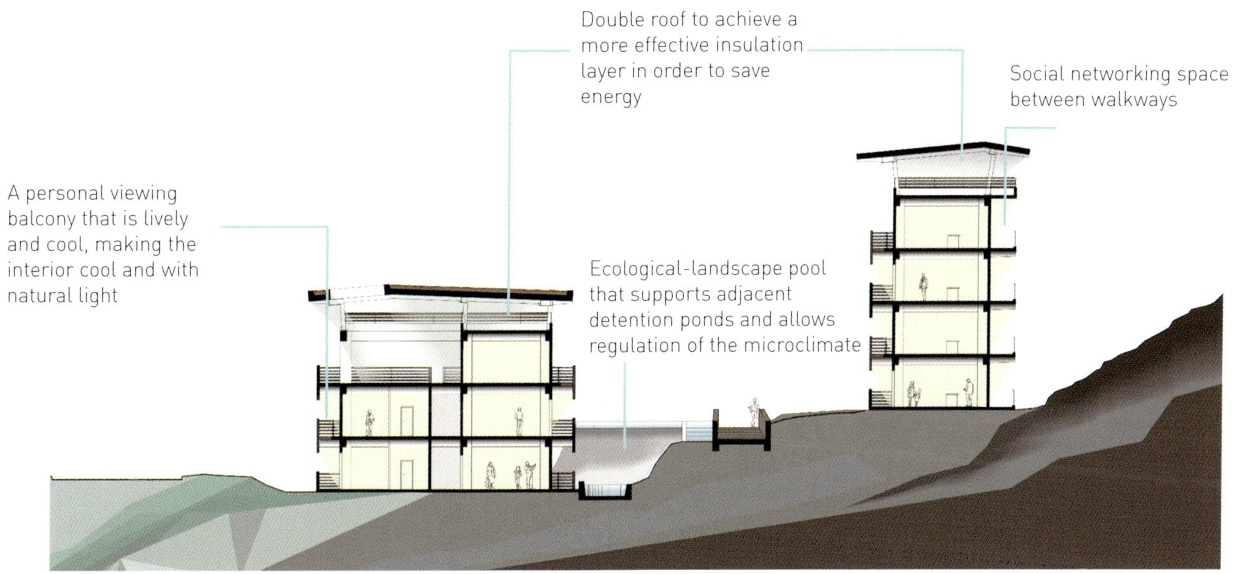

Left: Photo of the façade courtyard with the eco-pond, banana trees, and bamboo.

Above (right): The use of the eco pond allows for the retention of water on site.
Above: Explanatory section of the different strategies designed for a more efficient functioning building complex.

Left: Close-up view of the lively balcony façade.
Right: The different types of natural environments that surround the building.

TAIPEI FLORA EXPO PAVILIONS

TAIPEI, 2008

The design of the tri-pavilions used different corresponding technologies in order to achieve the best possible energy-efficient outcome.

The Future Pavilion, for example, is a large greenhouse that holds some of Taiwan's native plants indigenous to frigid, temperate, and tropical zones. This was made possible by an advanced temperature and humidity control system. For the plants from subtropical zones, water walls and air fans are used in place of an energy-consuming air conditioning system. The roof was fitted with advanced technology through the use of ETFT cushions which is transparent but insulated—it helps with the plants' photosynthesis.

The quality of the pavilion's indoor environment can also be controlled automatically, lowering energy consumption, and temperatures are reduced by the drencher curtain in the greenhouse. The hall is equipped with a mist spray and floor-cooling system instead of air conditioning. A light energy-saving green roof softens Taipei's skyline and reduces an urban heat island effect. Plants on the wall can contribute for a low maintenance requirement and thermal insulation. Solar panels placed on the inclined façade toward the courtyard provide sustainable energy. Meanwhile, rainwater is directed into a wastewater purification system where the aquatic flora absorbs the heavy metal in water and the gravel accelerates contamination precipitation in order to purify the water naturally—guaranteeing organic water purification. The 170-meter water purification path provides the courtyard of Xinsheng Tri-Pavilions with a clean source of irrigation, nourishes various aquatic flora, and administers a water recycling system.

INTERFACE
soft interface

Above: The surrounding nature: trees, eco-pond, vegetation, are all part of the building's interface.

Left: The façade's thriving green walls.

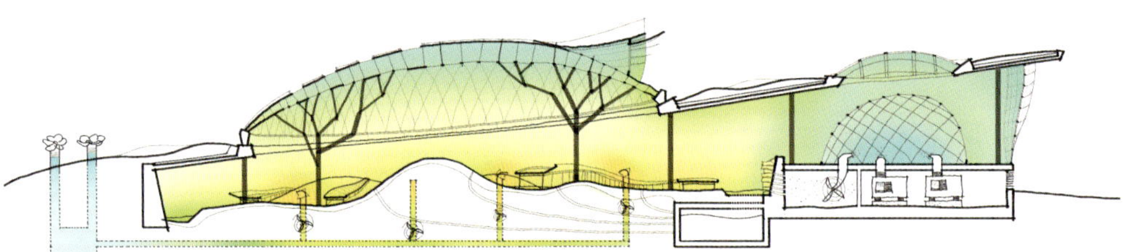

Above: The green roof overlooks the surrounding city.
Below: Section diagram representing the temperature inside the building during summer.

Left: The building smoothly ascends from the ground.
Left (below): Section diagram representing the temperature inside the building during winter.

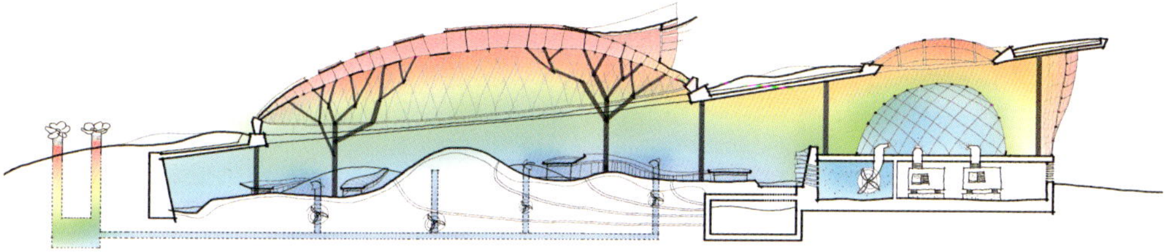

The green roof of the building not only helps reduce the heat island effect but also softens the skyline.

CHIAYI INDUSTRIAL INNOVATION CENTER

CHIAYI, 2011

This project introduced a distinctive and specific scale to each building according to their function. Intentionally each building block represents a different function and therefore has its own identity. The masses were designed to have distinct shapes, façades, floor heights and even structural baring capacities in accordance with their specific needs. The complex can be viewed as three different public buildings that share a plaza in the urban context.

The courtyard, defined by the three buildings, functions not merely as the physical connecting point but also as a comfortable space with a shared shadow which helps to reduce the summer heat. The northeast building mass blocks the cold wind during winter. The gap between the building blocks opens to the south, welcoming the summer breeze from the southwest.

Although the three buildings present separately, the entrance was placed in the exhibition center building mass which is covered by a large canopy of solar panels. From here a semi-outdoor network of walking paths were arranged to connect the public areas inside the buildings to the open space.

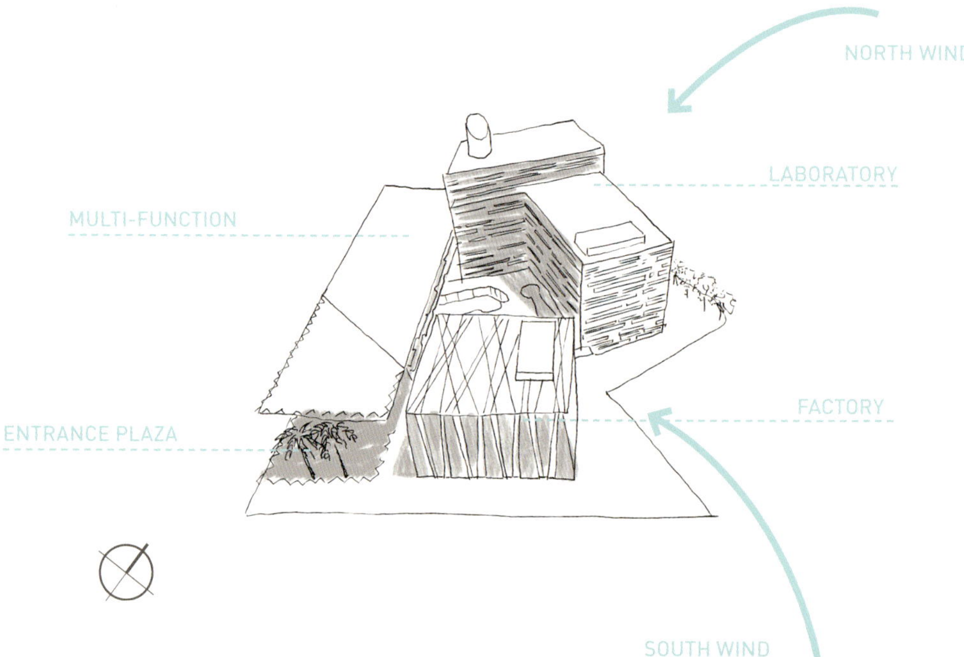
NORTH WIND
LABORATORY
MULTI-FUNCTION
FACTORY
ENTRANCE PLAZA
SOUTH WIND

Left (above): 3D drawing of the three buildings connected by a semi-outdoor courtyard.
Left (below): Street view of the building's façade.

Right: The façade is covered by green stripes in order to bring life into the complex.
Below: Close-up view of the plants that compose the green wall.

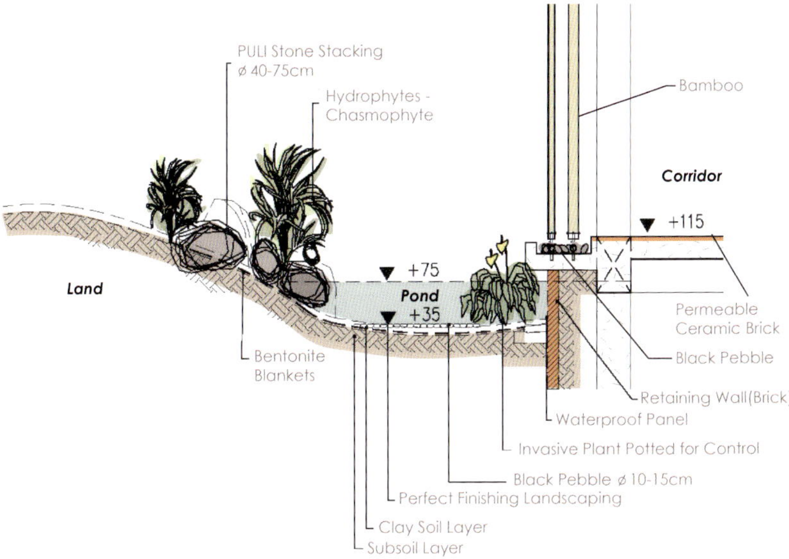

Above: Detailed drawing of the interface between the landscape and the covered galleria.
Right: Water and green spaces were combined to enhance the natural environment.
Below: The floor from the gallerias is covered with local Taiwanese tile.

Left: The courtyard viewed from the surrounding buildings.

TAOYUAN FUNERAL HOME

TAOYUAN, 2018 (COMPETITION)

The journey of life, from birth to death, is like everything in the universe. Spring, summer, autumn and winter: the universe and nature are endless.

This design intended to make the experience of a grieving person as peaceful and quiet as possible, using the integration of elements from nature that are the foundations of life.

The way through the landscape trail to the entrance of the complex is lined with greenery and extends all the way to the inner courtyard of the building and then vertically to the terraces on each floor.

Due to its singularity, the complex program was arranged according to the distinct demands and the flow is carefully designed for a variety of visitors.

The spaces were carefully designed, and the materials were chosen in order to create specific ambiance that suits the delicate moments.

The bamboo leaves from the atrium form a shadow, from movement of breeze, and reflect the sunshine. The light on both sides of the patio is filtered through the fine grid, making the interior room light and soft. The skylight of the patio overflows into the lounge with the warmth and softness from the wood.

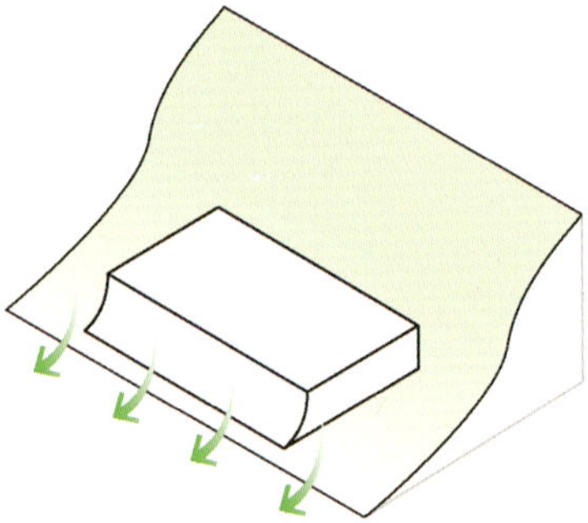

Adaption to the terrain, reduction in volume sense

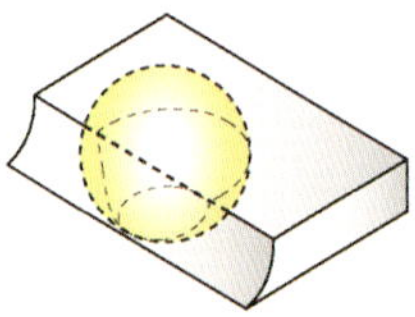

Rounded sphere

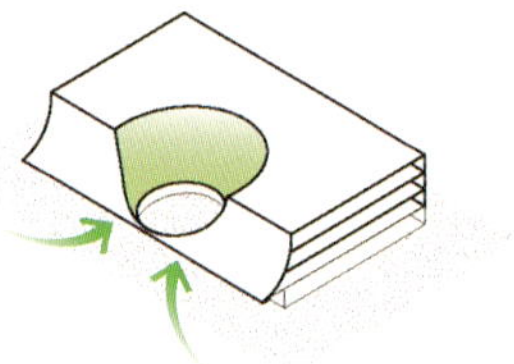

Three-dimensional open space

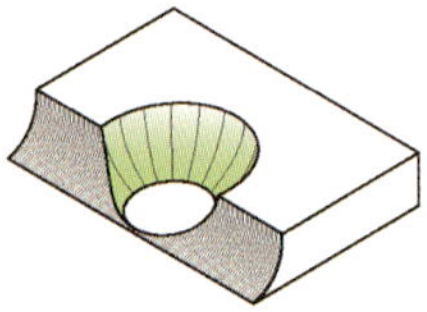

Planting corridor

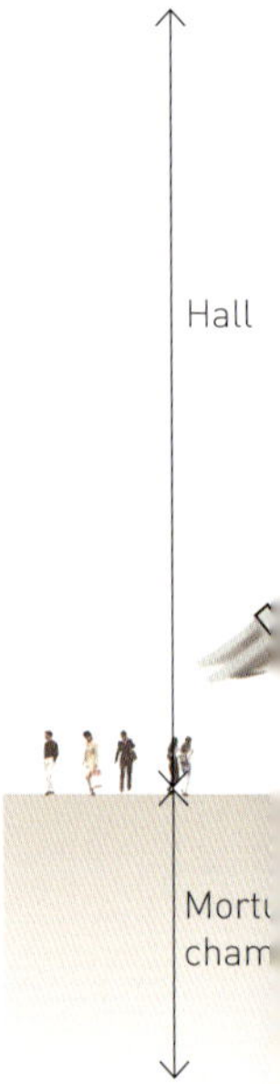

Above: Green spaces are incorporated along the building.
Below: Perspective section.

Left (above): Rendering of the main hall. The ecological conditions accompanied by the blue sky, greenery and lotus ponds create a life-long environment through the nutrients of the sun, air, and water.
Left (below): Concept diagrams.

social interface

Different species in any particular habitat develop a network of interdependency; each individual inhabitant contributes to and benefits from the network through an invisible interface. Every building benefits from the network of the city and, contributes to the city by being setback from the boundary line, growing vegetations in the open spaces, and providing beautiful façades and sky lines. Furthermore, an elaborately arranged approach to the main entrance can act as the social interface to further elevate the variety and liveliness of the city.

A well-designed social interface will slow down peoples' movement on approaching the entrance as the sense of space shifts from open to closed, from bright to shady, from hot to cool. Interface can also be functional: it can provide shelter for pedestrians from rain, it can provide space for public activities, or simply provide a space for people to rest or muse.

MIAOLI TRAIN STATION

MIAOLI, 2010

Taiwan Railways Miaoli Station is located in Miaoli City, in the northwest region of Taiwan. To advance Taiwan Railway's services and to develop tourism in Miaoli City, this station extends into the city that is originally separated by the north-south oriented train tracks. The station functions as a bridge that connects the east and the west ends of Miaoli City. The sloped roof design responds to the local mountainscape. Miaoli folk art is canvased on the ceiling to demonstrate their warm hospitality and agrarian culture with the choices of red-and floral-printed panels.

At the west end of the station, a transitional space, transforms into a stepped-performance platform. This is a flexible platform, as people who have traveled a long distance can simply rest on the big steps, or explore the framed view on the cutout walls while being entertained by the local buskers. To direct people to this stepped-performance platform, a ramp was constructed with a solar-paneled roof to invite various people of all ages. In the near future, this ramp will also connect the undergoing construction of the new commercial area in West Miaoli City.

The intention of this design was to create and construct without any interference of the existing train tracks. This floating sky lounge is bridged by a steel structure that complements the duration of construction and also complies with railway development for the future. On top of these achievements, Miaoli Railway station is an assortment of technology, nature, and culture that celebrates architecture in pursuit of sustainability.

INTERFACE social interface

Above: The different comfortable spaces can be found throughout the station where people can stop, rest, and appreciate the views of the trains arriving and departing.

Left: The interior hall of the station covered with the fabric-paneled ceiling.

BREAKFAST MENU
DAILY LUNCH MENU

FENGSHAN TRAIN STATION

KAOHSIUNG, 2017

Fengshan Station's design was inspired by the ancient streets and alleyways of its old town. The station's lower floors are accessible as open spaces that connect with the rest of the city, forming a continuous urban texture. A green corridor bridge connects the east and west side while the distinctive, green field and gigantic arched corridor respond to the axis of ancient waterway on the north and south side. This creates an all-around "heart of four-axis" concept, allowing Fengshan Station to connect to the essential urban features from four directions: Kaohsiung Bikeway in the west, Wetland Corridor in the east, Fengshan Cultural City in the south, and the commercial blocks in the north. It will be the new approach to the town of Fengshan.

In following the concept of using inspiration from the city's old urban streets and alleyways, Fengshan Station has a semi-outdoor commercial space on the third floor, reminiscent of the old Date Street, Furniture Street, Ju-Ren Alley, and old department stores like Cao-Dian-Tou. This will bring nostalgic vitality to the station and scale the commercial spaces back to a more traditional level. In addition, a cinematic-culture commercial chain was introduced in Fengshan Station, as a credit to the legendary film director Hsiao-Hsien Hou—also a local resident of Fengshan. This provides an entertainment and leisure space for local residents. By incorporating movie theaters and experimental studios, Fengshan Station becomes the central hub for transitioning commercial developments within the city and providing start-up spaces for entrepreneurial development.

INTERFACE social interface

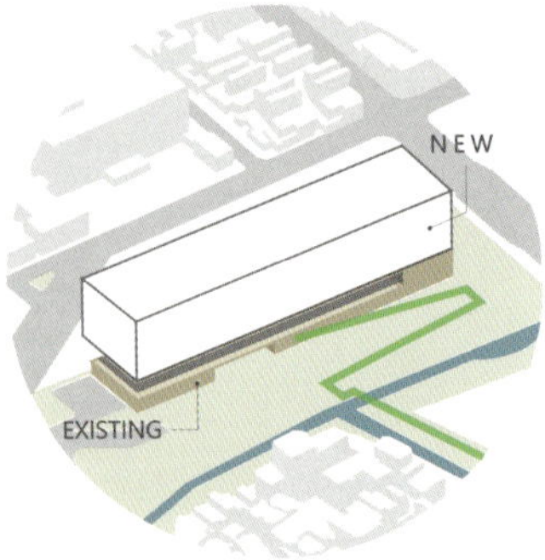

New building on top of existing building

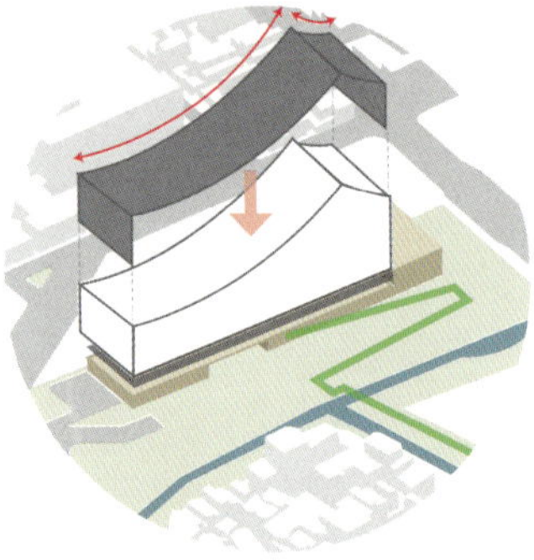

Historical architectural element in Fengshan -Dovetail Ridge

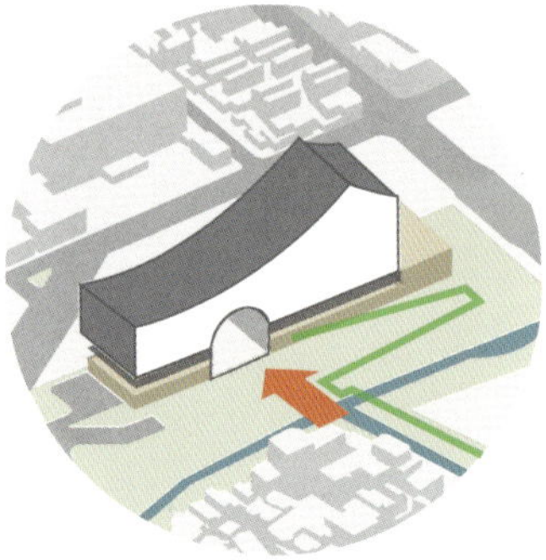

Expansion of the canal to build new gate

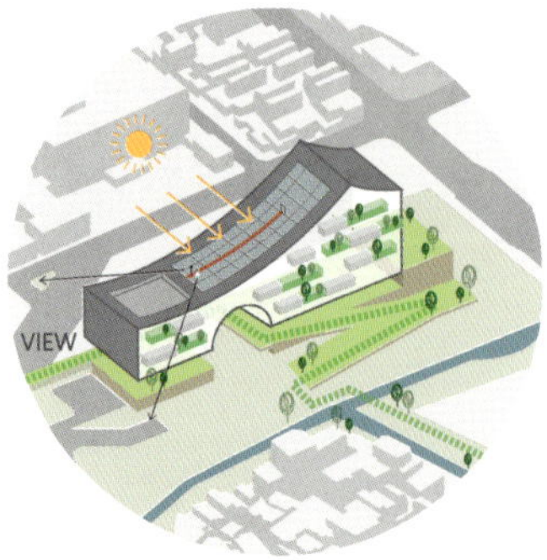

Extension of urban green space and vertical greenery/ rooftop solar farm

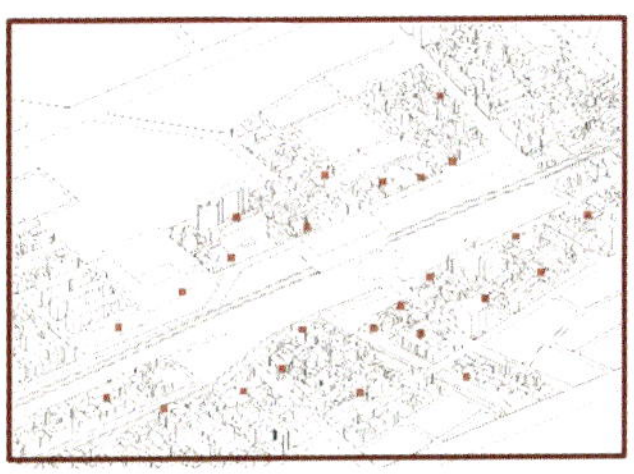

Before – Small, local businesses

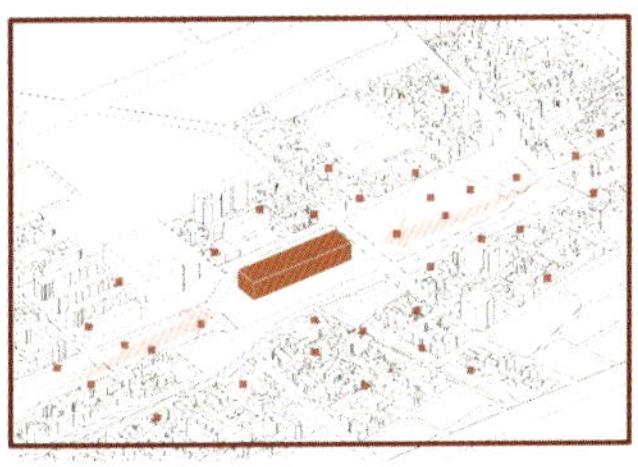

New Public space

New axis

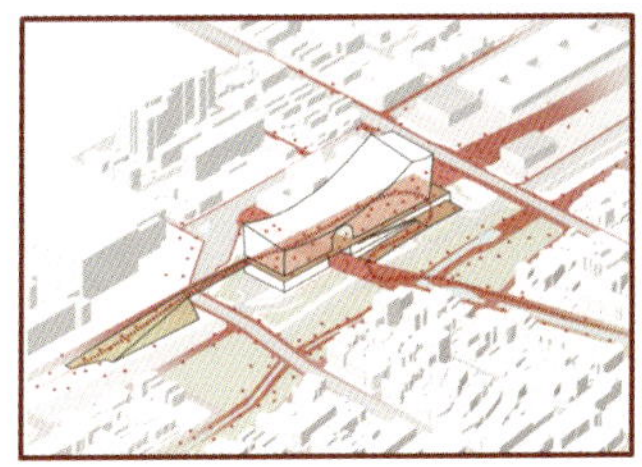

Social dynamic hub

Left (above): Arched corridor of the building on the north-south axis connecting the city to ancient waterways.

Above: Collage of the design concept where the station is a continuation of its ancient city.
Below: Diagram with the program.

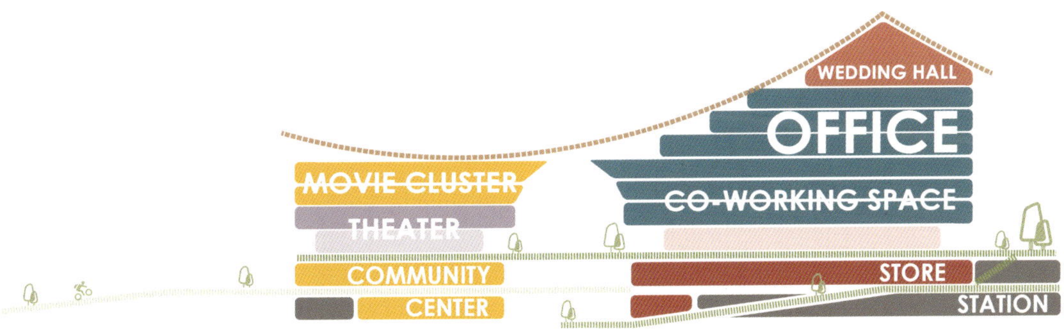

The open space of the lower floors of the station is continuously connected into the urban texture, and the railway corridor is connected to the underground by the empty bridge and the green corridor.

ART AND ARCH MUSEUM
TAICHUNG, 2012

Through art, a corporation can facilitate a strong connection with its urban environment; one can even make the argument that public art can be a very effective social interface. AAM (Arts and Architecture Museum) is a combination of JinRay Development Co.'s corporate headquarter, sales center, and art gallery.

Taichung City is situated in central Taiwan with accommodating weather year-round; and as such, the ground floor of this building, both the interior and exterior, features art spaces that are open to the public. The sales center is located on either side of the interior art gallery while the second floor houses the office space for JinRay Development. The open space along the side of the street is the sculpture garden, which can be a joy to view from the pedestrian walkway. The public entrance, facing the west, features a canopy made of polyester film that is floating in the air like a skirt; on one side it provides a necessary shade for the west-facing façade, and on the other side it transforms into an urban rest spot for viewing the sculptural pieces. The interior art gallery is an extension of the exterior sculpture garden, and works as a means of corporate social responsibility to elevate the cultural depth of the city.

The center of the interior gallery is an elevated void featuring seven diamond-shaped skylights in various sizes, allowing natural light to flow into the interior and infuse another layer of life onto the art work; not to mention the energy-saving benefits. These skylights imitate diamonds gracefully whirling in mid air; a metaphorical, representation of the corporate value of JinRay: quality, beauty, and affection.

INTERFACE
social interface

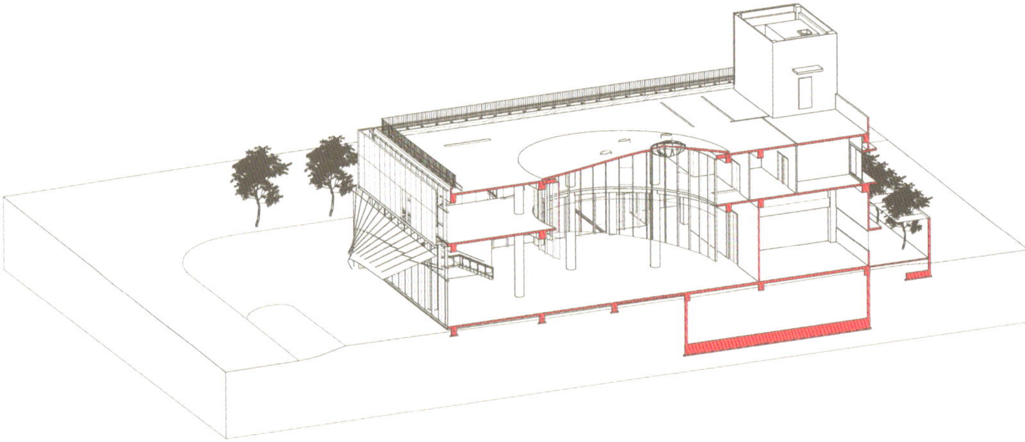

Above: Isometric section through the main hall.
Below: The diamond-shaped skylights during the day.

Right: Interior view of the main ground-floor hall and exhibition area at night.

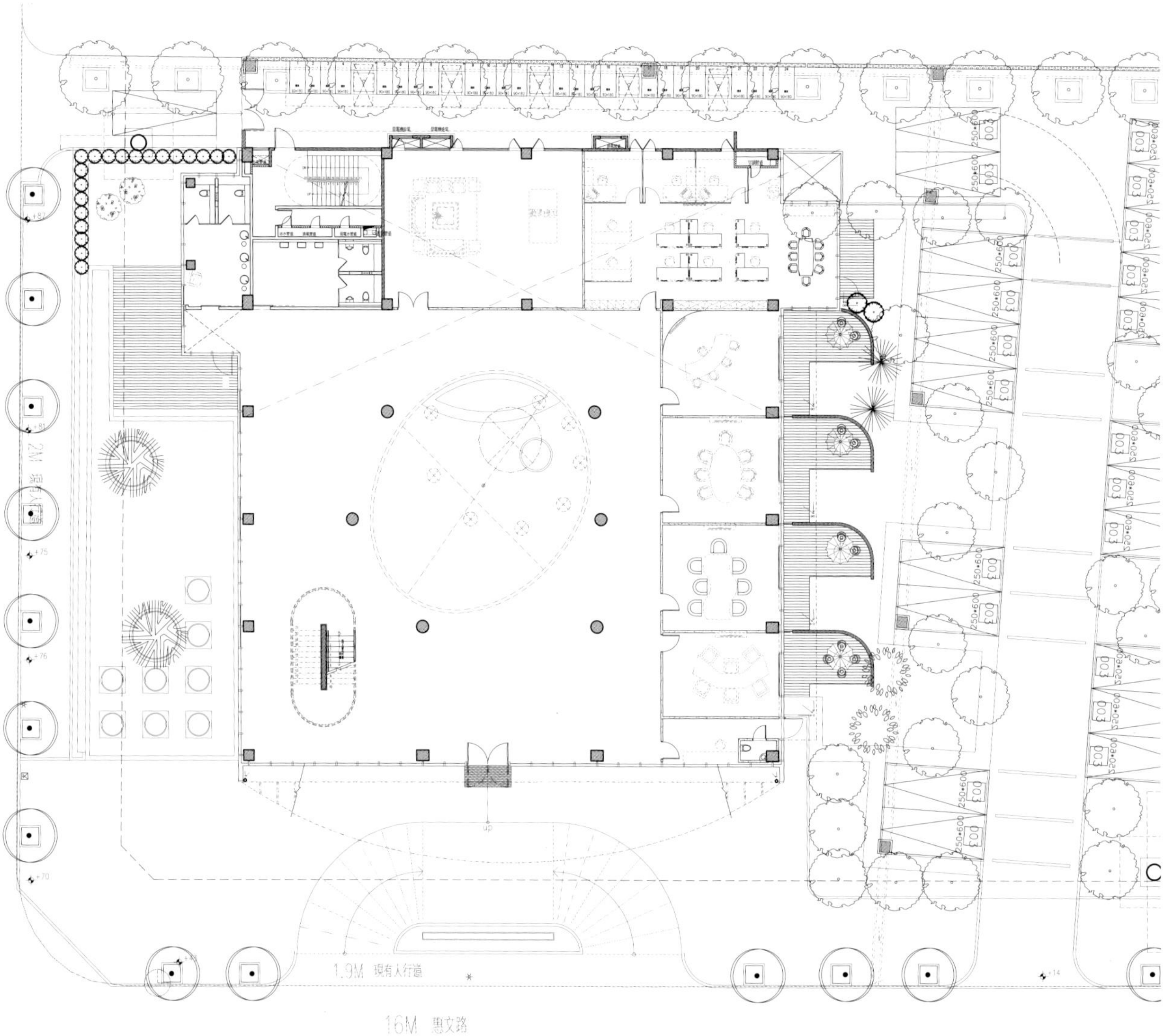

Above: Ground-floor plan of the Museum.

Right: The various interior spaces occupied by art and opened to the public.

NATIONAL CENTRAL LIBRARY AND NATIONAL REPOSITORY LIBRARY: SOUTHERN BRANCH

TAINAN, 2018

The concept of a library as a town was derived from the humility recognized in the context of creating a "town" as part of the town fabric. The guided route to the library was designed to be as seamless and effortless as possible to as a means of forging the library as an integral part of the community. Three main ideas drove the creation of this chance encounter: the integration of nature, the openness of learning, and the "museumization" of the library.

The 5.7 hectare site is currently used as a park and for sports activities. The trees are towering within the site and the golden shower tree boulevard is a landmark to the community. The placement of the massing was with utmost consideration in maintaining ecological diversity and integration with nature. We preserved almost 90% of the trees on site while carefully implementing the buildings in the zones without trees. This site has an existing ecosystem of which we worked to preserve and envisioned the built environment to coexist harmoniously and organically.

國家圖書館南部分館暨聯合典藏中心
The Southern Branch of National Central Library & National Repository Library

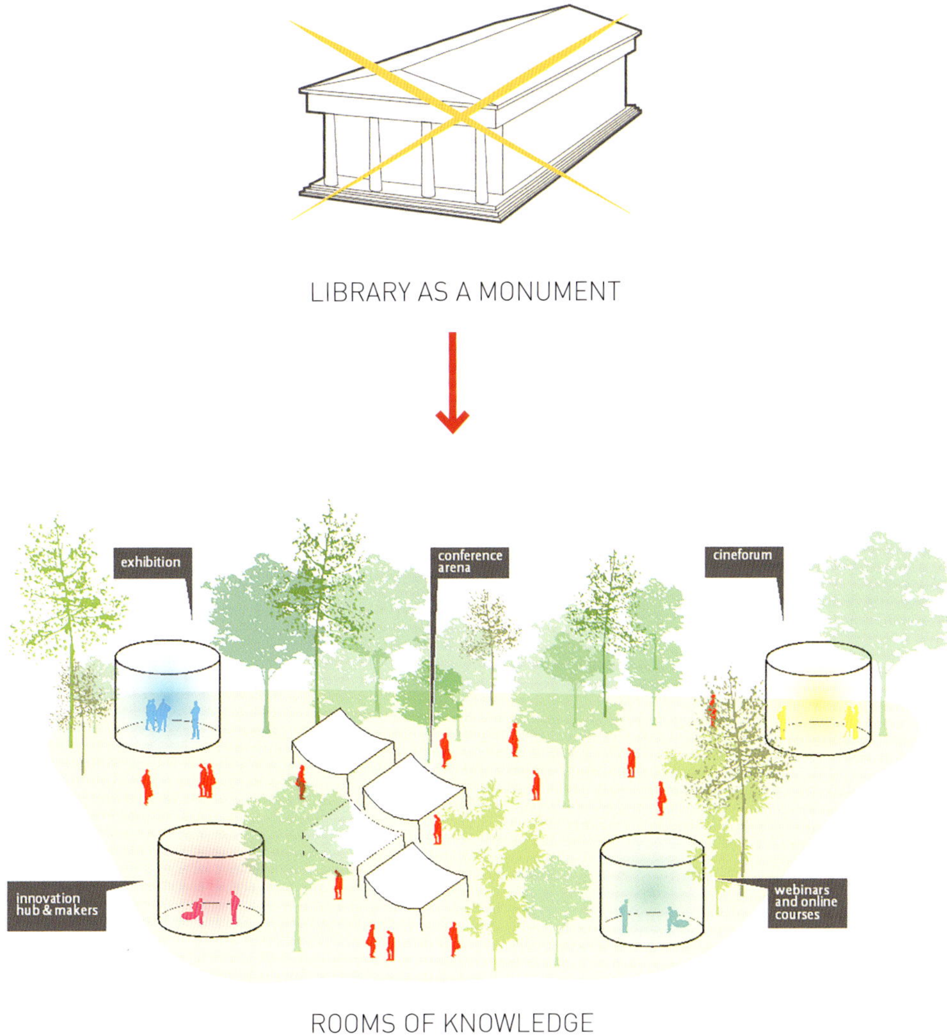

Above: Redefining traditional monumental library model to rooms of knowledge.

Left: Solar canopy creates outdoor agora and shading during hot summer.

長榮路二段 Sec. 2, Changrong Rd. (30M)
三興街 Sanxing St.(12M)
未開闢道路 Futrue St. (8M)
金華路一段 Sec. 1, Jinhua Rd. (40M)
典藏區
Repository
博物館
Museum
演講廳
Hall
圖書館
Library
自動化倉儲區
ASRS
N
圖例
人行動線 people
汽車動線 cars
機車動線 scooter
卸貨動線 truck
自行車動線 bicycle
建築物主要出入口 entrance
各館主要出入口 building entrance

Above: North entrance to the library through the park and the outdoor canopy.

Left: Site plan with the main connections to the surroundings.

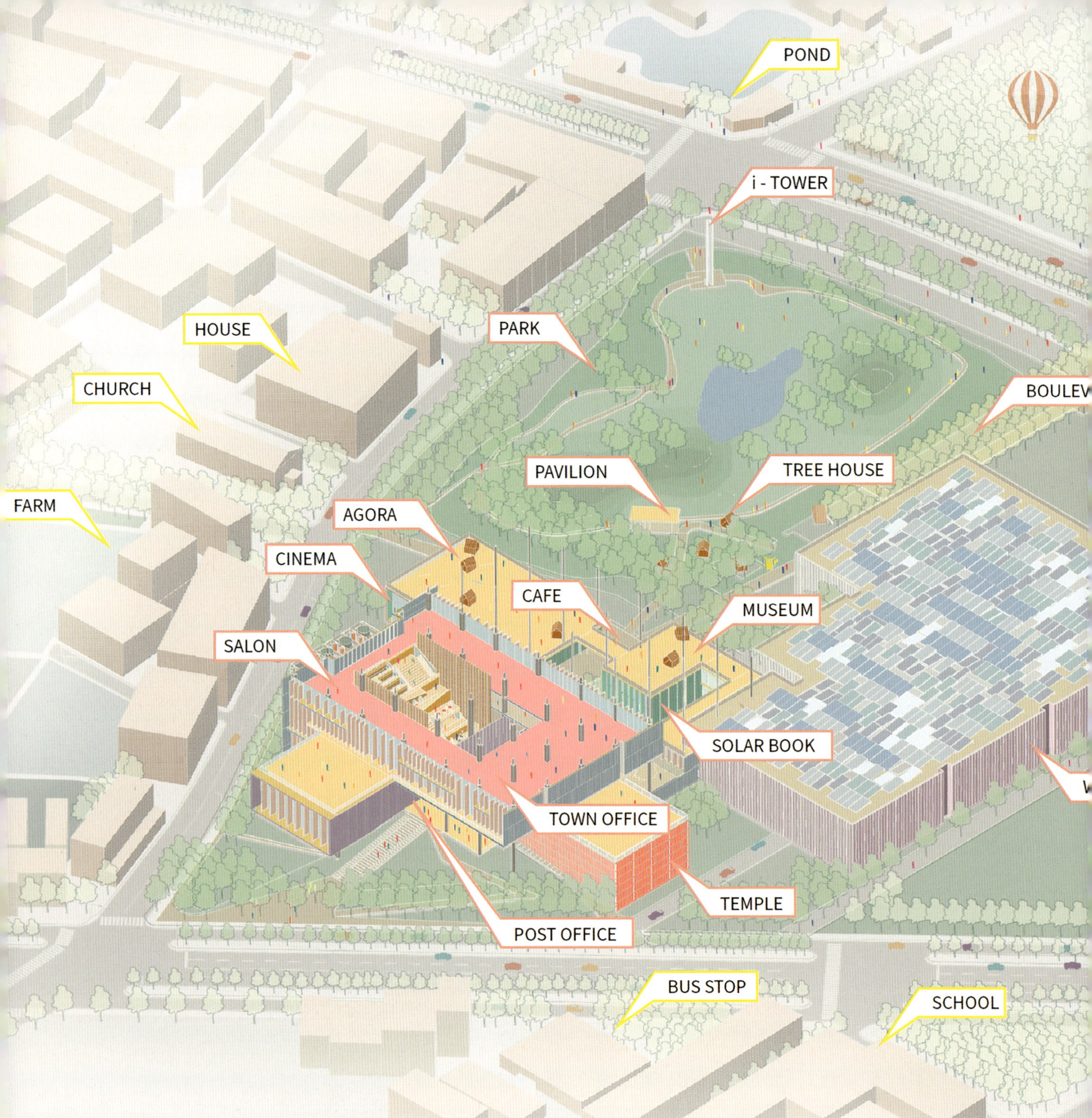

POND
i - TOWER
HOUSE
PARK
CHURCH
FARM
PAVILION
TREE HOUSE
AGORA
CINEMA
CAFE
MUSEUM
SALON
SOLAR BOOK
TOWN OFFICE
TEMPLE
POST OFFICE
BUS STOP
SCHOOL

A small town called XinYing,
once bustling with activities at the roundabout,
and trains passing through carrying sugar canes.
A small town, now, of culture and agriculture,
with kids running around the town,
and the farmers plowing in the field.
A small town will soon be the home for a big Library,
a big library that will be, yet another town.

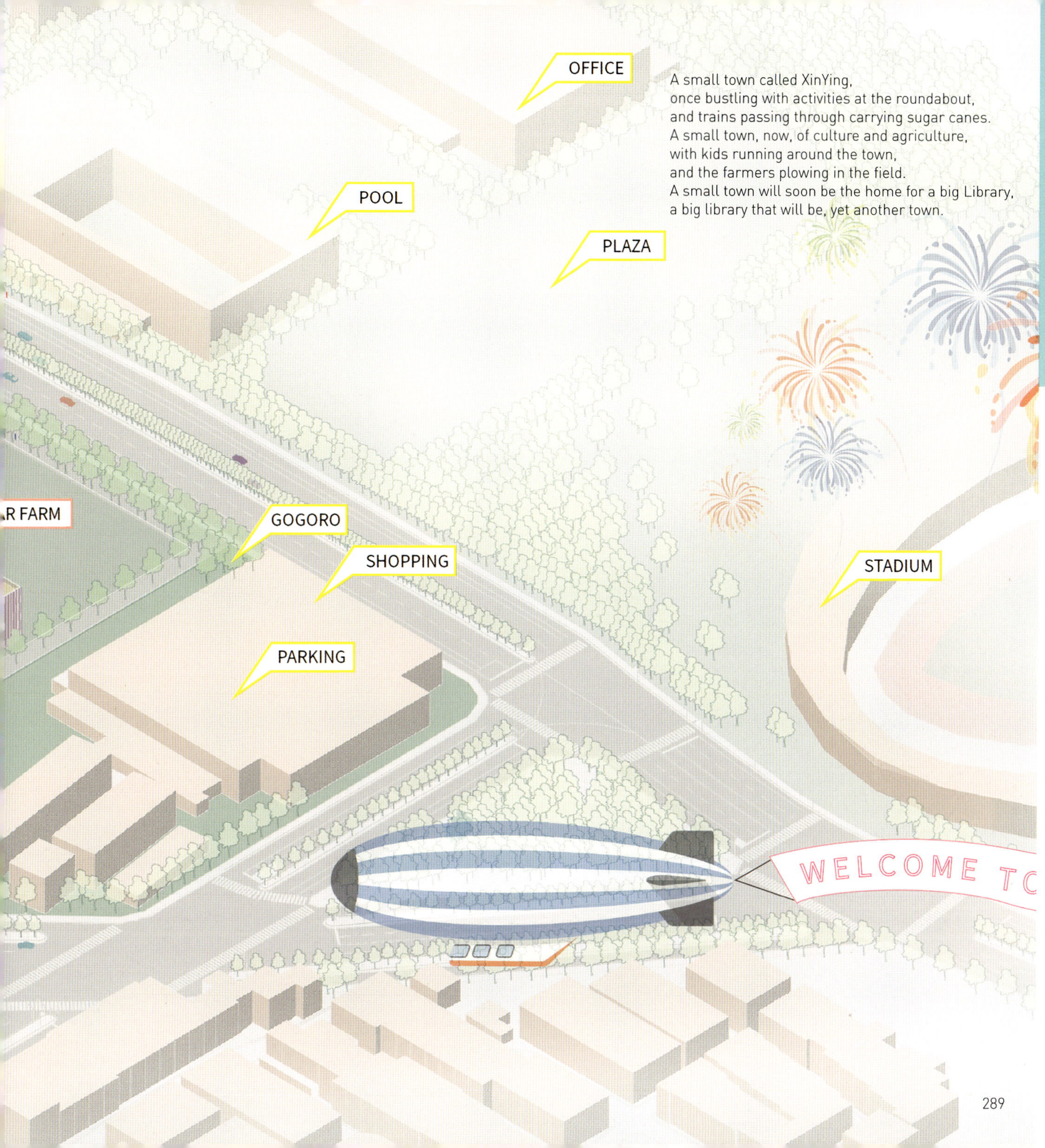

The network of life consists of many loops, big and small, all the information and materials are circulated, exchanged in these loops, either inside of lives or outside.

When everything is connected through these loops, the need for resources and waste are diminished; all the raw materials are assembled into something and disassembled afterwards within the loop. This is the formula to life's self-sustainability on this planet, and with limited resources for billions of years.

Architecture is also a network that uses materials from this planet and constructs built forms. These built forms should also be designed with a recyclable application: to deconstruct, disassemble, and reduced to its raw materials, to flow through the loop. A circular architecture embeds the principles of life's loops in all of its functions, establishing a system that is regenerative and restorative by design. In such architecture, the idea of waste is eliminated, with assets maintained at their highest levels of utility at all times and the use of digital technologies as a vital process enabler. A circular architecture aims to generate prosperity and economic resilience for itself and its inhabitants, while decoupling valuable creation and the consumption of finite resources.

CIRCULAR

CIRCULAR

TAIPEI FLORA EXPO ENTRANCE PAVILLION

TAIPEI, 2008

With a life-span of only one to two years, the amount of building materials that can be recirculated, at the end of their life cycle, relies heavily on the extent of consideration that was placed on the selection of these materials and the method of construction. Avoiding causing irreparable damages to the site has become the biggest challenge, especially when it comes to the building foundation and floor plates.

This temporary pavilion, built for the Taipei Flora Expo, was to function as an entrance/reception hall. Due to its temporary existence, it was carefully designed to be assembled and easily disassemble so that in the future it could be reused for another construction. This was the main objective that guided the design: using green materials and assembling them in a non-destructive way, allowing for a circular architecture.

Local natural materials, such as wood and, bamboo together with a lightweight-steel structure were prefabricated in the factory to be assembled on site.

The timber used for the columns came from the thinning method found in the forest, allowing for improvement in forest stability and, promoting the growth of more trees. The cedar timber can be found in the Taiwanese forest, making the material use low carbon as well as the bamboo and paper tube, also local materials that can be reused.

The identity of the project was also clearly enhanced by the inclusion of citizen participation in sustainable management like the green walls, vertical farms, roof greening and seedlings.

CIRCULAR

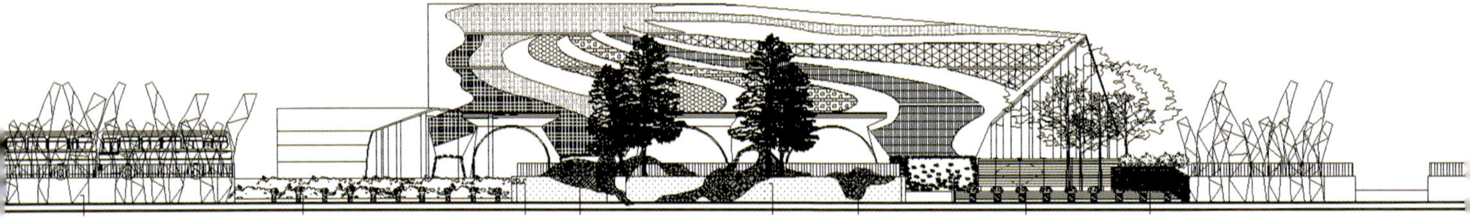

Above: The lively tilted slope roof invited visitors to walk along and enjoy the views over the park.

Left (above): The colorful rooftop meets the sky.
Left (below): Elevation drawing from the exhibition's main entrance.

Above: The wood columns create a forest-like space.
Below: Section drawing.

Right: The raw material with little processing retains its original appearance in order to preserve the best condition for reusing.

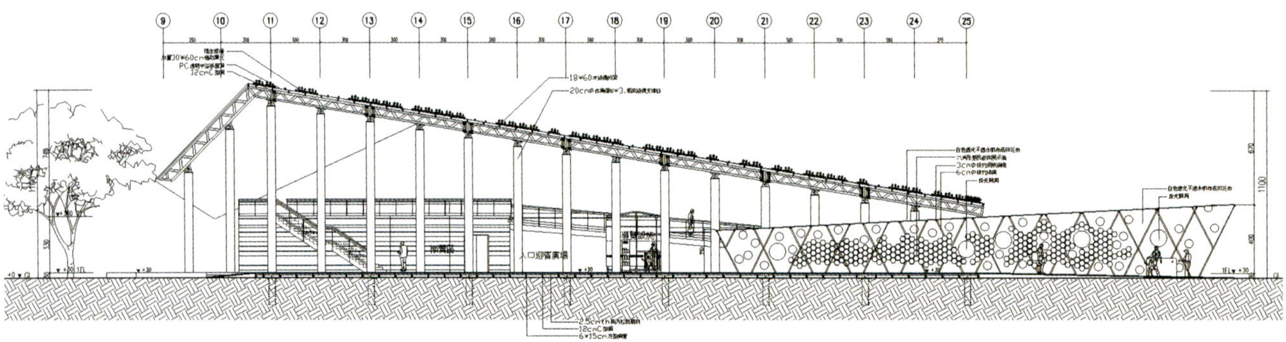

1

2

3

4

5

6

1 – Edge beam footing with a connecting plate.
2 – Timber columns with metallic joint.
3 – Composed column on top of edge beam footing.
4 – The upper joint that connects the composed column with the beams.
5 – Permeable bed of gravel.
6 – Pressing of the gravel floor.
7 – Pre-cast flooring system.
8 – Wooden flooring finish.
9 – Structure for the upper level floor.

Left: The local Taiwanese forest tree, more specifically cedar trees. To improve the stability of the forest the thinning method was adopted allowing for a reduction in the carbon footprint.
Left (above): The timber columns already on site are assembled in a way that allow for easy dismantling once the exhibition is finished.

Right: The pavilion's "natural landscape" benefits both the people as well as other species in the city.

TAISUGAR CIRCULAR VILLAGE
TAINAN, 2018

Modularization is crucial in larger scale urban developments to make fabrication assembly and disassembly more efficient and simplify the stocks of building material bank.
The "Circular Village" is made up of the three "Circular Blocks" where the living quarters are located, "Circular Field" where it consists of a "C-House," an "E-House" and a "C-Farm." The C-House functions as the living room of the village, the E-House as the kitchen, while the C-Farm is the garden where food is produced.
In the circular economy, materials are reused and virtually no waste is created. The design stage takes into account assembly in construction and deconstruction after use. Some of the materials used include recycled and green materials. For instance, the salvaged hardwood from TaiSugar's old dilapidated buildings were used as the main structure for the E-House while their recycled railway tracks were designed as fence on the ground periphery. Also, the wooden planks from the old buildings were treated and reused as the wooden frame for the pivoted door at C-House. As to reduce the carbon emissions, we have opted for green materials like CLT (cross laminated timber) and recycled LED glass insulation blocks for the façade and internal partition.
In order to design for disassembly, steel was chosen as the structural material rather than reinforced concrete.
Modular building components such as prefabricated PC boards, metal louvers for the façade, prefabricated floor panels for slabs were used in conjunction with BIM software to comprise the BAMB database. In order to further fulfill the spirit of circular economy, the ownership for the elevator, lighting, furniture, and sanitary fixtures were replaced with usership—so in other words, rented instead of purchased.

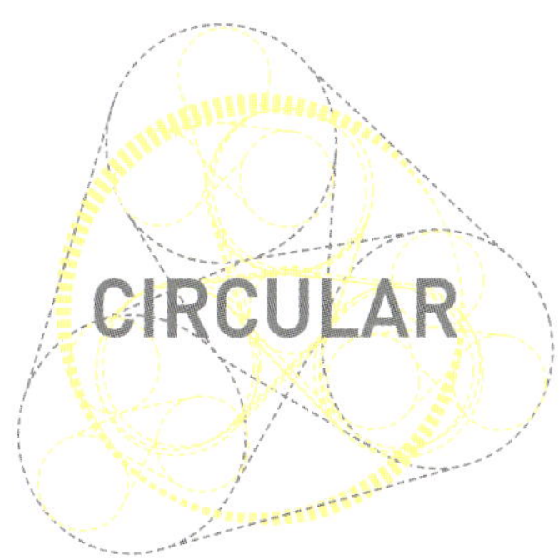

Left: The composition of "Taisugar Circular Village."
Below: Schematic diagram of the variety of "circularity" within the "village."

Right: Aerial view of the village complex.

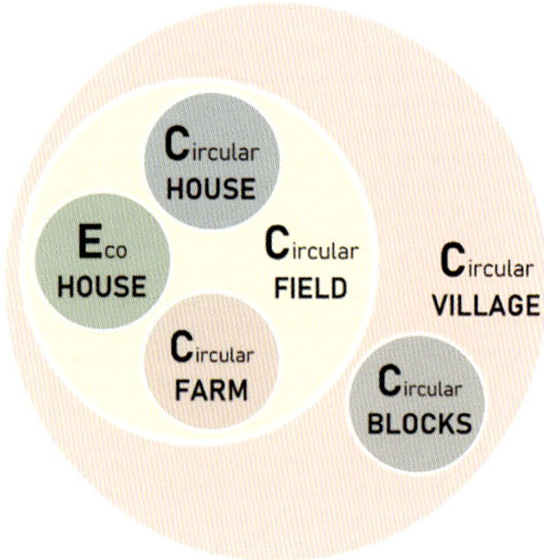

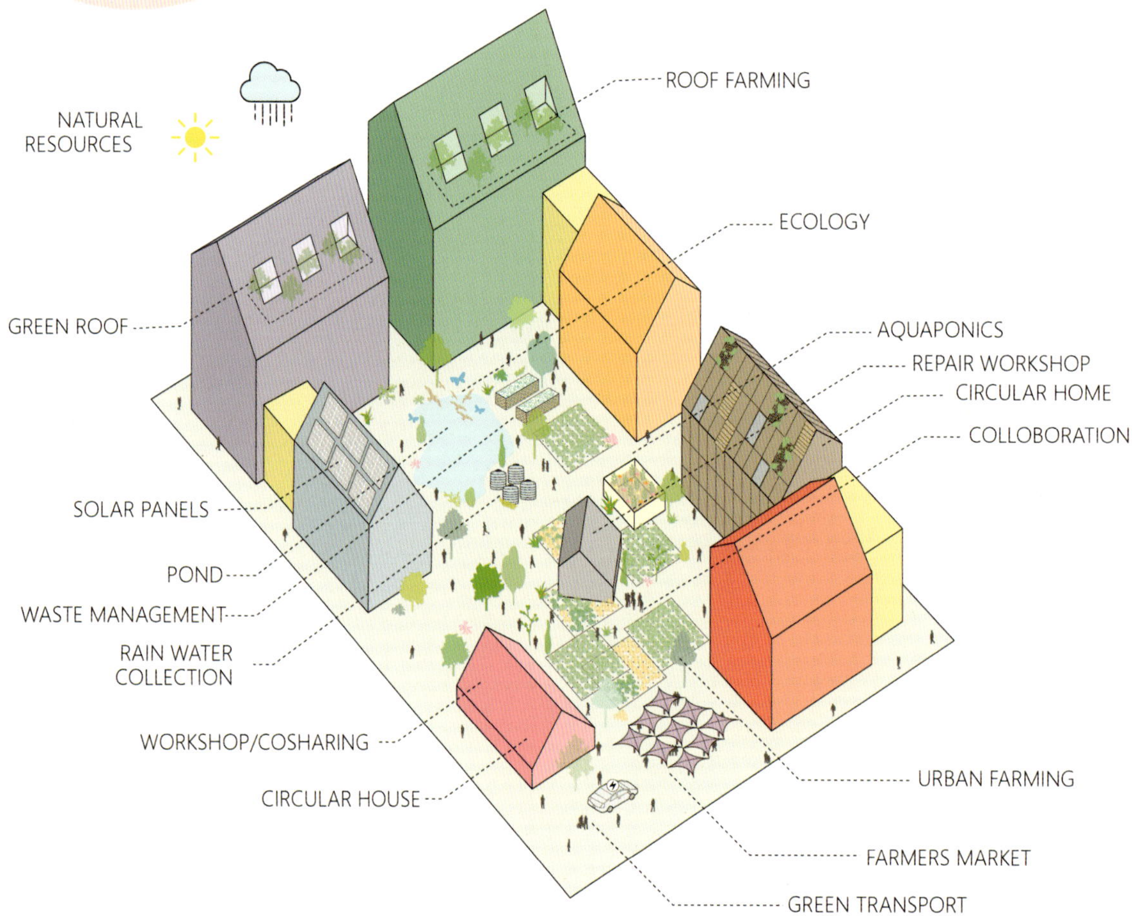

Above: Ground-floor plan of the Village.

Right (above): The roof garden is a circular farming space for residents to work together cultivating organic food.
Right (below): The interior and semi-outdoor public space is more than a social space and will become a collective memory place.

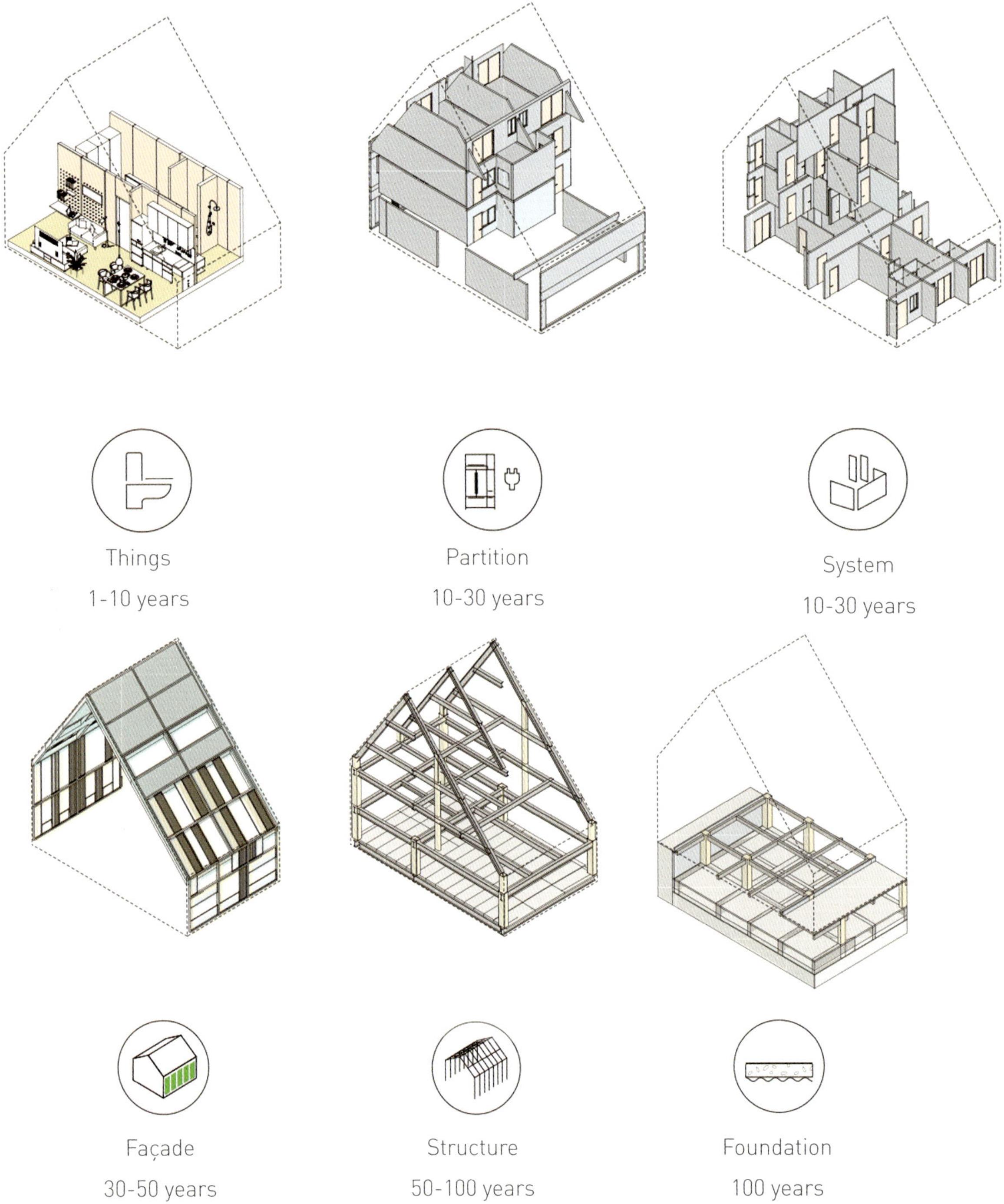
Things
1-10 years
Partition
10-30 years
System
10-30 years
Façade
30-50 years
Structure
50-100 years
Foundation
100 years

Left: Design with layers: the building is classified into six parts by material. The life cycle to access the different circularity and drive corresponding design strategies.

Above: Corner view of the "Circular village."

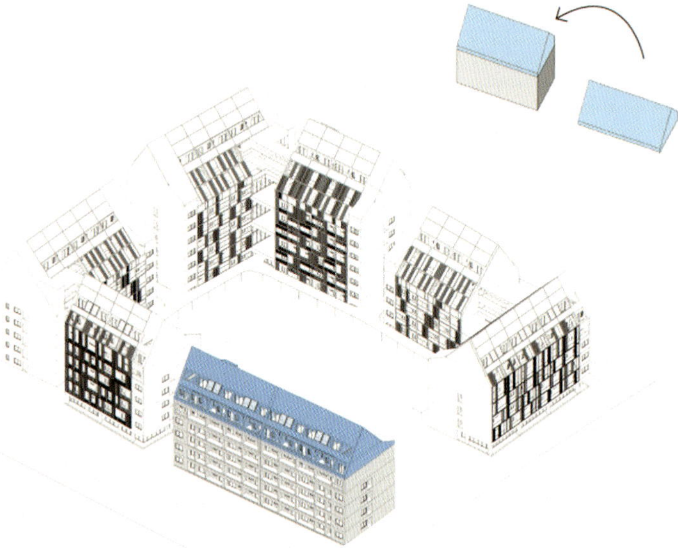

Left: The future possibility of amplifying the existing building (circular house).
Below: 3D section through the circular house and circular block.

Right (above): Exploded-isometric view of the one bedroom typology apartment. Rental service included with furniture and electrical appliances suppliers. The rental list includes elevator, furniture, lighting, appliances, bath and solar panels.
Right (below): Renting instead of purchasing could encourage users and manufacturers to maintain products more carefully to maximize the longevity of its life cycle.

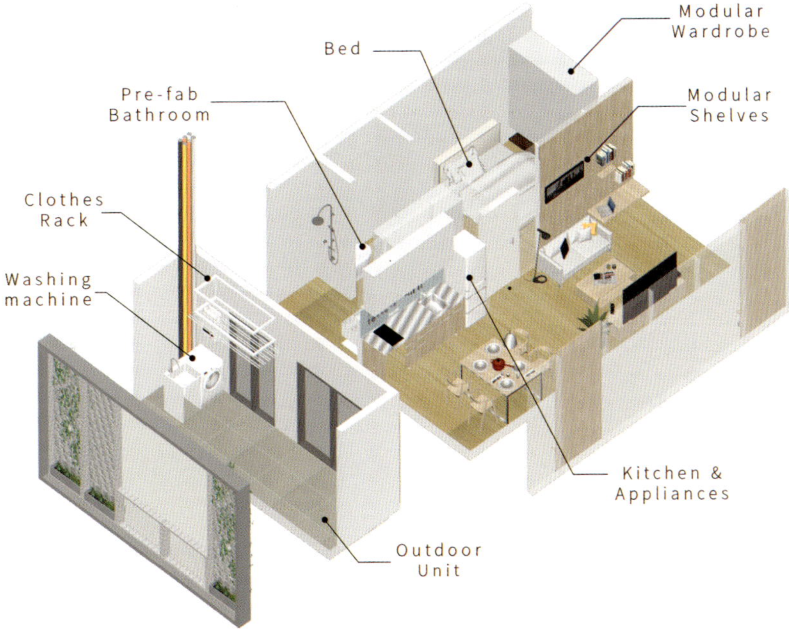
Modular Wardrobe
Bed
Pre-fab Bathroom
Modular Shelves
Clothes Rack
Washing machine
Kitchen & Appliances
Outdoor Unit

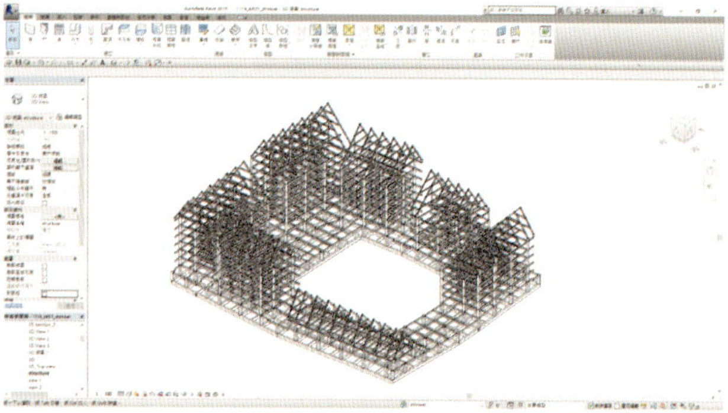

Structure

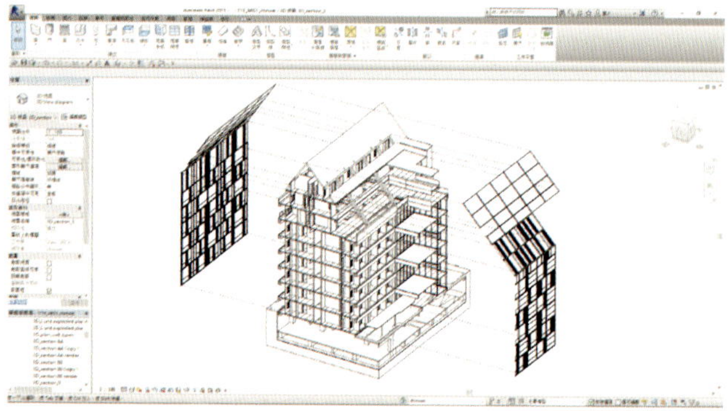

Façade/partition

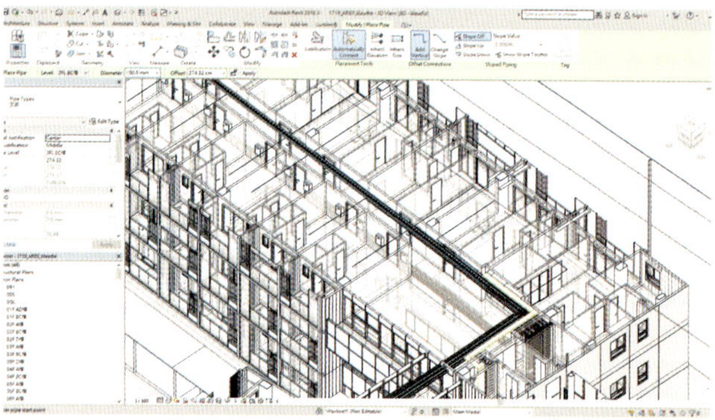

System (MEP/HVAC)

BAMB, building as material banks, is an idea to collect and store material in the buildings for the purpose of being circular the next life cycle.
BIM – application play as a platform in this "bank" to restore and manage an entire material data, from design phase to construction.
Below: BIM (Building Information Model) as a platform for "material bank," and "material passport."
Right (above): Pre-fabricated modular schematic elements of the façade (green wall) easy to install and disassemble.
Right (below) : The circular house is a flexible space for residents and visitors to share the knowledge, experience, and new technology.

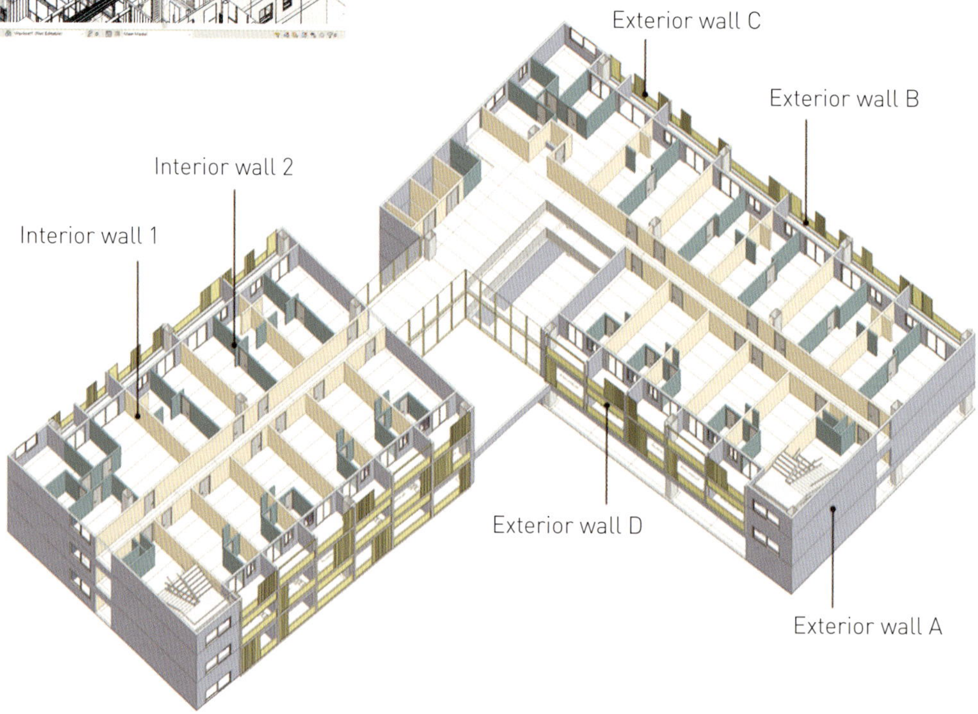

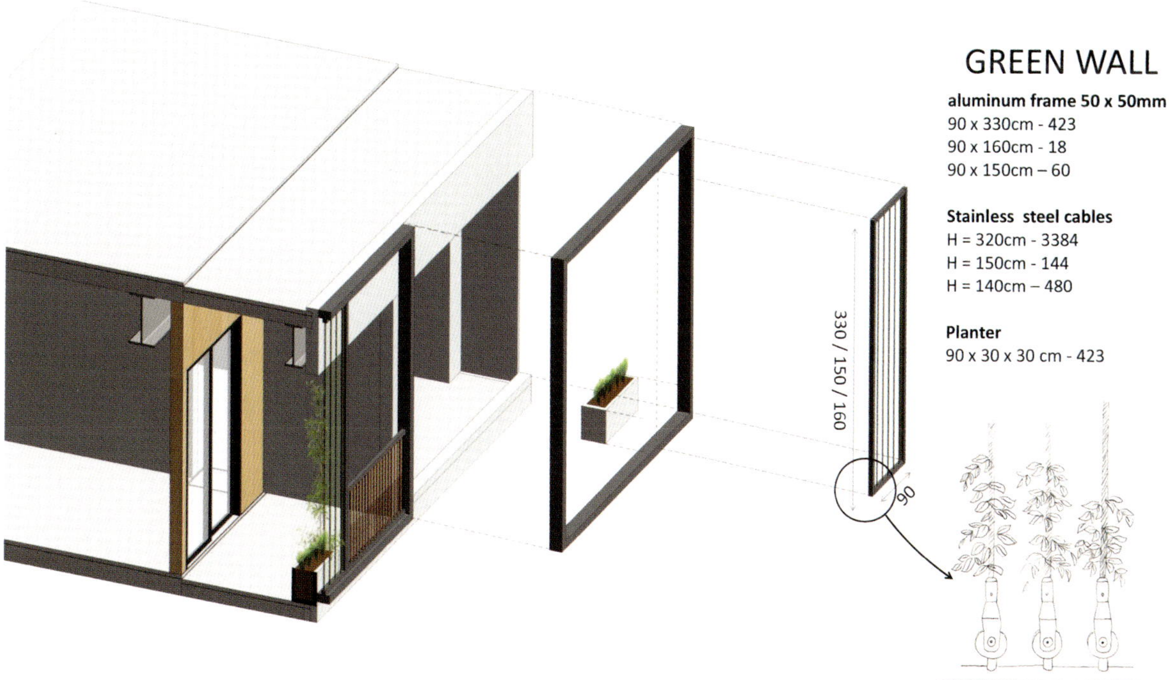
GREEN WALL
aluminum frame 50 x 50mm
90 x 330cm - 423
90 x 160cm - 18
90 x 150cm – 60
Stainless steel cables
H = 320cm - 3384
H = 150cm - 144
H = 140cm – 480
Planter
90 x 30 x 30 cm - 423
330 / 150 / 160
90

Left: 3D perspective section of the Housing block.
Below: The structural system.
Right: Diagram of renewable energy. This project aimed to increase the use of renewable energy by installing around 2,500 square meters of solar panels on the roof that will harness approximately 350 kilowatt-hours per year for the village. This energy is used to create a carbon neutral C-House. The heat loss from the centralized cooling system for the C-House is collected to power the domestic hot water for showering in the housing block.
Right (below): Fresh air ventilated spaces, brightly lit space, interior temperature control and non-toxic materials, circular village is a mentally and physically healthy living space.

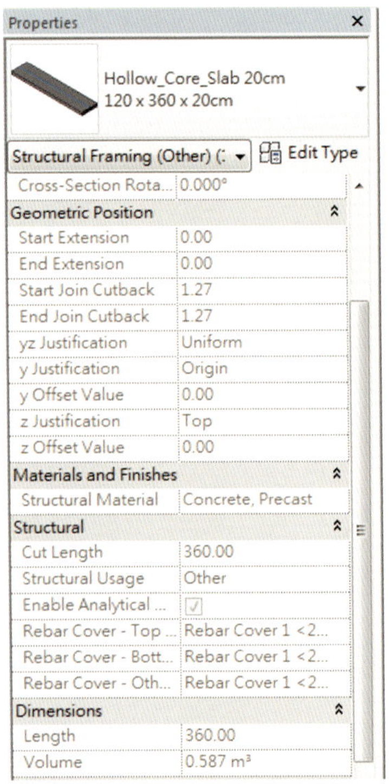

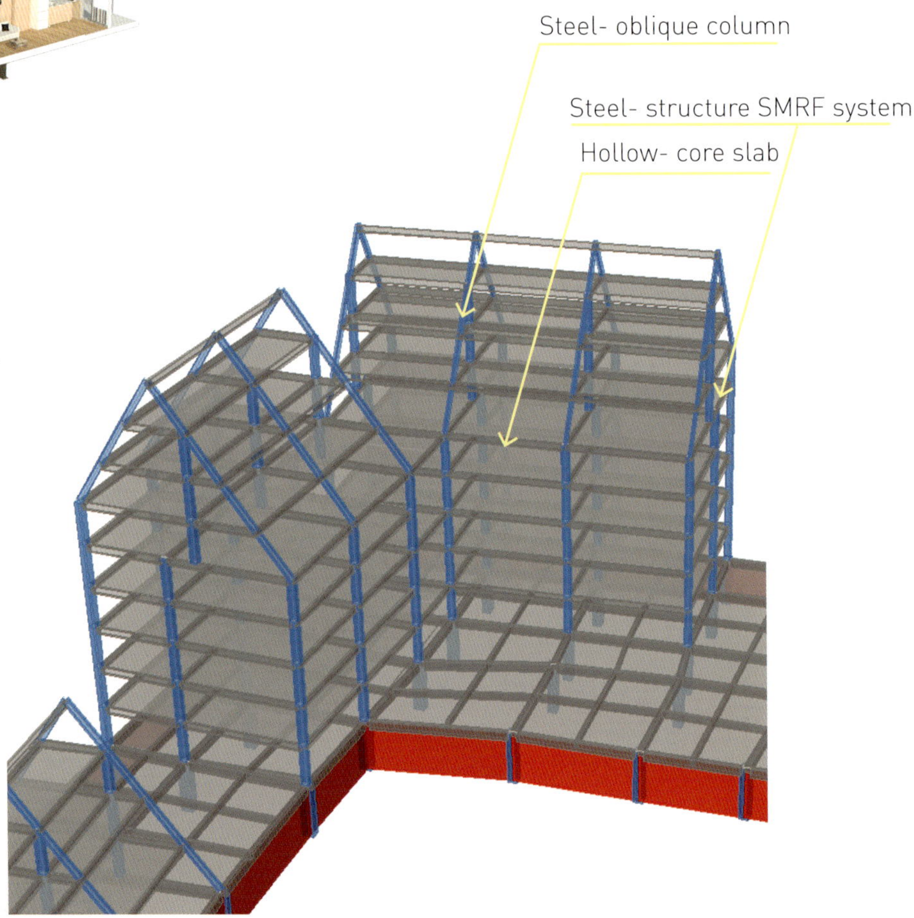

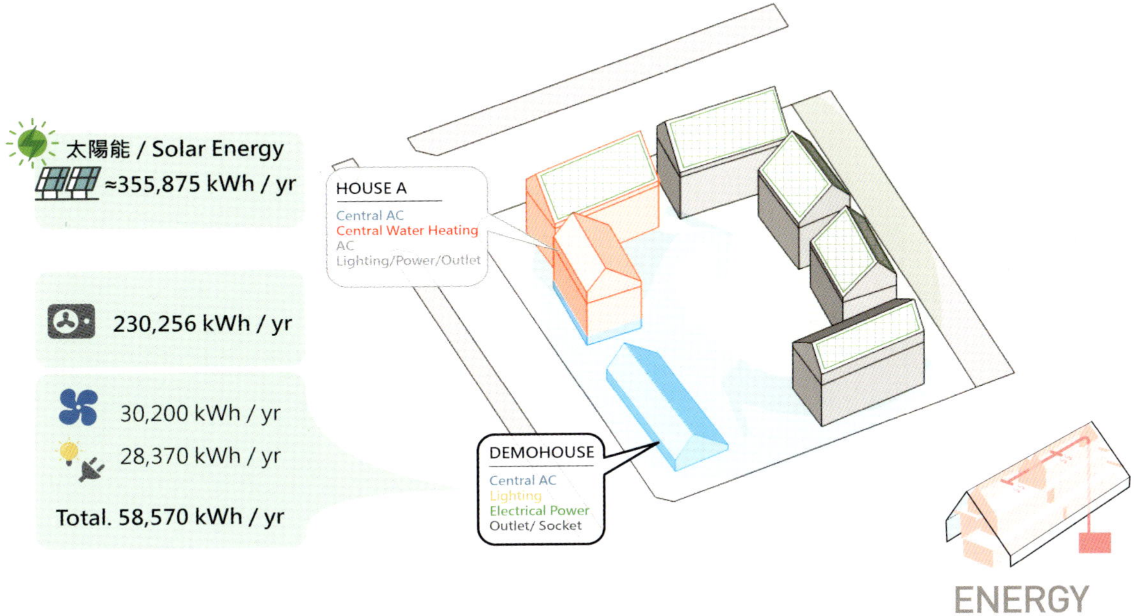
太陽能 / Solar Energy
≈355,875 kWh / yr
230,256 kWh / yr
30,200 kWh / yr
28,370 kWh / yr
Total. 58,570 kWh / yr
HOUSE A
Central AC
Central Water Heating
AC
Lighting/Power/Outlet
DEMOHOUSE
Central AC
Lighting
Electrical Power
Outlet/ Socket
ENERGY

SHIMEN CIRCULAR VILLAGE

NORTH COAST TAIWAN, 2018

Small-scale rural villages ultimately face nature's challenges like humidity, salt, insects, and other encounters. Therefore, the assessment of building materials, fabrication, and maintenance need a more stringent consideration compared to their urban counterparts. This residential area is deep in the forest (see page 110), where buildings are called "tree houses" due to their architectural style being similar to the structure of trees. They're raised from the ground in order to have a minimal footprint.

The main structure is a steel-modular skeleton with dry walls which will reduce waste throughout construction. The structural system has independent footing and the drilling positioned the precast foundations, the "tree house" concentrates the strength of the superstructure below the giant truss column and transmits the structural requirements to the earth through the foundation pile.

Shimen Circular Village adopted prefabricated construction methods in its entirety, and in order to minimize negative impacts in its surrounding environment and shorten the construction period, most building components will be hoisted on-site. Steel structure will be hot galvanized with a coat of fluorocarbon paint, the roof will be composed of titanium zinc metal paneling, hollow concrete panelings for the exterior walls to prevent sea erosion, and CLT boards will be used for the soffit to give the design a touch of warmth. Aside from the same, recurring sanitary fixtures, interior walls, ceilings, and floor panels are all modular and prefabricated to be assembled on-site.

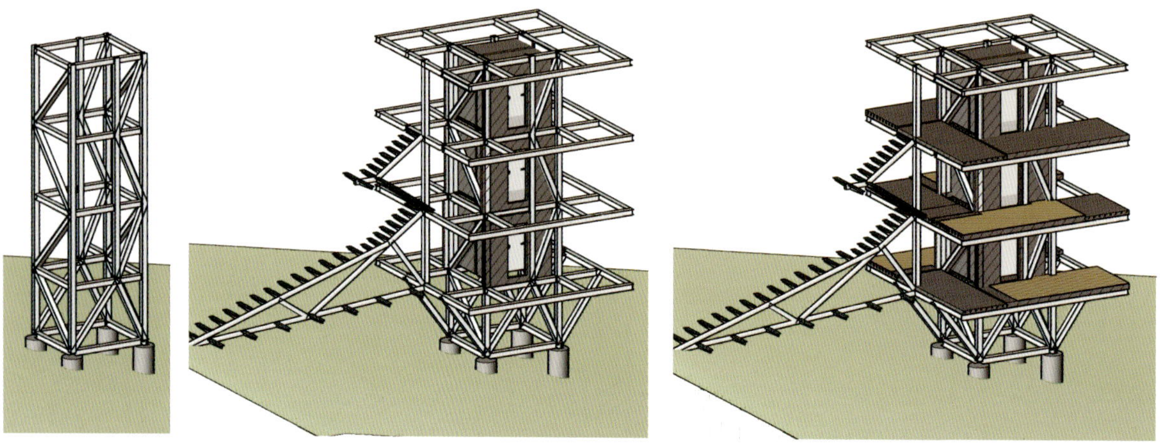

Above: Schematic elevation diagram.
Above (right): Before and after aerial photo showing the minimal footprint.

Below: Diagram showing the different construction modular layers, easy to assemble and disassemble.

Left (above): Perspectival section plan of the rooms modular prefabricated systems.

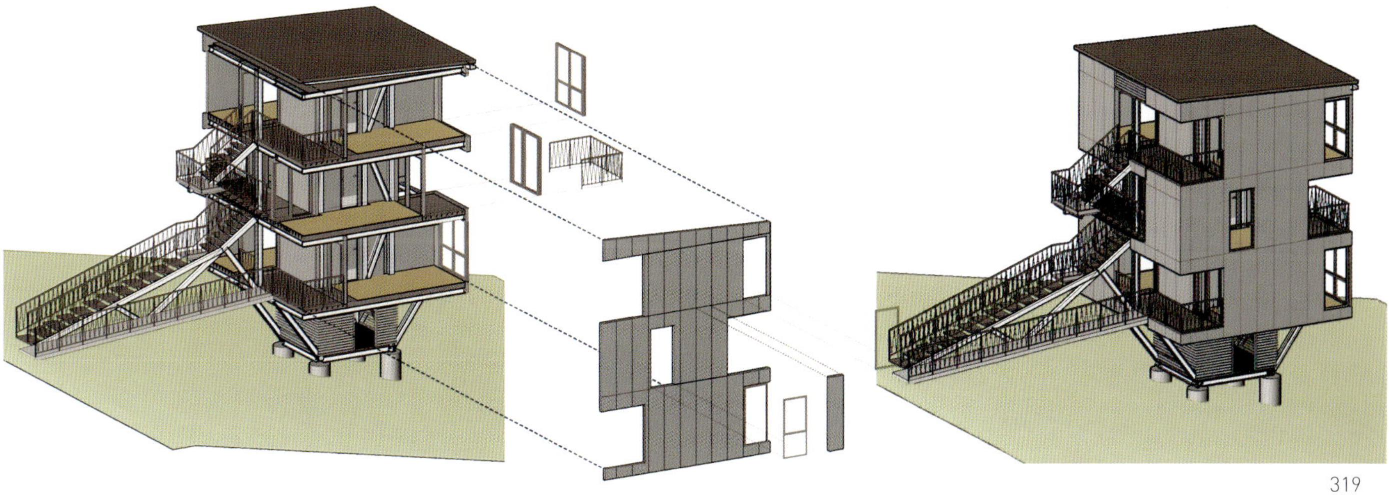

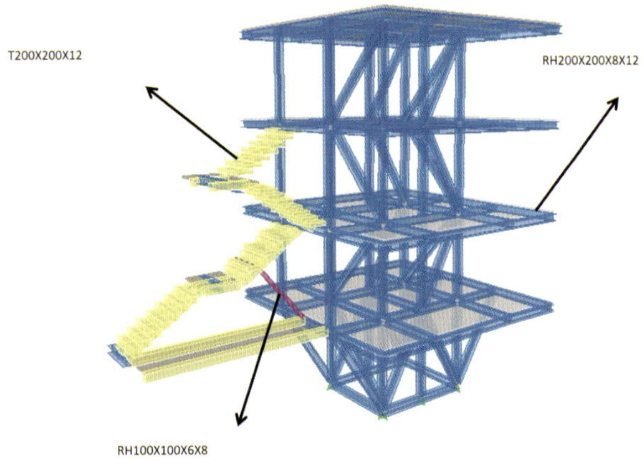

Above: Exterior rendering of the tree house from the access road, the façade expresses its modular system.
Left: The lightweight-structural system with a minimal foundation.

Right (above): Lifted from the ground, the tree house intends to have a minimal footprint.
Right (below): The floor plan expresses the concept of "bare necessity," with minimal dimensions.

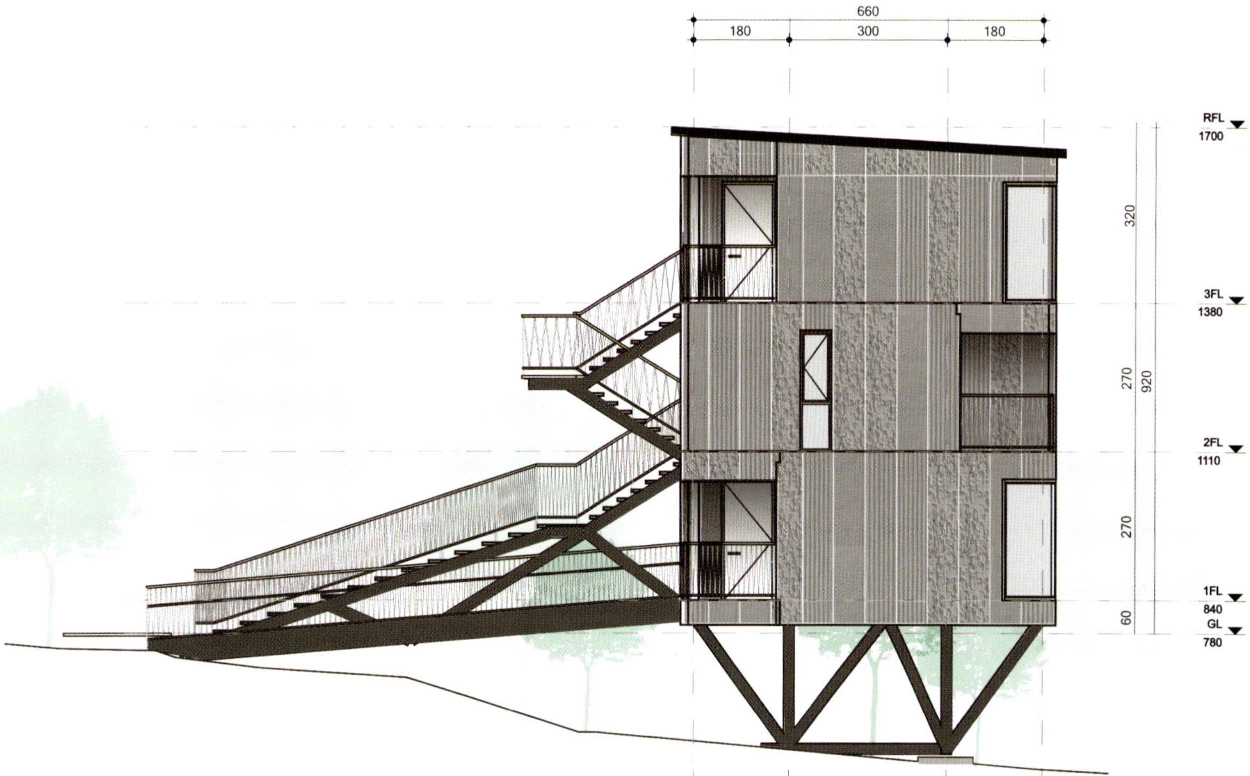

660
180
300
180
RFL
1700
3FL
1380
2FL
1110
1FL
840
GL
780
320
270
920
270
60

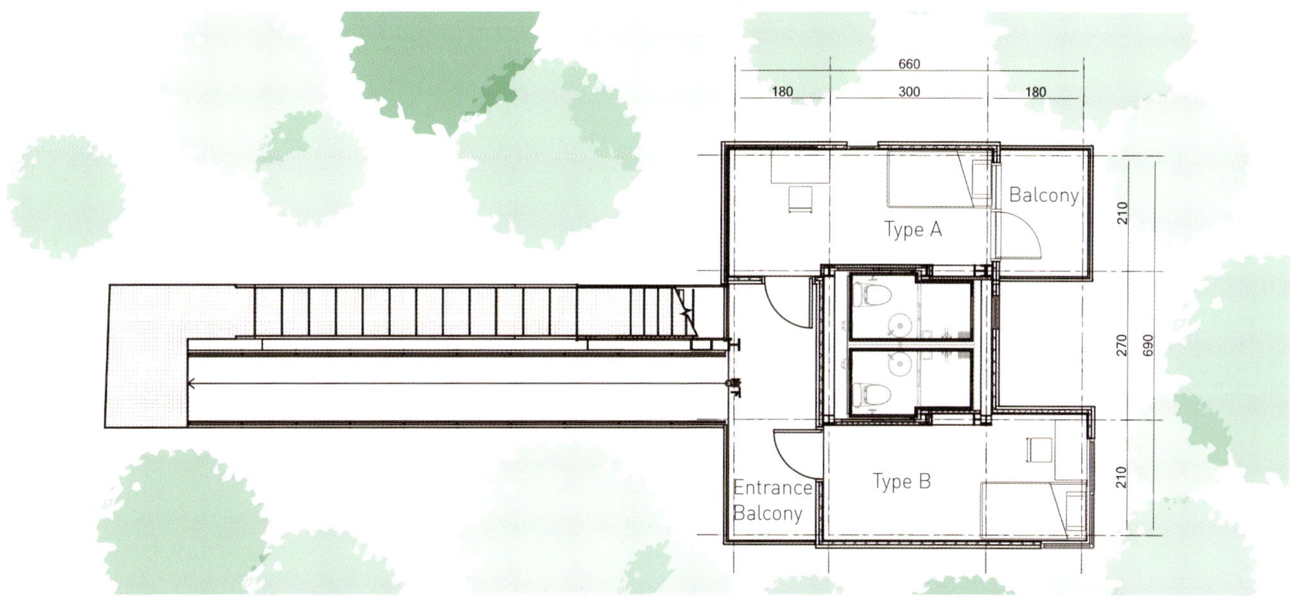

660
180
300
180
Balcony
Type A
210
270
690
210
Type B
Entrance
Balcony

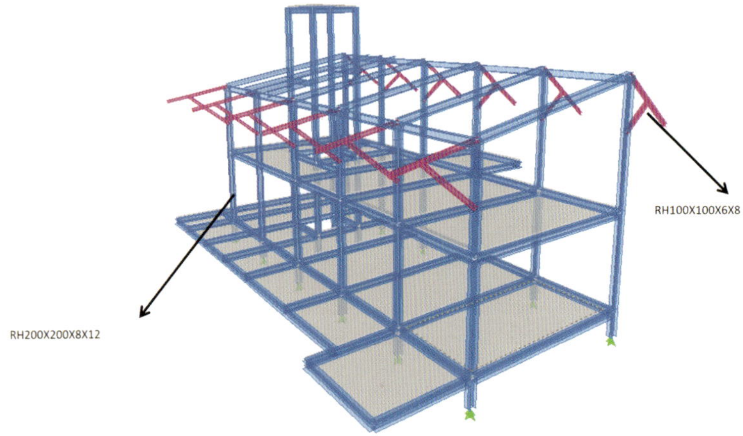

Above: Render view of the Village area.
Left: The lightweight structural system
Below: Independent footing– precast foundations.
Right: Diagram of the different construction modular layers of the buildings A1 and A2.

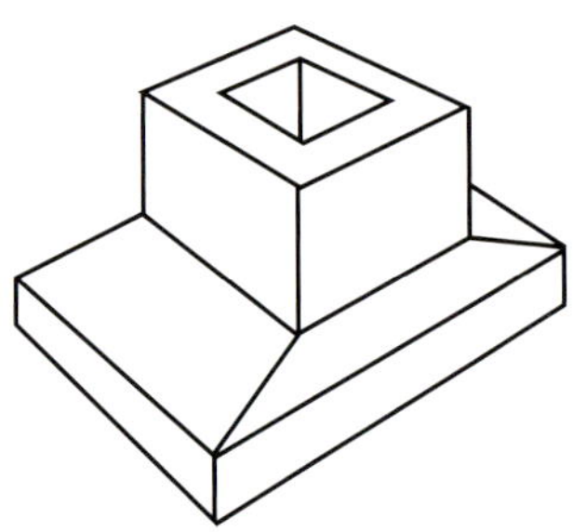

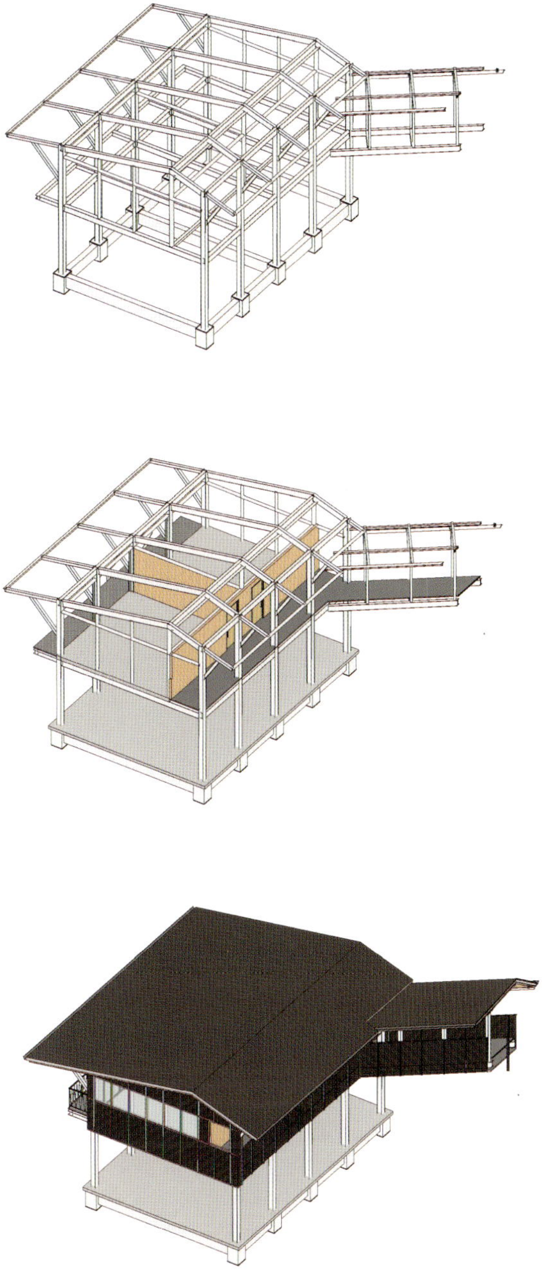

Building A1

Building A2

BaF'S WORKPLACE

TAIPEI, 2005

Since the life span for interior renovation is around five to fifteen years, it has become a suitable choice for Buildings As Materials Bank (BAMB). Since Bio-architecture Formosana has undergone three relocations since first established in 1999, we have made every attempt to preserve reusable building materials such as door panels, book shelves, cubicle partitions, ceiling fans, and even mock-up models from the construction site; employing minimal interior renovation, a unique interior environment that is rich in history and memories is achieved.

This interior design renovation was driven by three major factors: the use of green building materials (such as biodegradable flooring), the reuse of old furniture whenever possible, and the creation of an open-creative environment for work.

The space configuration reduced the walkway area and screen to separate the public and private areas, allowing the use of space to enhance the interaction between colleagues. The terrace was transformed into a green space where various plants are grown, becoming a place for employees to find respit during their workday.The office was equipped with the old ceiling fans for energy-saving purposes.

Carrying out our green philosophy in our own office renovation project guaranteed a more comfortable and healthier work environment.

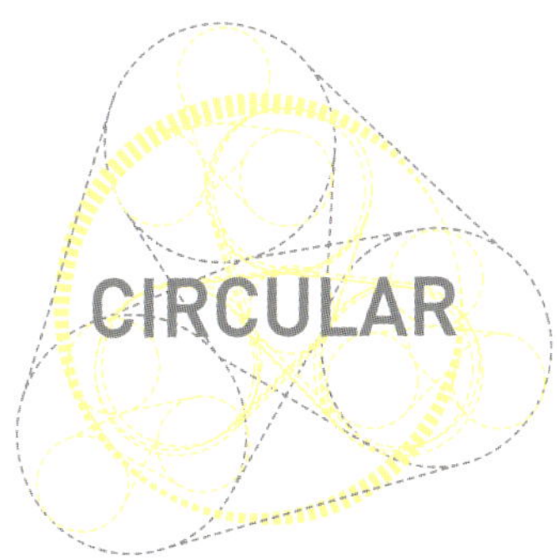

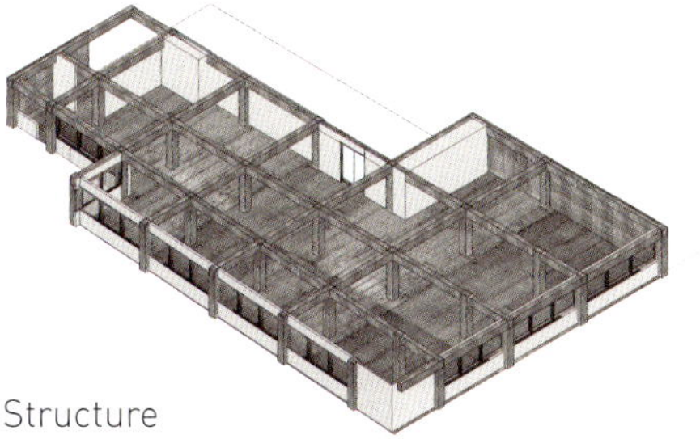

Structure

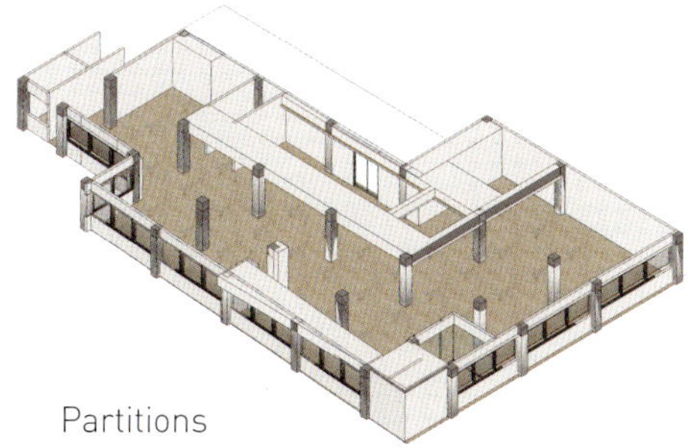

Partitions

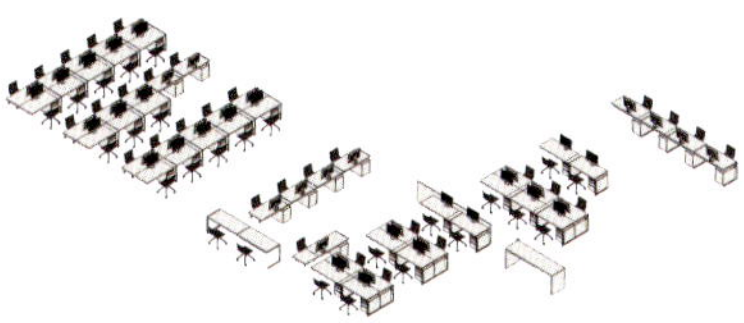

New furniture

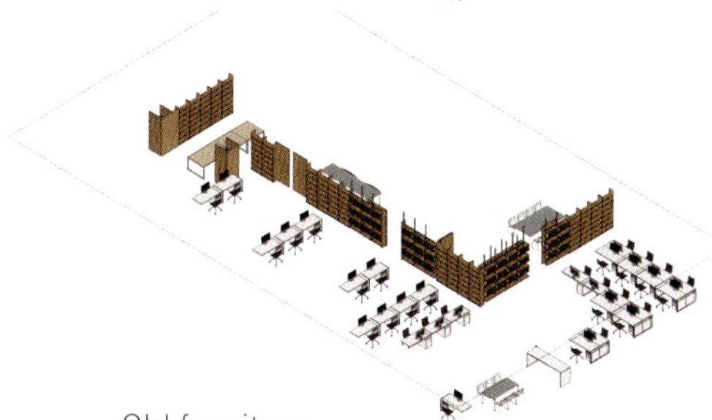

Old furniture

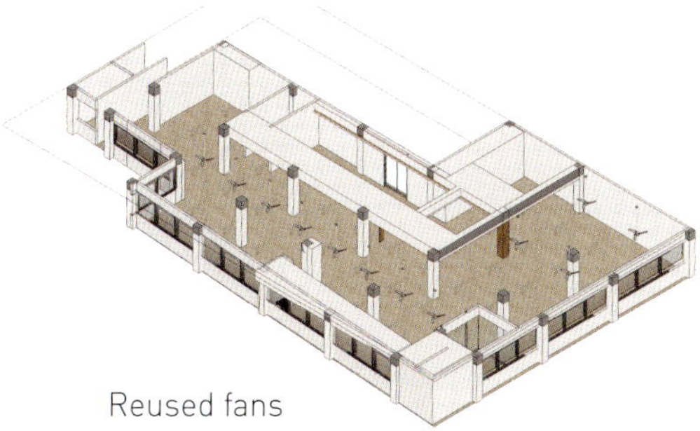

Reused fans

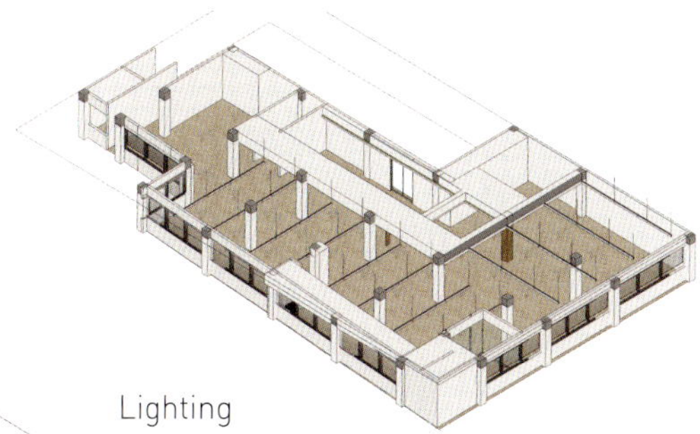

Lighting

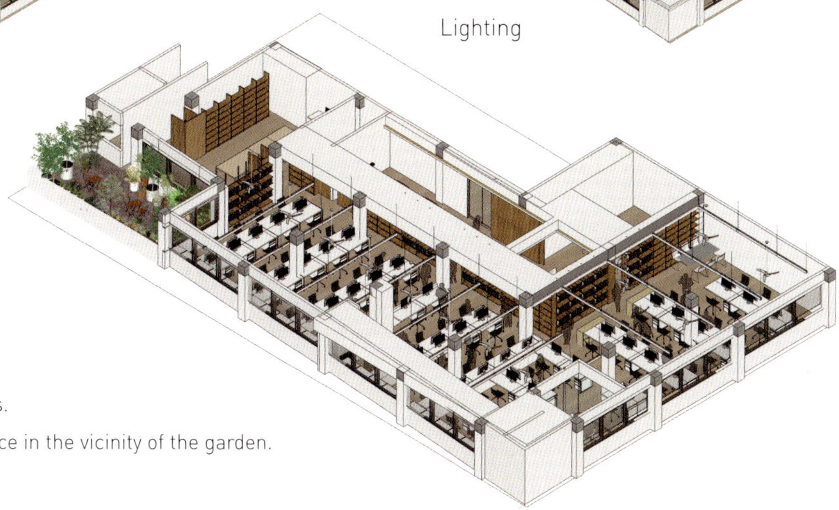

Above: Diagrams of the office space by layers.

Left (above): The galley and model-room space in the vicinity of the garden.
Left (below): Open space office.

Above: BaF's board of directors. From left to right standing: Wen Yao Wung (Director), Ching Huang Cheng (Associate Partner), Chin Wei Lee (Associate Partner), Chang Lien Lin (Associate Partner), Ching Hwa Chang (Founding Partner, Prinicpal Architect), Ying Chao Kuo (Founding Partner, Principal Architect), Sheng Liang Tsai (Associate Partner). From left to right seating: Po Hung Liu (Director), Pai Chi Lan (Director).

Right: BaF's garden.

AWARDS

2019

World Architecture Festival Awards
Future Projects – Culture Shortlist
Southern Branch of the National Central Library and National Depository Library

World Architecture Festival Awards
Completed Buildings – Civic and Community, Shortlist
Taijiang Administrative and Visitor Centers

FIABCI-Taiwan Prix d'Excellence Awards
Planning & Design Award
Taoyuan Chunglu Public Housing

FIABCI-Taiwan Prix d'Excellence Awards
Planning & Design Excellence Award
Taisugar's Circular Village

FIABCI-Taiwan Prix d'Excellence Awards
Planning & Design Excellence Award
Green Energy Technology Demonstration Site of Shalun Green Energy Science City

FIABCI-Taiwan Prix d'Excellence Awards
Planning & Design Excellence Award
Taijiang Administrative and Visitor Centers

2018

The 1st Excellent Intelligent Building Award
Chiayi Industrial Innovation Center

World Architecture Festival Awards
Residential–Future Project category, Shortlist
Taisugar's Circular Village at WAF Awards 2018

MIPIM AR Future Project Awards
Sustainability Entries
Green Energy Technology Demonstration Site of Shalun Green Energy Science City

MIPIM AR Future Project Awards
Offices Entries
MOXA Taoyuan Headquarters

S.ARCH AWARD
Completed Project –Finalist
TsingHua University Green Energy Building at S.ARCH AWARD 2018

Surface Design Awards
Sustainable Exterior Surface – Finalist
TAIJIANG Administrative and Visitor Centers

2017

Shopping Design – Best 100 Design : Best Architecture & Space Design
TAIJIANG Administrative and Visitor Centers

The 39th Taiwan Architecture Award — Finalist
Taitung Aboriginal Galleria

19th Chinese Society for Management of Technology (CSMOT) Best Enterprise Team
BAF – Technology Dept.

The 9th Best Practice Green Building Award, Ministry of Interior, Taiwan
TAIJIANG Administrative and Visitor Centers

FIABCI-Taiwan Prix d'Excellence Awards
Planning & Design Excellence Award
Xindian Public Housing on the North Side of Central Village

FIABCI-Taiwan Prix d'Excellence Awards
Planning & Design Excellence Award
Huwei Arts and Culture Leisure Park

2016

FIABCI World Prix d' Excellence Awards
Gold Winner
Central Taiwan Innovation Campus MOEA

Archdaily– Building of the Year Awards – Shortlist
Central Taiwan Innovation Campus MOEA

Archdaily- Building of the Year Awards – Shortlist
TAIPEI FLORA EXPO PAVILIONS

2015

Taipei International Design Award Distinction
Miaoli Train Station

The 8th Best Practice Green Building Award, Ministry of Interior, Taiwan
Miaoli Train Station

2014

The 36th Tiawan Architecture Awards – Honorable Mention
Miaoli Train Station

FIABCI-Taiwan Prix d'Excellence Awards – Planning & Design Excellence Award
Central Taiwan Innovation Campus MOEA

The 8th Far Eastern Architectural Design Award
Shortlist
TAIPEI FLORA EXPO PAVILIONS

Hong Kong Quality Building Award
Merit Winner
Chiayi Industrial Innovation Center

2013

The 7th Best Practice Green Building Award, Ministry of Interior, Taiwan
Chiayi Industrial Innovation Center

Chinese Institute of Civil and Hydraulic Engineering beautifying and Landscape Award
TAIPEI FLORA EXPO PAVILIONS

2012

International Awards for Livable Communities
Silver Award
TAIPEI FLORA EXPO PAVILIONS
World Architecture Festival Awards
Shortlist
Minquan Elementary School
Morakot post-disaster reconstruction

Kaohsiung City Barrier Free Public Building Certificate
Minquan Elementary School
Morakot post-disaster reconstruction

Green Building Award, Hong Kong
Merit Award
Minquan Elementary School
Morakot post-disaster reconstruction

The 36th Taiwan Architecture Awards
Honorable Mention
Minquan Elementary School
Morakot post-disaster reconstruction

Kaohsiung Green Building Award
Minquan Elementary School
Morakot post-disaster reconstruction

The 18th Yuan-Yie Award
Chiayi Industrial Innovation Center

2011

The 12th Awarding of Outstanding Architectural Studio in the ROC — BAF

The 12th Awarding of Outstanding Architect in the ROC
YING CHAO KUO – Principal Architect
World Gold Award for Design and Construction of Three-Dimensional Greening
TAIPEI FLORA EXPO PAVILIONS

The 6th Best Practice Green Building Award, Ministry of Interior, Taiwan
Dormitory for ITRI Southern Taiwan Campus

The 6th Best Practice Green Building Award, Ministry of Interior, Taiwan
DANSHUI ARTS WORKSHOP

FIABCI-Taiwan Prix d'Excellence Awards– Construction Management
DANSHUI ARTS WORKSHOP

2010

FIABCI-Taiwan Prix d'Excellence Awards – Planning & Design Excellence Award
TAIPEI FLORA EXPO PAVILIONS

The 9th Taipei Urban Landscape Award
1st Prize
TAIPEI FLORA EXPO PAVILIONS

The 32th Taiwan Architecture Award
TAIPEI FLORA EXPO PAVILIONS

Chinese Institute of Engineers Excellence in Engineering Project Award
TAIPEI FLORA EXPO PAVILIONS

Taipei County Government Public Construction Quality Award
DANSHUI ARTS WORKSHOP

2009

The 11th Awarding of Outstanding Architect in the ROC
CHING HWA CHANG - Principal Architect

The 1st Taoyuan County Urban Design Award
Honorable Mention
The Humanities Center at National Central University

2008

FIABCI Prix d'Excellence Awards
Shortlist
Taipei Public Library Beitou Branch

FIABCI-Taiwan Prix d'Excellence Awards – Planning & Design
DANSHUI ARTS WORKSHOP

The 9th Public Construction Golden Quality Award
DALIN train Station

2007

The 29th Taiwan Architecture Award
Taipei Public Library Beitou Branch

The 6th Far East Architecture Award
Shortlist
Taipei Public Library Beitou Branch
FIABCI-Taiwan Prix d'Excellence Awards
Taipei Public Library Beitou Branch

The 8th Public Construction Commission Golden Quality Award
Taipei Public Library Beitou Branch

The 6thTaipei City Innovative Quality Award
1st Prize
Taipei Public Library Beitou Branch

The 6th Taipei Urban Landscape Award
1st Prize
Taipei Public Library Beitou Branch

The 5th Best Practice Green Building Award, Ministry of Interior, Taiwan
Taipei Public Library Beitou Branch

The 5th Best Practice Green Building Award, Ministry of Interior, Taiwan
Taipei Public Library Beitou Branch.

CREDITS

ORIGIN

SITE

32–39; 246–253 TAIPEI FLORA EXPO PAVILIONS
CLIENT: Department of Economic Development , Taipei City Government
ARCHITECT: Ching Hwa Chang, Ying Chao Kuo
PROJECT TEAM: WenYao Wung, Chia Ju Li, Po Ru Chen, Ming Hui Lin, Chang Lien Lin, Chun Ting Lu, Ching Feng Chen, Chun Yu Chang, Po Hung Liu, Jui Lung Wu, Hsiao Hsian Wang, Jr Yuan Chen, Ting Hao Hsu, Jung Shan Lai, Hsing Hua Han, Li Chien Yang, Yu Ting Wei, Dah Yuan Lin, Chia Jen Yu, Tsu Chen Wu
SUPERVISION: BaF
STRUCTURAL ENGINEERING: Federal Engineering Consultant INC.
MECHANICAL AND ELECTRICAL ENGINEERING: Hander Engineering & Construction INC.
WATER ENGINEERING: Hander Engineering & Construction INC.
HVAC ENGINEERING: Archer Engineering Consultants Inc.
FIRE ENGINEERING: Yuan Dah Fire Fighting Engineering co., ltd.
LANDSCAPE: Ecoscape Formosana
GEOTECHNICAL ENGINEERING: Pan Asia Geotechincal & Engineer Association
GREENHOUSE: Department of Biomechatronics Engineering, NTU, Prof. Wei Fang
SMART BUILDING: Prof. Maolin Chiu
CONSTRUCTION: Fortune Construction co.,Ltd
PHOTOS: Rui Jsung Pan

40–47; 186–189 SONGSHAN PUBLIC HOUSING
CLIENT: Department of Urban Development , Taipei City Government
ARCHITECT: Ching Hwa Chang, Ying Chao Kuo
PROJECT TEAM: Wen Yao Wung, Chang Lien Lin, Yen Shiuan Chen, Yi Fan Chen, Pai Chi Lan, Zhen Chia Lee, Sheng Liang Tsai, Yue Lun Tsai, Jung Shan Lai, Yi Han Lee, Bo Wei Chen, Ling Xuan Su, Yi Syuan Chen, Chau Ching Chen, Ming Hui Lin, Wen Teng Tu, Chun Chieh Yu, Ching Hua Tung, Tzu Wei Huang, Tzu Hui Lo, Chen Wei Sun, Wei Hsi, Tsung Yu Lin
SUPERVISION: BaF
STRUCTURAL ENGINEERING: Federal Engineering Consultant INC.
MECHANICAL AND ELECTRICAL ENGINEERING: Taijie Technology Co., Ltd.
HVAC ENGINEERING: Taijie Technology Co., Ltd.
LANDSCAPE: Ecoscape Formosana
BIM: Sinotech Engineering Consultants,Ltd
HYDRAULIC ENGINEERING: Lu Chienlin Engineering Consultants Co.,Ltd.
TRAFFIC: GIS Engineering Consultants,Ltd.
CONSTRUCTION: New Asia Construction & Development Corporation
PHOTOS: Lucas K. Doolan (Studio Millspace)

48–57 HUWEI ARTS CENTER AND LEISURE PARK
CLIENT: Fabulous Group
ARCHITECT: Ying Chao Kuo, Ching Hwa Chang
PROJECT TEAM: Hsin Yi Chen, Yi Fan Chen, Ming Ching Li, Pei Lin Liao, Chi Li, Jia Lin Chao, Po Hung Liu, Ya Han Tu, Po Wei Lai
SUPERVISION: Fabulous Group
STRUCTURAL ENGINEERING: Strucpro Engineering Consultants co.,Ltd.
MECHANICAL AND ELECTRICAL ENGINEERING: Ming Cheng Consultant co.,Ltd.
HVAC ENGINEERING: Green HVAC. & R. Consultants
LANDSCAPE: Ecologue Landscape Architecture & Environmental Planning
CONSTRUCTION: Fabulous Group
PHOTOS: Yue Lun Tsai
IMAGE MAP: Tamkang University, Prof. Huang Jui-Mao

PROGRAM

60–67 ABORIGINAL GALLERY AND INNOVATIVE INCUBATION CENTER
CLIENT: Taitung County Government
ARCHITECT: Ying Chao Kuo, Ching Hwa Chang
PROJECT TEAM: Hsiao Hsian Wang, Hsin Yi Chen, Wen Yao Wung, Tzu Feng Chen, Hui Chen Chu, Yu Liang Chou, Yi Yan Siu, Yen Shiuan Chen, Yu Ting Wei, Zhen Chia Lee, Yue Lun Tsai
SUPERVISION: Ming Ji Engineering Consultants Co.,Ltd.
STRUCTURAL ENGINEERING: Strucpro Engineering Consultants co.,Ltd.
MECHANICAL AND ELECTRICAL ENGINEERING: Di-Ding Electrical Engineering Consultants co. Ltd.
HVAC ENGINEERING: Green HVAC. & R. Consultants
LANDSCAPE: Ecologue Landscape Architecture & Environmental Planning
CONSTRUCTION: Chang Hong Construction co., Ltd (Chu Bao Steel Industry Co., Ltd. Guan Jei Engineering Consultants Co.
PHOTOS: Lucas K. Doolan (Studio Millspace)

68–79 TAIJIANG NATIONAL PARK AND VISITOR CENTER
CLIENT: Taijiang National Park Headquarter
ARCHITECT: Ying Chao Kuo, Ching Hwa Chang
PROJECT TEAM: Jr Yuan Chen, Hsin Yi Chen, Yi Fan Chen, Yue Lun Tsai, Yu Tang Lien, Zhen Chia Lee, Chih Lin Tan, Hsing Hua Han, Wen Yao Wung, Po Ru Chen, Ming Hua Hsueh, Ming Hui Lin, Jui Lung Wu, Biophilia Architecture Association
SUPERVISION: BaF
STRUCTURAL ENGINEERING: Strucpro Engineering Consultants co.,Ltd.
MECHANICAL AND ELECTRICAL ENGINEERING: Ming Cheng Consultant co.,Ltd.
WATER ENGINEERING: Ming Cheng Consultant co.,Ltd.
HVAC ENGINEERING: Green HVAC. & R. Consultants
LANDSCAPE: Ecologue Landscape Architecture & Environmental Planning
CONSTRUCTION: Yung Cheng Construction co.,Ltd
PHOTOS: Rui Jsung Pan, Lucas K. Doolan (Studio Millspace) Guanting Chen

80–85 ZHONGSHAN PUBLIC HOUSING
CLIENT: Department of Urban Development , Taipei City Government
ARCHITECT: Ying Chao Kuo, Ching Hwa Chang
PROJECT TEAM: Po Hung Liu, Chin Wei Lee, Yu Ting Wei, Xin Yi Huang, Hun Tao Yu, Bo Yan Huang, Chan Ching Wu, Tzu Hsun Lin, Yi Shao Lin, Ren Chiao Guo, Jing Sin Chen, Ana Coelho, Kuan Yin Wang
COOPERATION: QUO Architecture Studio
STRUCTURAL ENGINEERING: Strucpro Engineering Consultants co.,Ltd.
MECHANICAL AND ELECTRICAL ENGINEERING: Wu Chien Hsing Engineering Consultants Co. Ltd.
HVAC ENGINEERING: Green

HVAC. & R. Consultants
LANDSCAPE: Environmental Arts Design
PUBLIC SPACE CONSULTANT: 9floor coliving
MONUMENT CONSULTANT: Prof. Hueyjiun Wang
PHOTOS: BaF

NATURAL FORCE

88–97 PUBLIC LIBRARY: BEITOU BRANCH
CLIENT: Taipei Public Library
ARCHITECT: Ying Chao Kuo, Ching Hwa Chang
PROJECT TEAM: Wen Yao Wung, Po Ru Chen, Chung Kai Hsu, Ching Huang Cheng, Yi Yuan Tseng, Chia Ju Li, Po Hung Liu, Hsin Yi Chen, Hsiao Hsian Wang, Meng Chuan Wu
SUPERVISION: BaF
STRUCTURAL ENGINEERING: Federal Engineering Consultant Inc.
MECHANICAL AND ELECTRICAL ENGINEERING: Ming Cheng Consultant Co.,Ltd.
WATER ENGINEERING: Ming Cheng Consultant Co.,Ltd.
HVAC ENGINEERING: Ming Cheng Consultant Co.,Ltd.
LANDSCAPE: Ecologue Landscape Architecture & Environmental Planning
CONSTRUCTION: Hau Bang Construction Co.,Ltd
PHOTOS: Jung Tai Chien, Miin Shyong Tseng

98–109 SHALUN GREEN ENERGY DEMONSTRATION CAMPUS
CLIENT: Industrial Technology Research Institute
ARCHITECT: Ying Chao Kuo, Ching Hwa Chang
PROJECT TEAM: Chang Lien Lin, Po Wei Lai, Pai Chi Lan, Sheng Liang Tsai, Chi Li, Klaudia Stefanowska, Meng Hua Chung, Andy Chang, Ko Ping Shih, Chiao An Hseih, Wen Qian Hu, Jing Sin Chen, Dylan Kuo, Meng Chuan Wu, Ya Chun Tsai, Wen Yao Wung, Po Ru Chen, Yen Shiuan Chen, Yi Ying Wu
SUPERVISION: BaF
STRUCTURAL ENGINEERING: Envision Engineering Consultant (EEC)
MECHANICAL AND ELECTRICAL ENGINEERING: Sinotech Engineering Consultants,Ltd
HVAC ENGINEERING: Sinotech Engineering Consultants,Ltd
FIRE ENGINEERING: Sinotech Engineering Consultants,Ltd
LANDSCAPE: Environmental Arts Design
HYDRAULIC ENGINEERING: Hong-Cheng Engineering Consultants Co.,Ltd.
TRAFFIC: Esco Tech Environmental Science Corporation
CONSTRUCTION: Reiju Construction Co., Ltd. (Architecture), Jiu Han Engineering Co., Ltd.(MEP)
WIND SIMULATION GRAPHICS: Building and Climate Lab, NCKU.
PHOTOS: BaF

110–119; 316–323 SHIMEN CIRCULAR VILLAGE
CLIENT: Anonymous
ARCHITECT: Ying Chao Kuo, Ching Hwa Chang
PROJECT TEAM: Ching Huang Cheng, Chien Shuo Pai, Shuan Hao Kan, Ren Chiao Guo, Hui Yun Chao, Vanessa Landazuri, Kurt Pollock, Ana Coelho, Po Ru Chen, Yen Shiuan Chen, Yi Ying Wu, Chan Ching Wu, Yi Syuan Chen, Yue Lun Tsai, Chi Jung Chen, Wen Qian Hu
STRUCTURAL ENGINEERING: Envision Engineering Consultant (EEC)
MECHANICAL AND ELECTRICAL ENGINEERING: Ming Cheng Consultant Co.,Ltd.
WATER ENGINEERING: Ming Cheng Consultant Co.,Ltd.
HVAC ENGINEERING: Green HVAC. & R. Consultants
LANDSCAPE: Ecoscape Formosana / Blue Racemosa
WIND SIMULATION GRAPHICS: Building and Climate Lab, NCKU.
PHOTOS: BaF

FORM

CIRCULATION

124–129 CENTRAL TAIWAN INNOVATION CAMPUS
CLIENT: Industrial Technology Research Institute
ARCHITECT: Ying Chao Kuo, Ching Hwa Chang
PROJECT TEAM: Chang Lien Lin, Wen Yao Wung, Yen Shiuan Chen, Po Hung Liu, Chi Chun Liu, Meng Chuan Wu, Pai Chi Lan, Yi Fang Chen, Hui Chen Chu, Tzu Feng Chen, Yu Ting Wei, Yu Tang Lien, Jung Shan Lai, Zhen Chia Lee, Yo Chia Chang, Kai Ting Chen, Kai Yang Chang, Chau Ching Chen, Chia Liang Hung, Ming Hui Lin, Chao Lung Wang, Yi Min Wang, Chih Chang Huang, Hui Cheng Chuang
COOPERATION: NOIZ
SUPERVISION: BaF
STRUCTURAL ENGINEERING: Federal Engineering Consultant INC.
MECHANICAL AND ELECTRICAL ENGINEERING: Sunrise Professional Engineering Corporation
WATER ENGINEERING: Sunrise Professional Engineering Corporation
HVAC ENGINEERING: EKC Energy And Environmental Control,Ltd.
LANDSCAPE: Ching-Fu Landscape Design Co.
CONSTRUCTION: Leeming Construction Co., Ltd. (Architecture), Jiu Han Engineering Co., Ltd.(MEP)
PHOTOS: Louis Liu

130–135 MOXA HEADQUARTERS
CLIENT: MOXA INC.
ARCHITECT: Ching Hwa Chang, Ying Chao Kuo
PROJECT TEAM: Po Hung Liu, Meng Chuan Wu, Zhen Chia Lee, Ting Yi Wu, Ya Ting Chuang, Tzu Hsun Lin, Yo Chia Chang, Ling Xuan Su
SUPERVISION: BaF
STRUCTURAL ENGINEERING: Strucpro Engineering Consultants Co.,Ltd.
MECHANICAL AND ELECTRICAL ENGINEERING: Ming Cheng Consultant Co.,Ltd.
HVAC ENGINEERING: Green HVAC. & R. Consultants
LANDSCAPE: Ecologue Landscape Architecture & Environmental Planning
CONSTRUCTION: Li Jin Engineering Co., Ltd.
PHOTOS: BaF

136–143; 282–289 NATIONAL CENTRAL LIBRARY AND REPOSITORY: SOUTHERN BRANCH
CLIENT: National Central Library
ARCHITECT: Ching Hwa Chang, Ying Chao Kuo
PROJECT TEAM: Chang Lien Lin, Chin Wei Lee, Yi Jung Lo, Wen Qian Hu, Chiao An Hseih, Hsiao Han Chen, Klaudia Stefanowska, Ling Xuan Su, Po Shun Wang
COOPERATION: Carlo Ratti Associati
STRUCTURAL ENGINEERING: Envision Engineering Consultant (EEC)
MECHANICAL AND ELECTRICAL ENGINEERING: Hengkai Engineering Consultants Co. Ltd.
HVAC ENGINEERING: Hengkai Engineering Consultants Co., Ltd.
LANDSCAPE: Ecologue Landscape Architecture & Environmental Planning
HYDRAULIC ENGINEERING: Sd

Technique Consultants Co.,Ltd.
TRAFFIC: Easygogo INC.
PHOTOS: BaF and Carlo Ratti Associati

STRUCTURAL SYSTEM

146–151 MINQUAN ELEMENTARY SCHOOL
CLIENT: Delta Electronics Foundation
ARCHITECT: Ying Chao Kuo, Ching Hwa Chang
PROJECT TEAM: Hsin Yi Chen, Ming Tse Lin, Yu Tang Lien, Zhen Chia Lee, Jr Yuan Chen, Feng Hsuan Chien, Yi Fang Chen, Yu Jung Liu
SUPERVISION: BaF
STRUCTURAL ENGINEERING: Strucpro Engineering ConsultantsCo. Ltd., Tomita Structural Design
MECHANICAL AND ELECTRICAL ENGINEERING: Ming Cheng Consultant Co.,Ltd.
HVAC ENGINEERING: Green HVAC. & R. Consultants
LANDSCAPE: Ching-Fu Landscape Design Co.
ENERGY: Architectural Environmental Programming and Control Group-Siraya, NCKU
CONSTRUCTION: Li Jin Engineering Co., Ltd. (Architecture), AD Engineering Corporation(MEP)
PHOTOS: Rui Jsung Pan

152–159 ABORIGINAL GALLERY AND HANDICRAFT SHOPS
CLIENT: Taitung County Government
ARCHITECT: Ying Chao Kuo, Ching Hwa Chang
PROJET TEAM: Hsiao Hsian Wang, Hsin Yi Chen, Wen Yao Wung, Tzu Feng Chen, Hui Chen Chu, Yu Liang Chou, Yi Yan Siu, Yen Shiuan Chen, Yu Ting Wei, Zhen Chia Lee, Yue Lun Tsai
SUPERVISION: Ming Ji Engineering Consultants Co.,Ltd.
STRUCTURAL ENGINEERING: Tomita Structural Design, Strucpro Engineering Consultants Co. Ltd.
MECHANICAL AND ELECTRICAL ENGINEERING: DI-Ding Electrical Engineering Consultants Co. Ltd.
HVAC ENGINEERING: Green HVAC. & R. Consultants
LANDSCAPE: Ecologue Landscape Architecture & Environmental Planning
CONSTRUCTION: Chang Hong Construction co., Ltd.
PHOTOS: Lucas K. Doolan (Studio Millspace)

160–165 CHENGGONG MARKET RECONSTRUCTION
CLIENT: Taipei City Market Administration Office
ARCHITECT: Ying Chao Kuo, Ching Hwa Chang
PROJECT TEAM: Chang Lien Lin, Yo Chia Chang, Shih Fan Yun, Wen Yao Wung, Jr Yuan Chen, Kai Ting Chen, Ju Hsien Yang, Sheng Liang Tsai, Yu Ting Wei, Chih Lin Tan, Yi Fan Chen, Jung Shan Lai, Pai Chi Lan, Chun Jung Chang, Po Han Wu, Yen Shiuan Chen, Po Ru Chen, Tsung Yu Lin, Ching Feng Chen, Chia Ju Li, Chien Po Liao
STRUCTURAL ENGINEERING: Strucpro Engineering Consultants Co.,Ltd.
MECHANICAL AND ELECTRICAL ENGINEERING: Ming Cheng Consultant Co.,Ltd.
HVAC ENGINEERING: Green HVAC. & R. Consultants
FIRE ENGINEERING: Snow Peak Fire Equipment Company
LANDSCAPE: Ecoscape Formosana
URBAN PLANNING: Kaishin Group
ENVIRONMENTAL ENGINEERING: Qian Da Eng.
TRAFFIC: Gis Engineering Consultants, Ltd.
PHOTOS: BaF

BUILDING MATERIAL

168–173 TAMSUI ART GALLERY
CLIENT: Urban & Rural Development Department, New Taipei City
ARCHITECT: Ying Chao Kuo, Ching Hwa Chang
PROJECT TEAM: Jr Yuan Chen, Yue Lun Tsai, Hsiao Hsuan Wang, Jui Lung Wu, Chun Ting Lu
SUPERVISION: Chun Yu Chang
STRUCTURAL ENGINEERING: Federal Engineering Consultant Inc.
MECHANICAL AND ELECTRICAL ENGINEERING: Ming Cheng Consultant Co.,Ltd.
WATER ENGINEERING: Ming Cheng Consultant Co.,Ltd.
HVAC ENGINEERING: Ming Cheng Consultant Co.,Ltd.
LANDSCAPE: BaF
CONSTRUCTION: Joint Construction Co., Ltd.
PHOTOS: Ko Chih Chang

174–179 TAMING HIGH SCHOOL OF THE APPLIED ART
CLIENT: Taming Senior High School
ARCHITECT: Ying Chao Kuo, Ching Hwa Chang
PROJECT TEAM: Chang Lien Lin, Tzu Wen Lin, Chia Ling Li, Hsing Hua Han, Hsiao Hsian Wang, Chi Chun Liu, Zhen Chia Lee, Sheng Liang Tsai, Chia Liang Hung, Po Cheng Chen
SUPERVISION: BaF
STRUCTURAL ENGINEERING: Tomita Structural Design
MECHANICAL AND ELECTRICAL ENGINEERING: Hong Mai Engineering Consultant Co., Ltd.
WATER ENGINEERING: Ming Cheng Consultant Co. Ltd.
HVAC ENGINEERING: Green HVAC. & R. Consultants
CONSTRUCTION: Reiju Construction Co., Ltd.
PHOTOS: Lucas K. Doolan (Studio Millspace)

180–185 LCY INDUSTRIAL CENTER R&D
CLIENT: LCY Chemical Corp.
ARCHITECT: Ching Hwa Chang, Ying Chao Kuo
PROJECT TEAM: Wen Yao Wung, Hsin Yi Chen, Ju Hsien Yang, Yo Chia Chang, Yi Yan Siu, Pai Chi Lan, Yen Shiuan Chen, Po Ru Chen, Chia Liang Hung, Meng Chuan Wu, Chi Chun Liu, Hsing Hua Han, Mei Chih Chang, Kai Ting Chen, Pei Shan Wu, Chia Hua Kuo, Chun Liang Hsu
SUPERVISION: BaF
STRUCTURAL ENGINEERING: Strucpro Engineering Consultants Co.,Ltd.
MECHANICAL AND ELECTRICAL ENGINEERING: Minginer Engineering Consultants, Ltd.
WATER ENGINEERING: Minginer Engineering Consultants, Ltd.
HVAC ENGINEERING: Green HVAC. & R. Consultants
LANDSCAPE: Ecoscape Formosana
CONSTRUCTION: Chung Yi Hsiang Construction Co.
PHOTOS: Louis Liu

190–195 AMBA HOTEL RENOVATION
CLIENT: The Ambassador Hotel Co. Ltd. Amba Hotels & Resorts
ARCHITECT: Ying Chao Kuo, Ching Hwa Chang
PROJECT TEAM: Po Wei Lai, Hsin Yi Chen, Yu Liang Chou, Yen Shiuan Chen, Po Yi Lee, Yi Yan Siu, Bo Yan Huang
STRUCTURAL ENGINEERING: Strucpro Engineering Consultants Co.,Ltd.
MECHANICAL AND ELECTRICAL ENGINEERING: I.S. Lin and Associates, Ming Cheng Consultant Co.,Ltd.
WATER ENGINEERING: Ming Cheng Consultant Co.,Ltd.
HVAC ENGINEERING: I.S. Lin And Associates, Ming Cheng

Consultant Co.,Ltd.
INTERIOR: T Group
CONSTRUCTION: Progiant Construction Co., Ltd
PHOTOS: The Ambassador Hotel Co. Ltd

196–201 FENGTAY AGRICULTURE R&D CENTER
CLIENT: The Fengtay Foundation
ARCHITECT: Ying Chao Kuo, Ching Hwa Chang
PROJECT TEAM: Sheng Liang Tsai, Po Wei Lai, Shi Jun Yu, Chun Hao Wu, Chieh Yu Liao, Wan Yu Chen, Chan Ching Wu, I Te Tsai, Ren Chiao Guo
SUPERVISION: BaF
STRUCTURAL ENGINEERING: Envision Engineering Consultant (EEC)
MECHANICAL AND ELECTRICAL ENGINEERING: Di-Ding Electrical Engineering Consultants Co. Ltd.
HVAC ENGINEERING: Green HVAC. & R. Consultants
FIRE ENGINEERING: Ld Fire Fighting Engineering Co., Ltd.
LANDSCAPE: Eco Orange Landscape Architecture Planning And Design Co.Ltd.
CONSTRUCTION: Feng Yu Group
PHOTOS: BaF

INTERFACE

HARD INTERFACE

206–211 NATIONAL ARCHIVES
CLIENT: National Archives Administration, NDC
ARCHITECT: Ying Chao Kuo, Ching Hwa Chang
PROJECT TEAM: Chang Lien Lin, Pai Chi Lan, Zhen Chia Lee, Ko Ping Shih, I Te Tsai, Meng Hua Chung, Ling Xuan Su, Yen Shiuan Chen, Yi Ying Wu, Kuan Yin Wang, Yue Lun Tsai, Wen Qian Hu, Chien Shuo Pai, Andy Chang, Chin Wei Lee, Yi Shao Lin, Ren Chiao Guo, Po Ru Chen, Sih An Yu, Chuan Wei Ting
STRUCTURAL ENGINEERING: Envision Engineering Consultant (EEC)
MECHANICAL AND ELECTRICAL ENGINEERING: Ming Cheng Consultant Co.,Ltd.
HVAC ENGINEERING: Green HVAC. & R. Consultants
LANDSCAPE: Ecoscape Formosana
PHOTOS: BaF

212–219 NTHU, GREEN ENERGY RESEARCH AND EDUCATION BUILDING
CLIENT: Dr. Weide Li
ARCHITECT: Ching Hwa Chang, Ying Chao Kuo
PROJECT TEAM: Wen Yao Wung, Hsin Yi Chen, Po Ru Chen, Yen Shiuan Chen, Meng Chuan Wu, Chi Chun Liu, Pai Chi Lan, Jui Chin Hsu, Yu Liang Chou, Hsin Yi Chang, Ju Hsien Yang, Yi Hsiang Chen
SUPERVISION: BaF
STRUCTURAL ENGINEERING: Strucpro Engineering Consultants Co.,Ltd.
MECHANICAL AND ELECTRICAL ENGINEERING: Ming Cheng Consultant Co.,Ltd.
FIRE ENGINEERING: Snow Peak Fire Equipment Company
LANDSCAPE: Ecologue Landscape Architecture & Environmental Planning
CONSTRUCTION: Leeming Construction Co. Ltd.
PHOTOS: Ko Chih Chang

220–225 GREEN ENERGY TECHNOLOGIES JOINT RESEARCH CENTER
CLIENT: Ministry of Science and Technology
ARCHITECT: Ching Hwa Chang, Ying Chao Kuo
PROJECT TEAM: Ya Ju Hsieh, Chun Chien Chang, Jie Chen, Chih Yu Ou
SUPERVISION: CECI Engineering Consultants, Inc.
STRUCTURAL ENGINEERING: Ceci Engineering Consultants, Inc.
MECHANICAL AND ELECTRICAL ENGINEERING: Ceci Engineering Consultants, Inc..
HVAC ENGINEERING: Ceci Engineering Consultants, Inc.
LANDSCAPE: Ecoscape Formosana
CONSTRUCTION: Reiju Construction Co., Ltd.
WIND SIMULATION GRAPHICS: Building and Climate Lab, NCKU.
PHOTOS: BaF

226–231 WANHUA PUBLIC HOUSING
CLIENT: Department of Urban Development , Taipei City Government
ARCHITECT: Ying Chao Kuo, Ching Hwa Chang
PROJECT TEAM: Wen Yao Wung, Po Ru Chen, Chia Ju Li, Tsung Yu Lin, Chang Lien Lin, Yen Shiuan Chen, Jr Yuan Chen, Yu Ting Wei, Zhen Chia Lee, Chi Chun Liu, Chi Li, Kai Ting Chen, Chia Ling Li, Peggy Shih, Yu Hsiang Wang
SUPERVISION: BaF
STRUCTURAL ENGINEERING: Strucpro Engineering Consultants Co. Ltd.
MECHANICAL AND ELECTRICAL ENGINEERING: Ming Cheng Consultant Co. Ltd.
WATER ENGINEERING: Ming Cheng Consultant Co. Ltd.
HVAC ENGINEERING: Ming Cheng Consultant Co. Ltd.
LANDSCAPE: Ecoscape Formosana
CONSTRUCTION: Cuo-Chi Construction Co., Ltd.
PHOTOS: Yue Lun Tsai

232–237 TAOYUAN WASTE TO ENERGY PLANT
CLIENT: CTCI Discover Reliable
ARCHITECT: Ching Hwa Chang, Ying Chao Kuo
PROJECT TEAM: Chin Wei Lee, Jhih Guo Wang, Jie Chen, Ming Tse Hsu, Zhen Chia Lee, Chiao An Hseih
LANDSCAPE: Ecoscape Formosana
PHOTOS: BaF

SOFT INTERFACE

240–245 ITRI SOUTHERN TAIWAN CAMPUS DORMITORY
CLIENT: Industrial Technology Research Institute
ARCHITECT: Ying Chao Kuo, Ching Hwa Chang
PROJECT TEAM: Wen Yao Wung, Hsiao Hsian Wang, Chia Hsing Hsieh, Ying Yi Chung, Meng Chuan Wu, Ting Hao Hsu, Jui Lung Wu, Pei Fen Lan, Hui Ching Huang
STRUCTURAL ENGINEERING: Strucpro Engineering Consultants Co.,Ltd.
MECHANICAL AND ELECTRICAL ENGINEERING: Ming Cheng Consultant Co.,Ltd.
WATER ENGINEERING: Ming Cheng Consultant Co.,Ltd.
HVAC ENGINEERING: Ming Cheng Consultant Co.,Ltd.
LANDSCAPE: Ecologue Landscape Architecture & Environmental Planning, Ching-Fu Landscape Design Co.
CONSTRUCTION: Chang Hong Construction Co. Ltd
PHOTOS: BaF

254–259 CHIAYI INDUSTRIAL INNOVATION CENTER
CLIENT: Industrial Technology Research Institute
ARCHITECT: Ying Chao Kuo, Ching Hwa Chang
PROJECT TEAM: Yao Tsun Wang, Hui Chen Chu, Meng Chuan Wu, Chia Ling Li, Wei Min Shen, Chang Lien Lin, Chia Liang Hung, Wen Yao Wung, Fang Chieh Chang, Yo

Chia Chang, Hui Ching Huang, Yue Lun Tsai, Chuan Hung Tai
SUPERVISION: BaF
STRUCTURAL ENGINEERING: Federal Engineering Consultant Inc.
MECHANICAL AND ELECTRICAL ENGINEERING: DI-Ding Electrical Engineering Consultants Co. Ltd.
WATER ENGINEERING: DI-Ding Electrical Engineering Consultants Co. Ltd.
HVAC ENGINEERING: Green HVAC. & R. Consultants
LANDSCAPE: Ching-Fu Landscape Design co.
CONSTRUCTION: Yih Shin Construction Co., Ltd.
PHOTOS: Ko Chih Chang

260–263 TAOYUAN FUNERAL HOME
CLIENT: Taoyuan City Government
ARCHITECT: Ying Chao Kuo, Ching Hwa Chang
PROJECT TEAM: Ching Huang Cheng, Po Wei Lai, Yi Yan Siu, Chien Shuo Pai, Wen Yu Liao, Man Chi Hsu, Han Yuan Chang, Yi Shao Lin, Ren Chiao Guo, Yu Heng Ko
STRUCTURAL ENGINEERING: Strucpro Engineering Consultants Co.,Ltd.
MECHANICAL AND ELECTRICAL ENGINEERING: Hengkai Engineering Consultants Co. Ltd.
LANDSCAPE: Ecologue Landscape Architecture & Environmental Planning
TRAFFIC: Gis Engineering Consultants,Ltd.
PHOTOS: BaF

SOCIAL INTERFACE

266–269 MIAOLI TRAIN STATION
CLIENT: Taiwan Railways Administration, MOTC
ARCHITECT: Ching Hwa Chang, Ying Chao Kuo
PROJECT TEAM: Hsing Hua Han, Jung Shan Lai, Yu Ting Wei, Chia Liang Hung, Feng Hsuan Chien, Yu Tang Lien
SUPERVISION: BaF
STRUCTURAL ENGINEERING: Strucpro Engineering Consultants Co.,Ltd.
MECHANICAL AND ELECTRICAL ENGINEERING: Ming Cheng Consultant Co.,Ltd.
WATER ENGINEERING: Ming Cheng Consultant Co.,Ltd.
HVAC ENGINEERING: Ming Cheng Consultant Co.,Ltd.
CONSTRUCTION: Fidelity Constrution Co. Ltd.
PHOTOS: Ko Chih Chang

270–275 FENGSHAN TRAIN STATION
CLIENT: Taiwan Railways Administration, MOTC, CECI Engineering Consultants, Inc.
ARCHITECT: Ching Hwa Chang, Ying Chao Kuo
PROJECT TEAM: Po Ru Chen, Yen Shiuan Chen, Po Wei Lai, Chang Lien Lin, Pai Chi Lan, Sheng Liang Tsai, Ko Ping Shih, Yun Chuan Liu, Ren Chiao Guo, Chiao An Hseih, Jie Chen, Shi Jun Yu, Zhen Chia Lee, I Te Tsai, Min Fang Tu, Jen En Hsieh
SUPERVISION: CECI Engineering Consultants, Inc.
STRUCTURAL ENGINEERING: Envision Engineering Consultant (EEC)
LANDSCAPE: Golden Park Landscape Architecture Planning & Design Consulting
PHOTOS: BaF

276–281 ART AND ARCH MUSEUM
CLIENT: Jinray Construction Co. Ltd
ARCHITECT: Ying Chao Kuo, Ching Hwa Chang
PROJECT TEAM: Hsin Yi Chen, Chia Ling Li, Meng Chuan Wu, Mei Chih Chang, Hui Ching Huang, Pei Shan Wu, Hui Chen Chu, Yo Chia Chang
SUPERVISION: BaF
STRUCTURAL ENGINEERING: Dayan Engineering Consultant
MECHANICAL AND ELECTRICAL ENGINEERING: Song Ling Engineering Consultants Ltd.
HVAC ENGINEERING: Green HVAC. & R. Consultants
LANDSCAPE: Ching-Fu Landscape Design Co.
INTERIOR: Daza Group
CONSTRUCTION: Jinray Construction Co. Ltd
PHOTOS: Ko Chih Chang

CIRCULAR

292–301 TAIPEI FLORA EXPO, ENTRANCE PAVILLION
CLIENT: Department of Economic Development Taipei City Government
ARCHITECT: Ching Hwa Chang, Ying Chao Kuo
PROJECT TEAM: Hsiao Hsian Wang, Chia Ju Li, Ming Hui Lin, Chang Lien Lin, Ting Hao Hsu, Wen Yao Wung, Jr Yuan Chen, Po Ru Chen, Ching Feng Chen, Po Hung Liu, Yue Lun Tsai, Chun Ting Lu, Jung Shan Lai, Hsing Hua Han, Yu Ting Wei
SUPERVISION: BaF
STRUCTURAL ENGINEERING: Federal Engineering Consultant Inc.
MECHANICAL AND ELECTRICAL ENGINEERING: Hander Engineering & Construction Inc.
WATER ENGINEERING: Hander Engineering & Construction Inc.
HVAC ENGINEERING: Archer Engineering Consultants Inc.
FIRE ENGINEERING: Yuan Dah Fire Fighting Engineering Co. Ltd.
LANDSCAPE: Ecoscape Formosana
CONSTRUCTION: Fortune Construction Co.,Ltd
PHOTOS: Rui Jsung Pan

302–315 TAISUGAR CIRCULAR VILLAGE
CLIENT: Taiwan Sugar Corporation
ARCHITECT: Ying Chao Kuo, Ching Hwa Chang
PROJECT TEAM: Chang Lien Lin, Chin Wei Lee, Yi Min Kuo, Lewis Hu, Klaudia Stefanowska, Yi Jung Lo, Wen Qian Hu
SUPERVISION: BaF
STRUCTURAL ENGINEERING: Strucpro Engineering Consultants Co.,Ltd.
MECHANICAL AND ELECTRICAL ENGINEERING: Ming Cheng Consultant Co.,Ltd.
HVAC ENGINEERING: Green HVAC. & R. Consultants
FIRE ENGINEERING: Snow Peak Fire Equipment Company
LANDSCAPE: Golden Park Landscape Architecture Planning & Design Consulting
TRAFFIC: Esco Tech Environmental Science Corporation
CONSTRUCTION: Feng Yu Group
PHOTOS: BaF

324–327 BaF's Workplace
CLIENT: BaF
ARCHITECT: Ying Chao Kuo, Ching Hwa Chang
PROJECT TEAM: Ya Chun Tsai, Yo Chia Chang, Chun Hao Wu, Hui Yun Chao
SUPERVISION: BaF
MECHANICAL AND ELECTRICAL ENGINEERING: Yo Chia Chang
WATER ENGINEERING: Yo Chia Chang
HVAC ENGINEERING: Yo Chia Chang
Interior: BaF
PHOTOS: Lucas K. Doolan (Studio Millspace)

EDITORIAL

Authors:
Ying Chao Kuo
Ching Hwa Chang

Editor:
Ana Coelho

Responsible Partner:
Ying Chao Kuo

Managing Partner:
Chin Wei Lee

Graphic design:
Ana Coelho

Translation:
Andy Chang, Pei Lin Liao

Contributing members:
Chien Shuo Pai, Klaudia Stefanowska, Yi Jung Lo, Yue Lun Tsai, Yi Shao Lin, Juanxin Chai

ORO Project Coordinator:
Kirby Anderson

THANK YOU

Ching Hwa Chang, Ying Chao Kuo, Pe Ju Chen, Wen Yao Wung, Jia Ru Li, Po Hung Liu, Yu Chih Ma, Chang Lien Lin, Hsin Yi Chen, Meng Chuan Wu, Yen Hsuan Cheng, Yue Lun Tsai, Tsung Yu Lin, Chao Ching Chen, Pin Wei Kuo, Po Cheng Chen, Ya Han Tu, Yi De Tsai, Ya Ju Hsieh, Chan Ching Wu, Pei Lin Liao, I Chen Pan, Ya Chun Tsai, Andy Chang, Tzu Hsun Lin, Wen Yu Liao, Chen Chia Li, Pai Chi Lan, Klaudia Stefanowska, Ko Ping Shih, Hun Tao Yu, Ting Chuang Ya, Bo Wei Chen, Po Yen Huang, Ching Huang Cheng, Chih Yu Ou, Shi Jun Yu, Yi Shao Lin, Yi Min Kuo, Chiao An Hsieh, Cheng Ling Lin, Jie Chen, Meng Ying Hsieh, Meng Hua Chuang, Yi Ying Wu, Wen Chian Hu, Min Fang Tu, Ling Hsuan Su, Hsin Yi Huang, Hsiao Han Chen, Yu Heng Ko, Chien Shuo Pai, Sheng Liang Tsai, Yi Jung Lo, Te Feng Liu, Chin Wei Lee, Jia Hao Tu, Ho Chen Hung, Jui Lien Chung, Shang Jung Wu, Pai Jung Hsieh, Vanessa Alulema, Yi Syuan Chen, Chi Jung Chen, Shao Yu Lu, Tzu Wen Lin, Yu Ting Wei, Jia Long Lai, Yu Wei Hsieh, Jen En Hsieh, Cheng Lin Ho, Ana Coelho, Kuan Yin Wang, Shuan Hao Kan, Cing Hua Dong, Tsai Neng Weng, Pei Ju Lin, Shu Wei Ho, Shih Han Jhang, Chih Kuo Wang, Li Chun Wu, Po Shun Wang, Shih Chang Chen, Ming Tse Hsu, Chih Yu Kuo, Lin Han Hu, Pei Chuan Tsai, Ching Hsin Chen, Ming Hua Hsueh, Hung Chi Hsu, Chun Yi Lin, Chen Li Hsieh, Chen Te Liao, Chia Wei Chang, Shu Ting Wu, Keng Wei Liu, Chun Hua Chiu, Li Ling Chen, Juan Xin Chai, Jia Hua Wu, Yu Jie Liao, Ya Pei Lin, Li Chi Yang, Yi Chi Wang, De Ming Yen, Calvin Lee, Shiau Lan Chiou, Ching Hung Chiang, Chung Chuan Cheng, Kuo Hua Liu, Hong Keng Kek, Shih Da Tseng, Yu Chung Wu

Yuan Yi Tseng, Yu Heng Tseng, Yi Fang Chen, Jui Lung Wu, Yi Ying Chung, Ching Feng Chen, Ting Feng Ho, Tsung Hsien Huang, Shan Ju Liu, Yi Ting Wu, Yu Chun Chang, Tsun Yao Wang, Hao Ting Hsu, Yu Tsung Wu, Hui Han Yang, Ping Yu Hsieh, Cheng Chung Ko, Chun Ting Lu, Wen Shou Lu, Chun Hsiung Chiu, Yen Ke Li, Yu Jung Liu, Ming Tse Lin, Ting Chang Lin, Ho Hsiang Lin, Hsiang Hsi Wang, Hui Ching Huang, Feng Hsuan Chien, Chia Yu Lai, Hao Chieh Chang, Fang Chieh Chang, Chuan Hung Tai, Yu Tang Lien, Hsing Hua Han, Heng Kang Hu, Wei Min Shen, Feng Ming Wang, Chen Ming Lien, Pai Jung Hsieh, Hsiu Wei Fu, Hua Hsin Chiang, Ming Hsien Hsieh, Chien Chih Chien, Ju Yi Lai, Chao Wen Yu, Yun Ping Li, Cheng Chung Lin, Jui Ying Hsiao, Chung Hsing Huang, Chien Nan Hsiao, Chi Tao Tseng, Yi Hao Chen, Chia Ling Li, Jui Chin Hsu, Chih Ming Chien, Ching Ti Tsai, Kai Yang Chang, Tzu Wen Lin, Hui Chen Chu, Mei Chih Chang, Yu Yu Chen, Cheng Fu Kuo, Tzu Feng Chen, Shun Ping Huang, Chia Hua Kuo, Ting Kuo Chiang, Cheng Ya Chang, Wu Hung Tsai, Pei Shan Wu, Chia Liang Hung, Chung Cheng Li, Ming Chia Li, Pi Na Wu, Ching Feng Chen, Ching Jung Chen, Hao Chang Hsu, Chien Po Liao, Yi Chia Tsai, Chin Sung Hsiao, Ssu Yuan Fang, Kai Ting Chen, Yu Ting Wei, Yu Tang Lien, Chih Chang Huang, Hsing Hua Han, Sheng Yun Hsu, Po Han Wu, Yi Hsiang Chen, Yi Min Wang, Chi Chun Liu, Yu Liang Chou, Hui Cheng Chuang, Chao Lung Wang, Chung Cheng Lu, Fan Yun Shih, Cheng Ping Chung, Cheng Hui Tai, Yuan Yu Chen, Ju Hsien Yang, Pei Chin Lin, Chih Yu Liu, Chen Chia Li, Hsiao Hsuan Wang, Po Yen Huang, Pai Chi Lan, Yu Wei Hsieh, Hsin Yi Chang, Yao Tung Su, Chia Chi Yeh, Ju Chun Hsiao, Ming Hui Chiu, Feng Chuan Li, Chih Lin Tan, Chia Pei Shih, Ming Hua Hsueh, Yu Hsiang Wang, Wei Hsi, Cheng Hui Tai, Shih Chin Wang, Shun Hsiang Chu, Yi Fan Chen, Yung Ching Tsao, Chih Yuan Chen, Chun Jung Chang, Liang Chun Liu, Ming Yueh Ho, Chun Chieh Yu, Cheng Hung Hsieh, Tsung Wei Yang, Yung Hsuan Chen, Chia Lin Chou, Yi Han Li, Pin Chih Liao, Teng Te Wang, Sheng Liang Tsai, Hsiang Yun Huang, Chi Li, Ho Fu Lai, Ching Hua Tung, Tzu Hui Tu, Ting Yi Wu, Wan Yu Chen, Chi Wen Liu, Hsin Yu Chen, Ming Ching Li, Tzu Wei Huang, Ching Chin Wang, Po Wei Lai, Chun Chien Chang, Ching Feng Chen, Yu Feng Chou, Sheng Wei Sun, Po I Li, Yun Chuan Liu, Hung Ta Liang, Yun Chung Chen, Wen Teng Tu, Yu Min Wen, Chieh Yu Liao, Chieh Shan Wu, Cheng Hung Li, Jung Shan Lai, Wei Tai Tang, Lin Han Hu, Yen Chun Lin, Yi Lun Wu, Yi Yan Siu, Chia Hsiang Li, Hao Chih Hung, Feng Chun Ting, Chia Yi Wu, Ming Tai Yeh, Chun Hung Chen, Li Hung Lin, Tzu Hui Lo, Mei Lin Sung, Chi Lin Ho, Ming Hui Lin, Shu Ping Huang, Han Yuan Chang, Chun Hao Wu, Ti Shou Chuang, Fang Chieh Chang, Chien Chou Chen, Hui Yun Chao, Man Chi Hsu, Hua Hsin Chiang, Yao Hsien Wang, Ren Ciao Guo, Ting Jung Ku, Hsiu Chi Huang, Chun Ming Chao.